THE GARRULOUS GRANDMA'S DAYBOOK

A PILGRIMAGE TO DISCOVER ACCEPTANCE, PEACE AND LOVE WITHIN

Contemplative Network
P.O. Box 941464
Houston Texas 77094-8464

Library of Congress Cataloging-in-Publication Data available from the Library of Congress.

Hard Cover   ISBN:979-8-9930806-0-4
Paperback   ISBN:979-8-9930806-1-1
epub   ISBN:979-8-9930806-2-8

Cover Photo by Dreamstime & Editing by Linden Price

Lovingly dedicated
to all the people who have joined
me on my pilgrimage:
Family, Family of My Heart, Friends,
Colleagues and Strangers.
Paul, my beloved husband and soulmate
for 32 joyful years.
The Holy Spirit for peacefully
dwelling within me.
She is my muse.

CONTENTS

FOREWORD

We met at a bar. It is inside our retirement community, a place where people are nearing the end of their spiritual journeys. People who have lived a full life, often without a spouse who is deceased. So it is how I came to know Jan over four plus years.

I read with delight her daybook. I thought I knew Jan but her book took me deeper. It is indicative of her style when writing her Garrulous Grandma newsletter column, which is relished by our community of over 1,000 retirees. I intuitively knew what garrulous meant but had to look it up anyway: "fond of talking or conversation." When we walk down the hallway together, she almost always suddenly disappears. When I look around, unannounced, she has stopped to talk to someone.

Here is the catch; her talk is never frivolous. She is always engaging the "other." She is a garrulously listening grandma. She is constantly applying her decades of wisdom to listening and analyzing. She meticulously keeps a balance between example and encouragement. She is never whiny or preachy but practical. Often sharing adjustments to her own thinking and reactions because she has learned from others; a gift difficult for most of us to learn. A God given gift.

In this daybook she lovingly shares her self-reflections with her readers. She often vulnerably shares her life's suffering and mistakes so she can share her lessons with her readers. A true act of humility. An avid reader, she selflessly enhances her words with many relevant, uplifting quotes from minors to mystics. Sometimes she slaps us with a different take on a situation that can initially draw a strong reaction of disagreement. But, if we read on, we realize it is we who needed to take a new view of things. I encourage you to ride her wave of a paradigm shift in thinking.

I highly recommend this book. Read it slowly and savor. I unabashedly share the not-so-secret ultimate climax of the book, which is in every month, day, and sentence: LOVE! She emanates the radiance of Holy Spirit dwelling within her. Her lesson is the peace of God's love dwells within you too.

Deacon Bob Hesse, PhD.
Cofounder and Chairman, Contemplative Network
Author: *Face to Face:*
Divine Encounters in God's Earthly Kingdom

ACKNOWLEDGEMENTS

As The African Proverb Suggests:
It Takes A Village

There are so many people I should acknowledge. With my unpredictable memory, I know I will miss some, but please know, I appreciate each and every person who contributed to my growth and understanding of me and my world. Friends encouraged me when I was tired and weary. Their wise words and emotional support always seem to come just when I need them the most. I am convinced there is a special place in heaven for those who lovingly walk with a searching soul as she staggers down life's path, especially when she is writing a book as she stumbles along.

The foundation of my obsession with writing is its twin obsession with reading; in my mind and life, they grew alongside each other. At an early age, my mother and grandmother introduced me to the joys of reading. Both always had a book close by their favorite chair, many on their shelves were well worn from frequent use. A peek at my bookcases would show the same. Mom and Gram introduced me to librarians who listened and suggested books to keep an only child entertained. Fun and fascinating stories in which a curious little girl met all kinds of "friends" who kept loneliness away. My book friends still keep me company. Thank you everyone.

All the teachers through sixteen years of a formal education who encouraged a curious student to read, read and read some more. Your words continue to motivate me in my eighth decade. I learned from every essay, term paper and book report assigned. The one teacher I remember distinctly is my high school freshman English teacher, Mrs. Ross. She was a task master who expected detail-oriented perfection in everything made of words. She is the only one who ever gave me an "F" on a composition. Why? I put "algebra" instead of "English" in the heading. Her note, "Details are critical." I never forgot the lesson.

I am thankful to the authors who struggle to find the right word, the perfect phrase, the realistic dialogue to bring a story alive. I am always a silent observer in the middle of the action. I consider your characters my friends and find the ending of a good book bittersweet. I want more. I wish I had kept track of all the books I have read through the years, it must be in the thousands. I learned to recognize and appreciate sound composition, the other kind too. Another valuable, ongoing lesson.

I am grateful to the participants in various book clubs and my on-going memoir-writing group. Your insightful comments offered other views of the message in both fiction and non-fiction stories. I appreciate your willingness to listen and respond respectfully to my opinions. You stretched my brain and made me think.

The people who suggested books they thought I might enjoy or maybe learn something to help me on my journey have a special place in my heart. A book recommended by a friend always sparks my curiosity. I have rarely been disappointed by your suggestions. Thank you.

The people who read my columns and feature stories in two newsletters encourage me to keep writing. If you didn't read my words and tell me honestly what you think, I would have no audience with whom to share my thoughts. I so appreciate you devoting your precious time to my efforts. You are the reason I work to inform, educate and entertain through my words. Thank you for your astute observations, especially the critical ones. I learned from every comment you shared.

I get encouragement and inspiration from a variety of people, places and conversations. I have had many muses through the years. Recently, I identified the primary source for everything I write; I couldn't do what I do without Her. Thank you, Holy Spirit.

There are two people in particular I want to thank. Each, in their own special way, introduced me to the Holy Spirit. Without Carolyn Rogas' and Bob Hesse's constant reminders the Holy Spirit dwells within me and works through my curated words and thoughtful messages, I would have never come to recognize Her as my Muse for everything I write. Thank you for one of the most powerful and meaningful introductions in my personal, spiritual and professional life.

A special thank you to the people who read this manuscript in various stages. Some read an essay. Some a column. Some listened. A few read the book in its entirety. All your comments and observations were given respectful thought and consideration. Patti Alexander, Pat and Karen Camerino, Bill Gorsky, Becky Ogle, Ann Smith, Carolyn St Pe, Lois Tatum, and Joe Teas took the time to read my scribbles thoughtfully and offered honest opinions. All are joyfully appreciated.

To my editor, Linden Price. His thoughtful comments from a male perspective were invaluable in making this book relevant for men in the audience. He made sensible suggestions, which caused me to seriously consider his viewpoint. Linden spotted questionable word choices, massaged my thoughts and made both better. He suggested appropriate quotes, which strengthened my message. This book wouldn't be in your hands today, dear reader, had it not been for his eagle eyes, endless patience and insightful comments. Every author should be as blessed to have an editor like Linden. Thank you is so inadequate.

A SPECIAL ACKNOWLEDGEMENT:

To my daughters, Barbara and Nancy, you have become cherished friends who inspire me with your loving ways, thoughtful words and continuing support.

To my sons, Brent and Mark, given to me when your dad and I married. A treasured gift, to be sure.

To my grandsons, David and Ryan, you give me joy with every smile, every hug, every game of Scrabble (even when you scoundrels beat me at my game!), you are the light of our family's future.

I am blessed beyond measure all of you are part of my life. You enrich my world with many priceless memories, but especially your love. Thank you.

INTRODUCTION

A Pilgrimage to Discover
Acceptance, Peace and Love Within

During a six-month period in 2022, a friend recommended two books: *The Shack* by Wm Paul Young and *The Café on the Edge of the World* by John Strelecky. Both had a profound effect on my perception of God, me and my purpose in the world. Before reading them, from time to time, I had quietly wondered if I was fulfilling my reason for being or just using up valuable natural resources. I had lovingly nursed my husband through the final years of his life. I had launched our four children; they are good, kind people living successfully in the world. I was available for friends who needed a listening heart and involved in volunteer projects for two non-profit organizations. I was facilitating a memoir writing group, editing books for three authors, helping promote a recently published book I had edited and writing essays for my memoir and columns for two newsletters. I was keeping a journal, which included gratitude entries. Occasionally giving the message at a Sunday worship service for residents in a nursing/rehab facility. But a nagging question kept intruding into my quiet time: Should I be doing more? Less? Is what I am engaged in the right involvement at this time in my life? Should I search for other projects? I never considered stopping, too much energy for that, also too much to share; I was just not sure I was devoting my time to the right people and activities.

These are scary questions at any time in life. But when the questioner is a 77-year-old widowed grandmother who has lived more years than she has left, it is terrifying! I am blessed to have a loving group of wise women and supportive men who are not shy about giving me a verbal kick in the posterior by suggesting a life-course correction and generously offering valuable advice. They are relentless with both praise and tough love. I would be lost without them. But ultimately, I knew I had to find the answers to my heartfelt questions on my own.

For several months, a nagging thought had been plaguing me. Could I write a book, an idea I have played with off and on for fifteen years? Maybe now is the right time to tackle that daunting project. If I did, what would the topic be? Do I have any answers to life's vexing issues? Immediate response: Heavens, no! I answer one set of questions, and another set pops up. One lesson I *have* learned: Life is not static. The world keeps evolving and so do we humans. Basic morality doesn't change, but how we interpret right and wrong seems about as firm as my flabby arms. Funny thing. Just like grandma's old-fashioned 20th century home remedies still work in the 21st century, sound judgment, basic morality and ethical behavior never goes out of style either. Each generation just needs to be reminded and educated.

Back to my question: If I were to finally write a book, and finish it, what would I talk about? How should it be structured? As I was thinking, my eyes casually glanced at the basket sitting by my favorite reading chair. Its contents a Kindle filled with fun reading, an electronic tablet and four books: an autobiography and three daybooks. As I pondered my current reading material, I realized the past several years, I have faithfully read daybooks. I rotate six volumes. When I come back to a particular book in two or three years, the thoughts spark different reactions because I am in a different place than the last time I read it. I learn new lessons from a book I read three years ago.

Bingo! My format became clear: a daybook using my thoughts and musings from memoir essays, previously shared columns and presentations offered in a new way.

The format: Brief daily passages to ponder. Each month has a theme. On the last day of the month, a gentle prod to think about: What have you learned? What have you already or plan to make a part of your life? What did you agree with, disagree with? Why? The month ends with a short prayer of gratitude, a practice I have learned improves my life in countless ways. So much so, I devote an entire month discussing the joy of keeping a journal and explaining how and why I add a note of gratitude to each entry.

Join me as I offer my views on a variety of topics using one of my favorite formats. Some reflections you will relate to; some you won't. Some observations you will agree with, some you won't. And that is okay. But, if read thoughtfully, all will make you think. In my world, always a beneficial exercise.

Jan

EDITOR'S NOTE:

It is always interesting others will sometimes see something in me I didn't recognize. That recognition, more often than not, will draw me into new life experiences. When the Garrulous Grandma asked me if I would edit her book, I probably gave her a blank stare before saying "Really? Me edit a pro writer?" What I didn't realize was she was honoring me by allowing some degree of male perspective in her work. I am thankful for the challenge. *A Pilgrimage to Find Acceptance, Peace and Love Within* is a thoughtful and soul baring work. Any reader, regardless of gender, will be drawn into this book by its talented and gifted author. Every daily entry is thought provoking and food for relationship growth.

Linden Price

DAYBOOK

*To journey without being changed
is to be a nomad.*

*To change without journeying
is to be a chameleon.*

*To journey and be transformed
is to be a pilgrim.*

Mark Nepo

JANUARY

Faith

"Be careful how you think;
Your life is shaped by your thoughts."

Proverbs 4:23

JANUARY 1

New Year's Day. The day many people make resolutions. Studies show only 8% of those who make these annual promises actually keep them. After stumbling on that enlightening tidbit a few years ago, I decided I would no longer list the ways I was going to improve myself with tactics I knew darn well I wouldn't follow and wouldn't work for me anyway. A little honest self-knowledge comes in handy here. No point wasting my valuable, and limited, time and mental energy.

What do I do instead? I settle in my quiet spot and have a friendly conversation with myself. What did I do right in the previous year? What could I have done better? Do I plan to continue what is working? Do I want to stop what isn't working? Why? Why not?

After answering these questions truthfully, I tell myself the new year is a blank page. How do I plan to fill my blank page? What do I want to do differently? How do I want to grow? Once I have the answers, I will spend the next few days outlining a broad plan of action, giving myself lots of wiggle room to determine what to do and how to grow throughout the year.

JANUARY 2

After taking time to reflect, I do an honest evaluation of the answers to the questions posed yesterday. This is not a self-flagellation exercise, but a reasonably objective look at how I fared with last year's promises to myself. This helps me decide if I want to continue practicing certain behaviors, spending time with the same people and staying engaged in the same activities.

An example may help. One year, I promised myself I would be bold, do things outside my comfort zone, say "yes" more often and consciously practice gratitude. While I did make modest forays into the first two, I decided I needed to devote a second year to both. I was still hesitant and frequently found lame excuses to avoid new experiences and stay in the safe familiarity of my comforting nest. I decided practicing gratitude had worked so well, I would give it a permanent and prominent place in my daily life.

I am gentle with myself. I am learning about me. I am trying to be a better me. I accept this is a thoughtful, life-long journey, not a hasty one and done weekend jaunt.

JANUARY 3

In order to make even modest changes in my approach to moving through my days, I have gradually learned I am more successful when I acknowledge God's presence in my life. I have always had a strong faith. I talk to God. I even get mad at my Deity sometimes. I ask the Holy Spirit for help and guidance every day; I have finally learned to listen to Her wise advice. Ultimately, I had to accept God works through me. Me!?! The insecure woman who messes up several times a day. I have no clue why me, but after much prayer and soul-searching, I finally accept God uses me, even if I don't understand why or many times recognize how or when.

It doesn't matter if you believe in God, Adonai, Allah, Buddha, or the Universe. Practice Judaism. Christianity. Islam. Buddhism, Hinduism. Stoicism. Another philosophy or faith tradition or none at all. God dwells within all of us. Female. Male. Single. Married. Widowed. Straight. Gay. Black. White. Brown. Yellow. Young. Old. In-between. Rich. Poor. Barely getting by. God dwells within you, me, everyone.

God is waiting for us, you and me, to ask for help and guidance by any name we know Him and Her, in whatever way we are comfortable doing so. Acknowledging, accepting and turning to our Higher Power is the only way we will be successful making even the tiniest change in our behavior. Our relationships. Our lives.

JANUARY 4

Six years ago, I was attending a caring neighbors meeting; my mind was wandering; I was doodling. A woman was asking for volunteers to help at an inter-denominational Christian worship service at our community nursing/rehab center. She said it was an ideal place to "bloom where we are planted." I had heard the expression before, but for some reason, her heartfelt request spoke to me in a way I couldn't ignore. I turned up the next Sunday. And kept returning for almost three years.

I learned it doesn't take much to be a light in someone's day: escorting an unsteady person down the hall; helping her settle in a chair; fetching his dropped song book. I also learned having a cheerful attitude with a smile that showed in my eyes and was heard in my voice had a subtle, but visible impact ... On both of us.

My adventure is an example of how we can, no matter our age and stage in life, education, income level or particular talents, make a difference in our fractured world when we bloom where we are planted. And studies show helping others enhances our well-being and adds meaning to our life. A win-win in my book.

Find a cause. Give of your time, talent and treasure. When you take the focus off yourself, you too will benefit in immeasurable ways and bloom where you are planted.

JANUARY 5

Researchers who study human behavior strongly suggest a successful day begins with a morning routine. After much trial and error, fits and fretting, stops and starts, I finally settled into one that works for me.

The first thing I do is make the bed. There is a certain satisfaction knowing I did one productive thing and only five minutes after I woke up. After I make a mocha smoothie and get comfortable in my favorite reading chair, I ask myself: What will I be brave about today? My answer gives me my challenge for the day. I pray for the people in my life and thank God for a special few who lovingly keep coming back and putting up with me. I continue my morning ritual reading self-composed prayers, verses from favorite psalms and biblical passages, reflections from three daybooks and daily meditations written by various spiritual teachers. I review emails for the news of the day and thoughtfully respond to personal and business messages. This quiet time devoted to my inner life and discovering what the outside world is up to, anchors my heart and my head in reality so I can go about the rest of my day with confidence and courage.

I understand being "retired" gives me freedom and flexibility not everyone has, but I encourage you to develop a morning routine that works for you. The only criteria: Say one heartfelt prayer and acknowledge your God's loving presence in your life. Both *will* make a difference in your day.

JANUARY 6

Even though I live alone, in order to be in the right frame of mind to quietly begin my day, I knew I needed the right space. So, I arranged a special corner in my small study. To accomplish my goal, I needed to downsize the contents of the room. A large bookcase and a wooden filing cabinet were donated to our community non-profit resale shop. The contents of the cabinet were scrutinized and either shredded or stored in a smaller box in the closet. The books were relocated or donated. The two pieces were replaced by an eighteen-inch, round, revolving side table designed to hold two shelves of books. It nestles next to one of my favorite recliners. With a floor lamp behind and a comfy throw draped over the back, I sit comfortably, with my feet up or down, and focus on my morning ritual. The only cost was sixty dollars for the table/bookcase, thoughtful planning and searching plus a few additional hours to assemble the table and move things around.

An Interesting benefit I didn't anticipate: The corner has evolved into my favorite spot for thinking, meditating, praying, reading, listening to music and quietly unwinding (sometimes napping). I find myself wandering to my quiet space whenever I need a break from my busy day or the world is too much with me. I'm spending more and more time here. I'm beginning to believe my Inner Spirit knew, before I did how much I need this space, how often I would retreat here (I'm typing this reflection on my tablet in my special space), and how much I would cherish its comforting presence. Perhaps you should consider creating your quiet spot. It is good for the body, the psyche, the soul.

JANUARY 7

What I decide to face bravely today may be as simple as leaving my safe, cozy apartment and venturing out the door. Some days that decision takes a lot of courage. I reside in a senior living community. It is in many ways a nurturing environment. The residents are friendly and look out for each other. The staff is caring and helpful; truth be told; they spoil us silly. But as a closet introvert, sometimes I just don't want to interact with anyone, friendly or not. I want to complete whatever the errand, with as little human contact as possible. On those days, I need to convince myself the task is more important than my desire to avoid people.

What to do? I remember the promise to myself to be brave today. I take a deep breath, hide my desire to be invisible, say a quick prayer for courage and walk out the door with a smile to deal with whatever the outside world puts in my path. Do my preparations always work? More often than not, they give the fearful little girl lurking inside a gentle nudge, enough to complete the errand.

We all have times we need a little, or maybe a lot, of courage to meet our challenges with a positive attitude. This is when we should lean into our faith and ask for help. Our God promises to be with us to comfort, encourage and strengthen.

JANUARY 8

I am an inveterate list-maker. My super busy, super organized schedule would collapse without detailed lists. These days my Google calendar and note-taking app are two of my best friends. I would lose that thought or catchy phrase, forget what I was supposed to do, overlook important dates and be late for every appointment without my electronic executive assistants. But the most important to-do list I read during my morning ritual is the one which reminds me what it means to have a successful day and gives me concrete directions on how to make it happen.

Count my blessings, an easy one; done during prayer time. *Practice kindness*. Many times, all that requires is a warm, loving smile and a cheerful nod as I pass someone in the hall. *Let go of what I can't control*. Being a "fixer," this can be a challenge. Acknowledging my Higher Power is in charge means I don't have to be. I turn everything over to Him or Her and concentrate on not snatching them back. *Listen to my heart*. If I tell myself to walk through the day with a positive attitude, I am automatically tuned into this one. *Be productive.* Made my bed; check this one off.

In my mind, the next three work in tandem. If I remember to a take a breath, it will induce a feeling of calm, which gives me permission to "be."

Breathe. Find my calm. Be. A gentle, reaffirming way to successfully navigate my day.

JANUARY 9

Compassion, kindness, and discriminating awareness are the essential teachings of Buddhism. One other important list I read every morning comes from several Buddhist spiritual teachers. I compiled ten tenets from the Zen practice, which seems to succinctly sum up their philosophy.

Today, I will

> Live without pretending.
> Carry a heart that never hates,
> A smile that never fades,
> A touch that never hurts.

Today, I will:

> Give before taking.
> Understand before deciding.
> Listen without defending.
> Think before speaking.
> Speak without offending.
> Love without depending.
> Remember *Namaste.*

If you think about these suggestions, they compose a positive, loving way to move through, not only our day, but our life.

JANUARY 10

Many would call what I do every morning meditation and in some ways, that is what my ritual is all about. Taking time for myself, quieting my mind, turning to my loving God for inspiration and guidance. After saying favorite prayers and reading encouraging reflections, I add one more element to my ritual. Centering Prayer. Some know it as Oneness Prayer.

I settle into a comfortable position, sit up straight, feet flat on the floor, hands relaxed in my lap. Close my eyes. Clear my mind. Gently let all those pesky thoughts float away. When thoughts, sounds, other distractions interfere, I focus on a sacred word or image. At the end of twenty minutes, I slowly and silently say a short prayer, gradually open my eyes and once again engage with the outside world.

My goal with Centering Prayer is to open my inner world to "hearing" God's message. This is not an easy practice. My mind refuses to shut down for more than a few seconds at a time. Even so, when I open my eyes, I am calm, serene, at peace. Occasionally, I have an insight about a vexing issue or a gentle feeling I need to do something or a soft nudge to contact a friend. My Inner Being, the One who knows me better than anyone, is gently encouraging me. It took me a long time to recognize the messages; I am still amazed I am offered this Divine guidance. Smarter, more spiritual people than I, assure me I am being guided by the Holy Spirit. I am learning to accept this gentle presence as the gift from the God She is. I am training myself to stop asking, "Why me, Lord?"

JANUARY 11

We have reached the 11th day of the new year. Our blank page is no longer blank; it has ten notations. Now what? Good question. Let's see what we have accomplished to date.

We have established a morning routine that works for each of us. Yours may have a few elements of mine, maybe not. That's okay. I only shared mine so you would have a place to start, proven actions to ponder. It is your ritual, not mine. It should fit you and your life. It will change over the years as your life and circumstances change. That is as it should be. You are growing, so your ritual should adapt to whoever and wherever you are on your personal path. Mine at 77 is definitely different than it was at 57. Don't even want to remember what it was when I was 37! Thank goodness, my unreliable memory keeps me blissfully in the dark about those long-ago times.

If you haven't already set it up, you are planning your special spot. You are deciding where it will fit, what you will include and how you will use it. And enjoying the anticipation of its soothing presence in your home, in your life.

We are learning what it means to be brave. We have discovered bravery is found in the little things, the minor actions, the quiet moments: Taking the first step. Smiling. Reaching out. Being who you are. We have made real progress. Celebrate!

JANUARY 12

Even though I have a good understanding of many words, I was surprised when I looked up the definition of faith and discovered it has several meanings. The online *Merriam Webster Dictionary* says it is: "fidelity to one's promises; belief, trust and loyalty to God and the doctrines of a traditional religion; firm belief in something for which there is no proof."

The meanings tell me there are subtle nuances to faith depending on its context, but no matter how it is applied, it requires *belief*. Whether referring to someone or something, if I have faith, I believe in whom it refers and for what it stands. If I believe my friend will be on time for our lunch date, I have faith he will keep his word. If I believe my boss will treat me fairly and with kindness, I have faith in her integrity. If I believe in myself, I have faith I will make good choices. If I believe in a Higher Power, I have faith He and She lives, even though I can't see, touch or physically interact. I believe my God will keep promises, answer prayers and lovingly guide me to the right decisions.

Faith requires knowledge of the subject and implies acceptance of the promises. It also requires me to keep my promises, behave with integrity and remind myself God loves me.

By the way: He loves you too.

JANUARY 13

One promise I made shortly after my beloved husband died: Show up for myself every day. What does that mean? I get out of bed, even on those days I would rather stay snuggled in my safe sleeping spot. As soon as my feet are on the floor, I make the bed. That way I am not tempted to crawl back in during the day. Why? Since I don't like looking at a rumpled bed, I will be forced to make it again. Waste of time and energy doing the same chore twice (or more), so I stay up.

Now that I am more or less awake and moving, I start my morning ritual. When I am finished, I break my fast, shower and dress. Most days I stay in and work on one of the various projects in progress. I derive satisfaction devoting time to organizations and causes I believe in. That includes writing columns for two newsletters, letters to pen pals, entries in my journal and essays for my memoir, researching and reading and composing these reflections. Other days, I venture into the outside world. Sometimes it is to complete errands essential to keeping my household operating efficiently; other times to meet a friend for shopping or antiquing; another choice is joining someone special for lunch or dinner. Occasionally, I wander around my community greeting people, fetching the mail, picking up a meal for later. My point: I *do* something every day.

Your day is different than mine, but the message is the same: Show up for yourself. Get up. Get dressed. Do something. If you follow this simple agenda, you will be productive *and* make a difference in your corner of the world. Isn't that what we all want? As the psychologist, Brene Brown said, "Courage starts with showing up and letting ourselves be seen."

JANUARY 14

Habits. We all have them. Some are good. Some not so good. According to people who study these things, it takes three months for a habit to become part of our daily life. From that premise, I figure it should take three months to overcome one. I've learned it depends on the habit.

When I decided to start using cloth bags while shopping, I needed to make it easy for myself. I stash the large bags in my trunk. The smaller ones that fold into themselves, I keep in a compartment on the dashboard. In the beginning, I frequently forgot to bring the bags into the store. When I realized I left them in the car, I stopped, parked the cart and fetched them. Adding a few of my quickly diminishing minutes to a chore I don't especially like, but now I remember the bags every time, like auto pilot. It took about three months to make the habit stick.

Smoking. A thirty-five-year habit I definitely needed to stop for reasons we all know. It took close to two years to break free, especially from the automatic ones. On the phone. With coffee. With wine. After dinner. Chatting with a friend. Used everything from gum to patches to hypnosis. And a lot of patience, persistence and prayer. I kept trying because I knew I was improving my health and lengthening my life with every cigarette I didn't smoke.

Two habits. One good. One not good. Making the good habit part of my routine took far less time than ridding myself of a destructive one. Point of the story. Try not to get yourself entangled in bad habits, but when you do, keep working to break free. You will feel better about yourself. You might even improve your health and lengthen your life. We can all use a self-esteem boost now and then.

JANUARY 15

Take action. When I read that admonition, I wondered what one woman could do, which would affect anything in our complicated culture. How could I make a difference? As we briefly discussed January 4th, small, quiet moments between two people change both and cause a ripple effect for the rest of their day. Being kind to ourselves makes a difference because we face the world refreshed and renewed and pay the kindness forward. As the politician, Dick Dirksen said, "A billion dollars here, a billion dollars there, pretty soon you're talking real money." So it is with kindness. One gesture here, one gesture there and pretty soon we have created a kinder corner of the world.

Getting into the habit of showing kindness to ourselves and everyone we encounter, leaves warm feelings wherever we go. A smile for the overworked cashier in the market makes her day a little brighter. A brief thank you note to a teacher tells him he is appreciated. A nod to a police officer or a firefighter lets them know we are grateful they keep us safe. A hug for a distressed child calms their fears. Loving attention for a friend struggling with what seems like an unsolvable problem gives them a safe place to talk through their issue.

All of these gestures are small in and of themselves, but when done habitually, with love, *will* have an impact *and* make a visible difference in your world. As Mother Theresa said, "Not all of us can do great things. But we can do small things with great love."

JANUARY 16

For hundreds of years, Native Americans have practiced a seemingly simple approach to living with and being respectful to each other and our fragile planet. Their traditions have long fascinated me.

> Listen to the wind, it talks.
> Listen to the silence, it speaks.
> Listen to the heart, it knows.

I don't remember where I read the prayer above, but it spoke to me, quietly, forcefully. Its message stays with me; I read it during my morning ritual. It reminds me there are many ways to listen for inspiration as we go about our days. The only requirement to hearing what we need to guide us through our hectic lives is to listen to all the sources speaking to us. To recognize when we are given a special message for our heart only. When we are being given our sacred daily duty, if we don't listen, hear, accept and carry out the tasks assigned by our Higher Power, those tasks won't get done. I don't know about you, but I don't want to face my Maker at the end of earthly life and try to explain why I haven't used the gifts given me.

How will you use your gifts today?

JANUARY 17

In Sanskrit, mantra means "sacred utterance." Its message provides clarity or guidance. They are a positive way to show ourselves gentle kindness. I have several, depending upon my particular need at the moment. My favorite is *One Day at a Time*. Regrets about yesterday are a waste of time; can't change what we already did. Concerns about tomorrow are a second waste of time; worry never prevented anything. All we have is today, now, this moment. We are not even promised this afternoon. This one helped me keep my sanity when my husband was dying and I couldn't fix him or change the situation. Hence, *One Day at a Time* became my go-to mantra. I use it these days because I finally acknowledged a few years ago, I have no idea how long I have on this earth and do not want to waste a precious second pondering and fretting about things I have no control over.

Accepting my memory isn't as reliable as it once was, my second mantra is *If it ain't wrote down, it ain't real and it ain't happin.* Lousy English, but it succinctly sums up how I manage to keep my life operating more or less efficiently. I enter everything either in my electronic calendar or add it to one of the innumerable lists and reminders on my phone (that mini-computer most of us carry). I admit it may take me a minute (or two or ten) to find what I am searching for, but eventually I locate it with a relieved sigh at my wise decision to write it down.

I suggest you devise one or two mantras to help keep your life on track, organized and reasonably calm. Permission to use mine until you find your own.

JANUARY 18

Affirmations are different than mantras. These short, positive phrases are a quick lift whenever we need a hug and no one is nearby to give us one. They come in handy when the world is encroaching and there is no lifeboat to take us away to a safe place. They form our own private cheering section when we need a shot of confidence, encouragement, love. No matter what is happening around us, we can silently say one or more of our special affirmations to help us navigate our restless inner world and unpredictable outer world. Until you come up with your own, you may use mine.

A few of my go-to affirmations in no particular order of importance or frequency of use:

> I am on time.
> I am ready.
> I am knowledgeable.
> I am confident.
> I am calm.
> I am composed.
> I am serene.
> I am special.
> I am worthy.
> I am content.
> I am blessed.
> I am loved.

JANUARY 19

I was raised in an ecumenical environment before the term was known and used by laypeople. Because of those early experiences, I am comfortable in any house of worship. During the years I was searching for a church home, I visited many congregations of various faith traditions. As a member of the interfaith committee in my current community, I visit different faith groups to learn about and pray with them.

One Friday evening, I joined our Jewish community for Shabbat, their weekly worship service. The reception I received was warm and welcoming. The group quickly made me feel comfortable. After several months of regular attendance, their matriarch said, "You are one of us." I was surprised and honored I had been accepted into this loving faith family. I teasingly call myself their token gentile.

Experiencing the wonder of their acceptance showed me one of the things I had been missing as I wandered from church to church: a permanent faith family where I was known, accepted and loved. During my searching, watching and listening, I confirmed humans are wired to believe in a Higher Power. One doesn't have to belong to a particular church, temple or mosque to worship God, however you know Him and Her, but having community acceptance and support makes a real difference in my life. Eventually, I rejoined the church of my youth partly because of the example of "my" Jewish community. I continue to attend Shabbat as my schedule permits and I am always welcomed with love and joy.

I learned God is everywhere. We just have to open our mind and heart to the possibilities.

JANUARY 20

What is a miracle? The *American College Dictionary* definition: "an event that appears inexplicable by the laws of nature." The key word: *appears*. As St. Augustine of Hippo said, "Miracles are not contrary to nature, but only contrary to what we know about nature." I tend toward the saint's definition because it more closely mirrors what I believe.

To me, miracles happen every day: the sun rises and sets; the ocean tide comes in and goes out; flowers bloom and trees bud; birds chatter cheerfully; a healthy baby is born; children laugh joyfully; flashes of intuition; a lightbulb moment; a genuine smile, a warm hug; love given, love reciprocated. All these everyday happenings are miracles. They are part of our life, yet we rarely take a moment to acknowledge their power and impact. Or whisper "thank you."

When I began to consciously notice the wonder and awe all around me, my attitude shifted. I am no longer always caught up in what I think I need. I tell myself to appreciate what I already have. To take time to really see, hear, feel and experience the miracles and magic in the world. To stop and smell the roses that have always been on my path. I didn't pay attention to them before. Now I do. It changed my perception. It calmed my inner life.

What will you see, hear, feel and appreciate today?

JANUARY 21

We have been practicing a morning ritual for sixteen days. It is time to develop an evening routine. Mine is a lot more flexible than the one in the morning. It depends on how I spent my day and what intake I may be trying to process or ignore. Being an introvert, I need more quiet, alone time than most and many days I only find it after the sun goes down. There are evenings I just shut off the world; I don't think about anything more complicated than what to have for dinner. Many days, after eating and tidying up the kitchen, I plop (not sit, plop) in one of my favorite chairs. I have two: one in my special space in the study and one in the living room. I am not much of a television watcher, but occasionally I turn it on; sometimes I may even pay attention to the program. How do I spend my downtime? I read for fun. Or write in my journal. Or play solitaire on my tablet. I find coloring apps very relaxing. I may call a friend. I may sit and stare into the void. I let my body and my mind decide what they need and follow their lead.

The only things I do every night is take my medications, brush my teeth and make sure the door to the apartment is locked. My body prepares for sleep between 10:00pm and midnight. Sometimes I am unable to shut my mind off and I am up until 2:00am or later. I go to bed when I am sleepy, not when I am tired. Big difference. Most nights I am tired by ten or so, but not sleepy. I have learned there is no point going to bed until my eyes are so droopy, I can't keep them open. If I do, I end up staring at the revolving ceiling fan, hoping it will hypnotize me into a restful state. It never does. Some nights I toss and turn. When that happens, I get up and read or meditate. Eventually my tired body wins the battle with my active mind. And I sleep.

Most sleep experts would tell you I really have no bedtime routine. I disagree. What I do may not be prescribed in the official sleep manual, but it works for me. You have to find what works for you. What helps you turn off the day and prepare for the necessity of restorative sleep? Listen to your body and pay attention to your mind; do whatever they tell you; they know best.

Sweet dreams.

JANUARY 22

I have never understood why it seems we must undergo pain in order to evolve emotionally. I had experienced the phenomenon growing up, but in college I began to study and sort of understand.

The concept of life lessons was a hot topic, especially during lively discussions in the student union. (I learned as much or more from these conversations as I did in the classroom.) Details are sketchy. What I do recall is our brain requires stimulation to grasp complicated issues. Apparently, most of us learn more from negative experiences than positive ones. At 77, I still don't understand why. I just sigh and accept.

Lessons come to us in many ways. Consequences from making good and not so good decisions. Helping a friend navigate a scary medical diagnosis or an unstable relationship. Silently observing society grapple with challenging issues. The important thing is to learn from these situations. Sometimes what to do. Sometimes what not to do. Just pay attention. Decide what is relevant for us and integrate the lesson into our interactions with others, with the world, with ourselves. It isn't easy, but it is essential in order to grow into the person we are meant to be.

JANUARY 23

Do I want to be a victim or a survivor? Tough question with, at first glance, an obvious answer. Most of us would say, unequivocally, "Survivor!" But is it really that simple? As we all know, you have to experience the lows to appreciate the highs; it is the same with moving from victim to survivor. How can we say we are a survivor if we have never had to live with and navigate through a challenging time in our life?

From the outside, I had a happy childhood and wonderful young adult years. Parents who stayed together through the rough times. Educated at one of the best girls' private prep schools in the state. The finances to obtain a college degree with no student loans. Marriage to a bright, ambitious man. Two healthy children. Yet if we pull back the privacy curtain in both houses, we see alcohol addiction, frequent fighting, unstable relationships. The first thirty-two years of my life were chaotic, unpredictable and sometimes downright scary.

When I finally found the courage to remove my girls and me from the toxic environment in which we were living, I was faced with raising two tweens on my own with limited financial resources. But I found ways to make it work for us. Was it easy? Heavens no! I lived through many uncertain days and dark nights. But with my unwavering faith and eventually the support, encouragement and unconditional love of a good man in a second marriage, I made it. Even though my soulmate died several years ago, he continues to walk with me, in my mind, my heart, my soul.

I am a survivor because as the British statesman, Winston Churchill said, "If you're going through hell, keep going." I kept going. So can you.

JANUARY 24

Never give up on someone, especially you. As it says in the Talmud, "Such is the way of creation: first comes darkness, then light." As I told you yesterday, I am a survivor. Why? Two immutable reasons: my faith in God's unconditional love and never giving up on me.

I am eternally grateful to a lot of people who helped and encouraged me on the rocky road to the me I am today. And I like me. I am comfortable in my skin, extra pounds, wrinkles, eccentricities and all. Am I perfect? Good grief, no! After prayerful thought, I decided not only will I never be perfect, but while I keep striving for that pinnacle, I don't really want to get there. Perfection is God's domain. I just want to be the best me I can be. When I inevitably mess up, I not so jokingly say, "If I ever get my act together, watch out world!" I say it because I know I won't pull it off. There is always room for improvement.

A relevant incident many years ago stays in the back of my mind. One of my kids messed up. After discussing how to learn from and avoid repeating the infraction, I apologized for not being a better role model. As young people frequently do, he said something, which caused me to pause and contemplate. "Why do you always think everything is your fault? It isn't you know." I was taken aback by his wise words. I have never forgotten his astute observation. I am passing it along to you.

JANUARY 25

As I have hinted, I am my own worst critic. I am better than I used to be, but too often I still try to take responsibility for someone else's improper behavior, mean comment or hurtful actions. Somehow it must be my fault. I wasn't a good role model. I didn't say the right things. I didn't show enough love.

Gradually, I have come to recognize I do not have control over anyone except myself. I am working on accepting that truism. It is a mighty struggle. As far back as I can remember, I have been the buffer, the mediator, the grown-up in the room. As a child, when my parents argued, each looked to me as a reason to stay together. Among my friends, I was the one who listened to both sides and often cast the deciding vote. In my professional life, I was assigned to create the action plan to ensure the project was completed on time within budget.

It became second nature to take on the responsibilities for making my corner of the world neat and tidy, better. The longer I carried the burden, the heavier the load became. Eventually, I couldn't separate what was mine and what wasn't. Trying to control everyone and everything took a toll mentally and physically. I developed serious digestive problems, suffered migraine headaches and frequently fell into deep depressions, which I refer to as "the black pit."

With the help of pleading prayers, loving friends and many productive sessions with mental health professionals, I finally faced my demons. It was not easy and it was a painful process, but I am on the mend. As with any addiction, and the need to control my world is indeed an addiction, I am in recovery. It is an everyday battle.

Whatever your demons, and we all have them, stop, take inventory, ask for Divine and human help. Be kind to yourself as you walk the road to recovery. As with anything worthwhile, it is a life-long journey, not a brief weekend jaunt.

JANUARY 26

The last few days, we have been looking at how we view essential parts of us. Who we are. How we define ourselves. We have asked difficult questions about areas we usually don't visit. We avoid them because they can be confusing, hurtful, even scary. But in order to grow emotionally and spiritually, we need to confront our demons, however they manifest themselves. Some call this process introspection. Some contemplation. Many know it as "the dark night of the soul." Whatever label you use, please accept the pain, confusion and uncertainty are worth it. When you emerge from this essential stage of growth, and you will emerge, you will be stronger, more content, wiser.

Unfortunately, no one can predict how long you will walk this part of your journey. It is different for each of us. I am not going to suggest you will enjoy the process, but you will have critical insights into who you are now and learn ways to become who your God created you to be. You will be closer to your Higher Power.

Definitely a goal worth reaching for, no matter the pitfalls and side trips along the way.

JANUARY 27

As a Christian who honors and appreciates my Jewish heritage, I decided I should learn a bit about the third belief of the Abrahamic faith traditions. Islam is misunderstood by many. It is a theistic faith. Its name is an Arabic word meaning surrender, submission, commitment, peace. Allah is the Arabic word for God; it is neither masculine nor feminine. Just knowing this much about Islam increases my understanding of the faith and tells me its basic tenets are much the same as Christianity and Judaism. We may worship in different ways and some of our beliefs differ, but it is the same God we love, honor and try to obey. So why should I dismiss Islam out of fear because of a few adherents who misrepresent and misuse it?

In my quest to learn about and understand my image of God, I strive to know more about other faith traditions and spiritual philosophies. It puts my belief in perspective. It reinforces there is only one God. There are just a lot of roads to reach Him and Her. It helps me overcome my fear of the "other." It encourages me to accept the marvelous diversity God created and recognize how very tiny my role is in the grand scheme of the universe and eternity. More importantly, knowledge of God in all the iterations leads me to love and appreciate my image of Him and Her so much more.

Learning about the Divine is always positive. I plan to continue my pursuit of knowledge until I take my final breath. Besides, I'm curious about the how and why of the world and its flora and fauna, especially humans and their motivation for good and evil. Helps me understand me too, scary as that may be.

JANUARY 28

Nirvana, as defined by the Buddhist teacher, Thubten Chodron, is a "state beyond death and rebirth." For those who believe in reincarnation, it is a straightforward definition. For those who believe in eternal life with a Higher Power, it carries a different connotation.

When I read the Buddhist word, my Abrahamic mind immediately translated Nirvana as the "state after earthy death that brings me into God's presence forever." I am still working on understanding what "forever" actually means. Since theologians and scientists are debating the concept, I will leave it to more learned minds than mine to figure that one out. Until they do, I trust if I live my life loving God and all His creations, caring for our earthly home and sharing when and how I am able, I will be granted the honor of a home with God forever. Simple, childlike understanding, but it comforts me when I am having grownup doubts about my purpose in life and if I am doing what my Creator expects me to do. I don't know about you, but a childlike faith is a comfortable blankie I use to help me function in the crazy world around me. My blankie is soft and blue. What color is yours?

As it says in Matthew 18:3, "Unless you change and become like little children, you will never enter the Kingdom of heaven."

JANUARY 29

I read somewhere until a person's faith is tested, he or she has not matured in their belief system. For me, in order to grow in my faith, it is necessary to question, to listen, to understand, to fully embrace. Our faith is always evolving as we walk our path, no matter its direction, its obstacles or how we view its ultimate destination. My journey is different than yours. I am sharing mine to encourage you to reflect on yours. If we don't know where we are going, how do we know which path to take to get there? How will we know we have arrived?

Over the years, I have gained wisdom from reading books and essays by theologians, ministers, priests, philosophers, psychologists, scientists, poets and everyday people with a compelling story to share. I have been privileged to have many enlightening dialogues with thoughtful people of both eastern and western faith traditions who were willing to share their experiences. I have questioned. I have listened. I have studied. I have absorbed. Some concepts I made my own. Some I have been living all my life and wasn't aware of it. Some I respectfully rejected for various reasons. I slowly came to realize the basic tenants of most faith traditions and spiritual philosophies have much in common: love and honor your Higher Power, respect and be kind to all creatures, live a life of service, care for the earth. How these guidelines are practiced may vary, but every commandment of most traditions flows from one of these universal tenets.

The purpose of this daybook is not to convert you to any particular religion, faith tradition or philosophy. My goal is to present different viewpoints for you to consider. Take some, all or none, but at least think about the ideas and concepts. I firmly believe everyone needs a strong moral and ethical foundation on which to base their choices, their treatment of each other, their way of life.

JANUARY 30

Faith is the theme for January. Faith in a Higher Power. Faith in ourselves. We opened our minds and hearts in an effort to invite more positive energy into our lives and to discard the negative.

Our goal for each day is to strive to become a better me than I was the day before.

Questions to Consider:

- Do we accept a Higher Power working in our life? Why? Why not?
- Does our morning ritual start the day with positive feelings? Does our evening routine end the day gently?
- What have I made my own? What do I plan to carry into February? Into the rest of my life?

GRATITUDE ENTRY: I am grateful I am reading this book. It is providing realistic, doable actions to help me be a better me.

Reader: Add at least one thing you are grateful for as a result of reading, and contemplating the January reflections.

JANUARY 31

God, grant me the serenity to accept the people I cannot change, the courage to change the one I can and the wisdom to know it is me.

I don't remember where I read this version of the Serenity Prayer, but I immediately added it to my morning prayers. It describes one of the major goals in my life. When added to my daily query, "What will I be brave about today?" it causes me to pause and reflect on the messages I am sending to myself. Both focus on me and what I can do. Not the outside world. Not other people. Me, myself and I. It reminds me the only person I can control is me, my thoughts, my behavior, my reaction to whatever I encounter on my personal path. Everything I do, or don't do, summed up neatly in thirty-five, easy-to-remember words.

FEBRUARY

Belief

"Knowing others is knowledge.
Knowing yourself is wisdom."

Lao Tzu

FEBRUARY 1

What we believe to be true forms the foundation of our character. How we perceive those beliefs is the basis of our personal ethics. When the two align, we are in harmony within ourselves. We grow into who we were created to be. When they are out of alignment, chaos reigns and we are unable to be all we were meant to be; unable to complete the Divine assignments which are entrusted to us. This state frequently results in uncertainty and confusion; our life seems unmanageable, out of sorts. Misalignment can also lead to physical and mental health issues, both of which will escalate if we don't have, and live by, a set of beliefs.

The first step in preventing misalignment is to identify, define and understand just exactly *what* we believe. If we have no guidelines, how can we know if we are behaving appropriately in any area of our life. Just as when we instruct children in acceptable behavior, so too we as adults need a set of instructions, a belief system.

Many find their foundation within a faith tradition. Others in spiritual philosophies. Some from the hard lessons taught by life. Most of us combine parts of all three, even if we don't realize we are. The important message is to create a belief system we accept and follow.

Most of us continue to learn all our lives. At 77, I am still questioning, absorbing, growing. I am not a finished product and don't expect to be until I take my final breath. You won't be either.

FEBRUARY 2

Humans are wired to believe in a Higher Power. Ancient civilizations worshipped entities they found mysterious, frightening, unknowable. The sun. The moon. Water. Mythical beasts conjured out of fear. As humanoids developed a thinking, reasoning brain, cultural beliefs gradually became more sophisticated. I am not going to attempt an historical time-line; suffice to say the idea of a Higher Power came to be part of our essential human needs. As it says in the *Fundamentals of the Torah*, "The foundation of all foundations, and the pillar of all wisdom, is to know there is a First Existence."

Today we call our Supreme Being Adonai, God, Jesus, Allah, Buddha, and many other names. We worship in diverse ways in many places: temple, mosque, church. Some of these structures are simple, others are grand, some are not buildings, but forests and fields. The point is humans have an ingrained need for a Higher Power to look to, follow and worship. We also find it handy to blame life's gifts and challenges on an entity "up there" somewhere in a different dimension. After all, successes and misfortunes can't possibly be the results of anything *we* did or didn't do, said or didn't say. No, of course not.

So, at the top of our list of beliefs is God, whatever you call Him and/or Her and however and wherever you worship your Deity.

FEBRUARY 3

Many of us shy away from discussing, or even admitting, we believe in the supernatural, while others embrace the concept wholeheartedly. Having experienced visits from my dad and my husband after they passed into eternal life, I am firmly in the latter camp. Those of you who believe the entire idea is absurd, out there in woo-woo world, stay with me please. At least be willing to listen and consider my understanding of the phenomenon.

As a child, I was taught there are angels, each group has a specific divine job. God assigned one to be with me while I was nestled safely in my mother's womb. This guardian will walk with me all the days of my earthly life. While I am fuzzy what happens after my earthly pilgrimage is done and I move to my eternal reward, I am comforted knowing I have her with me now. When I was young, I remember vaguely thinking she would keep me out of trouble and would literally catch me if I was falling. As I learned about free will and taking responsibility for my actions, my thoughts about my angel gradually faded into the background. Occasionally, I would remember and say a quick prayer to let her know I hadn't really forgotten her. Today I admit I took her presence for granted. Sorry, Sarah (the name I gave her), I failed to appreciate you as the gift from God you are.

As I learned more about the Divine Plan listening to the biblical passages on Sunday and studying sacred scripture, I was introduced to other angels, whose mission was to bring messages from God to we humans. Gradually, I began to understand and accept their presence and purpose. They took their proper place in my belief system. They are an integral part of my Creator's promise to be with everyone always. That thought has been a comfort many times over the years.

FEBRUARY 4

Belief in authority is an important element in our sense of safety, although the shenanigans of the last few years have sorely tested us. Assigning people, the role and responsibility to make laws, enforce them and interpret them when people disagree, creates a more or less stable, predictable order in our public and private world. When that stabilizing force goes awry, our feelings of safety and security are threatened.

When our world becomes unmanageable and frightening, we react in various ways. Many people pull into themselves, keep quiet and only venture into the outside world when absolutely necessary. Some take to the streets in peaceful demonstrations. Others react in frustrated violence and destruction. There are those who organize and work within the system to affect needed changes, which will hopefully benefit everyone.

My goal is not to judge; neither should yours be. None of us has the right or responsibility. Judgement is God's domain. Our goal should be to do what helps us, our family, friends and neighbors live in a peaceful, loving way with good will in our heart for everyone. Be the change you want to see in the world or as Gandhi actually said, "As man changes his own nature, so does the attitude of the world change toward him."

FEBRUARY 5

I believe in the strength of blood kin, family by choice and close friends. If we stand together most problems can be solved before they become seemingly unmanageable catastrophes. Whether we are addressing personal grievances between two people or major challenges which require community cooperation, we need to stay calm and listen more than we talk to find solutions everyone can abide by and live with.

Minor issues can usually be addressed by a sincere conversation, attention to the needs of each person and a willingness to compromise. Bigger challenges require more complicated solutions. They too can be solved by discussing and agreeing on reasonable, workable steps to changing and improving the situation. Are either of these conversations easy? No, they are not. But if we want to avoid unnecessary confrontations and live in a peaceful environment, it is imperative we adopt some form of these approaches appropriate to the group and the situation.

FEBRUARY 6

In order to successfully function in society, it is necessary for business and social colleagues, strangers on the street and anyone we encounter adhere to similar standards of behavior. They don't have to be carbon copies of our beliefs, and most likely won't be, but they do need to complement each other. Through the years, all cultures develop acceptable ways of interacting. These behaviors keep society running reasonably smoothly and help avoid unnecessary conflict. They also make our world a much nicer place to be.

A Pollyanna view? Maybe. But I honestly believe we humans are capable of respecting each other's humanity. If we make it a major mission in life to find the good in everyone, we will. If we expect the bad, we will find it. A valuable lesson I learned long ago: No one is all good or all bad, but a bit of both. What we unconsciously decide to "see" and respond to is what determines how we treat the people with whom we interact. If I look for, expect to find and only respond to the good, it makes my world better. It also makes the world around me better for everyone else. A kinder place. A peaceful place. If only for a moment. For me, that moment is worth searching for the good, the humanity in everyone.

FEBRUARY 7

We all inhabit the same universe. Live on the same planet. Interact with Mother Nature. What we believe our responsibilities are to each determines how we care for, or don't, this place called earth. If we respect our fragile ecosphere and accept all parts work in harmony, we will work to not do anything to harm our environment. We will learn and practice ways to keep the air, water and land clean and healthy. We won't shrug off preservation of our natural resources, caring for our flora and fauna. We will employ scientifically proven methods of growing and harvesting food sources. We will carefully protect and propagate animals, fish and birds to prevent over population and over hunting.

All parts of creation are interwoven, each dependent on the other. They are God's gifts for man to use, not abuse. We must learn to appreciate the necessity and the beauty of every animal, fish, bird and plant with which we share the earth. One is not more important than the other. Each has a place and a function.

As the highest form of earthly creation, it is humans' responsibility to care for all other forms of nature.

How are you doing your part?

FEBRUARY 8

In order to successfully function in the world, we need to believe in ourselves and respect what we each have to offer. I am not advocating a selfish, arrogant, it is-all-about-me view. I am talking about a realistic appreciation of our strengths and weaknesses and what each of us brings to the table of life. My experiences are different than yours. Which means we all have a unique perspective on our society and everyone and everything in it. I learn from you. You learn from me. Knowledge is not diminished when shared, it grows exponentially.

In past generations, people seemed to know that maxim and worked together to accomplish whatever needed to be done. In most cases, there was no individual praise or blame because everyone took responsibility for their particular part. Barn raisings come to mind. Community planting and harvesting collaboratives. Watching whichever children were around with the understanding whatever adult present was in charge, their word was law for all the kids.

When we truly live in community, the strengths of the individuals combine to make a stronger, more effective whole. No one is lost.

Everyone is valued. What a marvelous goal for us all to reach for and work toward.

FEBRUARY 9

Humility is an attitude most of us don't give much, if any, thought to. It is usually not on our radar screen. Until someone or something brings our ego to an uncomfortable crash. Rarely is it a grand public humiliation. What usually happens is a small, private realization we are not the center of the universe...anyone's universe. It doesn't matter how we are forced to confront unrealistic thoughts about ourselves. What matters is how we react. What lesson we learn. How we change our view of me, myself and I.

Pride, the granddaddy of most of what is wrong in the world and the root of all human failings, is the opposite of humility. Bold statement, I know. But if we think for a moment, we know it is also a true statement. The only person I have control over is me. The only actions I can control are my own. The moment I forget or ignore that reality, trouble is brewing. My world becomes more frustrating and unmanageable. It doesn't take long for my life to spin out of even my control. I am forced to stop, take stock, change my behavior and alter my reaction to the situation. On the way, make amends to whomever I may have used, abused or offended. Humility returns because of a dose of reality and its very real, unavoidable consequences.

FEBRUARY 10

A close friend controls his pride by loudly announcing his greatest virtue is his humility. He says it in jest, but he really uses the statement to remind himself he is not in control of anything or anyone, sometimes not even himself. It is his unique way of working to keep himself humble. He has a lot of which to be proud, but he makes sure to give the real credit for his accomplishments to the Divine Spirit. He becomes a living example of humility and doesn't even know he is.

Another close friend is humility personified. He too has much of which to be proud. He loves his wife without restrictions or reservations. He is a supportive father, uncle, grandfather and great grandfather. A thoughtful friend. He is quiet and unassuming. He doesn't talk much, but when he does offer an observation, it is measured and well thought out. He doesn't want or seek the spotlight. His is a different example of humility.

When I am in their company, I am in awe of both men. They are almost opposite in personality and their way of interacting with the world, but both show me what humility is. Both love unconditionally. Both exude joy, no matter what may be happening in their private part of the world. I am a better person because they are members of my family by choice. I adopted them as the brothers of my heart. I hold them close. I thank God every day for the gift of these two special men.

FEBRUARY 11

The Abrahamic faith traditions each have a set of rules handed down through the Torah, the Christian Bible and the Koran. You should learn, understand and live by these principles. If you don't have a set of rules by which you live and operate in the world, your life will be total chaos. You will have no sense of right and wrong. You will have no clue how to treat other people. Your world will be out of sync with reality. If you want to crash through life causing mayhem and dissention, leaving pain and destruction in your wake, then skip this reflection. In fact, stop reading this book altogether. But if you want to be a kinder, gentler person, think about the guidelines of your belief system, decide how you can adopt them as your set of rules. Adhering to your belief system's guidelines will improve your life and the world around you.

This is another area in which honesty plays a huge part, honesty with yourself. It doesn't matter what age and stage you may be in, it is never too late to develop better ways to live, to treat others, to treat yourself. Surprised I added the last one? I learned the hard way, if I don't respect myself and treat me with love, I am unable to treat anyone else with love and respect. If I don't understand I am human and mess up all the time, I can't extend the same courtesy to others. What we feel inside is what we show outside. It is how we relate to everyone and everything in our world. Let me repeat that: If we don't love and respect ourselves, treat ourselves with kindness and patience, we are unable to offer this humane treatment to others. Learn to be your own best friend and you will radiate confidence and spread happiness. You will go a long way in creating a kinder, gentler world for everyone. Now isn't that a grand goal.

FEBRUARY 12

Honesty is the foundation for my personal ethics. My acceptance of this fact began with my dad's expectation of my behavior. We were very close; he was my best friend and biggest booster. The only behavior he absolutely demanded was to always tell the truth, no matter what. Because I never wanted to disappoint daddy about anything, I took that promise very seriously. I rarely lie to anyone about anything. If I tell you something, you can take it to the bank, as the old saying goes. It's that simple. In my eighth decade, I still live by that rule.

Is it always easy? No, it isn't. But being honest has become a large part of who I am. If I give my word, I will go beyond reason to make sure I follow through. I would rather say, "I can't tell you," then lie or make up a plausible story. Plus, I have learned over the years, it is so much easier to remember what I told you and you and you if it is always the truth. My memory is stretched enough without having to remember whom I've told what.

Wouldn't life be so much easier and work so much smoother if we all followed my dad's rule? Fewer disagreements. Less strife. Fewer angry confrontations. More acceptance. A more respectful society. More love in the world. All because everyone of us always tells the truth. An idea to ponder.

FEBRUARY 13

Honesty is about more than always telling the truth. It includes not stealing: a possession, an idea, or damaging a reputation. It is treating everyone with respect, even people we don't like. It is honoring a commitment. It is a huge part of living an ethical life. Giving someone your word, and sticking to it, is the foundation upon which trust is formed, nurtured and treasured. And trust is the backbone of every relationship: personal, business, social.

Honesty has guided me all my life. It has kept me from hurting others as well as myself. It's freeing. I don't have to worry if people believe me or take me at my word or wonder what my ulterior motive is. If I conduct myself with honesty in all my interactions, people want to associate with me. People will want to be around me because they feel valued and respected. Most important, it's the right thing to do, the right way to live, the right way to treat people.

Integrity is critical to living a life with a well-defined set of values. Integrity is knowing you did the right thing every day, in every situation, no matter what. It's knowing you can look in the mirror at the end of the day, and not only like, but respect, the person staring back at you. If you don't respect yourself, you will be lost in our fractious world. You need one person you can rely on to always tell the truth, always be honest; the person you can't hide from. You.

FEBRUARY 14

St. Valentine's Day. Some cynics claim this day was devised by the greeting card companies to sell cards, the candy companies to sell chocolate, the florists to sell roses. While these enterprises do make a handsome profit, we don't have to buy into the hype and promotion. (Pun intended.) There is a better way to celebrate this day of love.

Let's commit to being aware of our words and how we use them. Words are powerful tools. They can lift up. They can put down. Once said, they cannot be unsaid. Once read, they cannot be unseen. Maybe because I use words to share thoughts and ideas as a columnist and feature writer for two newsletters, essays for a memoir and verbal messages for a senior population, and edit other writers' words, I am acutely aware of their reach, their power.

One of my favorite parables is the pebbles in the water; we will never know how far the waves go and whom they touch. Not only does it apply to our actions, but in some ways, it applies even more to our words. As Maya Angelou said, "I've learned that people will forget what you said, people will forget what you did, but people will never forget how you made them feel." We all carry the meaning of the message with us, even if we don't remember the actual words or deeds. In our minds, in our hearts, we incorporate both positive and negative impressions into our sense of self and carry those beliefs forever. Negative ones are the hardest to give up.

While I strive to always tell the truth, I also strive to be the bearer of uplifting messages. I want people to feel better when we part, whether in person or on paper. Not to make me feel better, because I have no way of knowing how my words affect anyone, none of us do. I choose words to offer hope to the reader and the listener, to give them food for thought and maybe help them be a bit better than they were before they read the words or listened to the presentation. It is a goal we can all work to achieve, no matter how small or large our audience. I firmly believe this one change in our interactions with others will spread love in our corner of the world. What an uplifting idea.

FEBRUARY 15

Forgiveness. This concept took me a long time to truly understand and even longer to embrace and practice. *The American Heritage College Dictionary* says to forgive is to "to excuse for a fault or offense; pardon; to renounce anger or resentment against." Forgiveness is "the act of forgiving." Forgiving is "providing for an error or shortcomings." The dictionary gives multiple examples of what, why and how to forgive. I was surprised when I read all the entries. I knew it was a powerful concept, but had no clue how many ways to view it. It made it even more important to understand what the word really means. How we can apply it in our lives.

The general message in all the definitions is to pardon the offender. They tell us in order to forgive, we need to "excuse, renounce, avoid resentment." Wow. A lot to swallow. When someone hurts us, it is a challenge to do any of those things. The larger the hurt, the harder it is to forgive, but also the bigger the reason to pardon, the more relief we will feel. Seems counterintuitive, but it is how forgiveness works.

More importantly perhaps, please note the definitions do *not* say we need to forget. I have learned to excuse unacceptable behavior, without having to condone it. For the most part, I can renounce my anger and learn to let go of the resentment for being treated in a hurtful, disrespectful manner. What I have never been able to do is forget. With some of the hurts I believe I would feel better if I *could* forget. Time does soften the sting, but scars remain. Sometimes it doesn't take much to rip the wound open, which means I have learned to recognize the warning signs. I have decided the inability to forget is my psyche's way of helping me avoid getting into similar situations. If I do, I have hard-learned lessons to call on to help me deal with and remove myself from the potentially harmful encounter. When I listen to my cautionary Inner Voice, that is exactly what I do. I think of it as self-preservation. With a little practice, you can learn to do the same.

FEBRUARY 16

As the motivational speaker, Tony Gaskins, poignantly tells us, "I can't let my forgiveness become foolishness." That statement stopped me. I thought I had figured out and accepted what forgiveness means, when and why I should apply it and its potential personal benefits. Now this suggestion comes along and causes me to take a second look.

What does he mean? How does forgiveness morph into foolishness? Even scripture says, "to turn the other cheek." After contemplating this idea, I decided one way it happens is when forgiving the same action over and over is actually enabling the person to continue destructive behavior. When a loved one uses my forgiveness to continue taking drugs, using alcohol, stealing to support the habit, abusing me and others, my forgiving over and over is actually harmful. Harmful to me. Harmful to society.

Harmful to the person who uses it to continue unacceptable, hurtful behavior.

Remember, forgiving does not mean condoning. It does not give absolution. It does not give permission to ignore the behavior, especially when it continues to cause hurt and destruction. Depending on the offensive behavior, there are steps we can take to help the person help themselves overcome, change and learn from the consequences of their actions. This is the loving response to forgiving. Show understanding. Show compassion. Lead them to the help they need to start over. Loving the offender in spite of the severity and frequency of the offense says we remember, "To err is human, to forgive is Divine." We are calling our Inner Spirit to forgive. To me, this response translates to true forgiveness.

FEBRUARY 17

I'm sorry. Two words, yet so very difficult for many people to think, let alone say out loud. There are people who say it even when they were not responsible for the incident. Some say it when they don't really mean it. Why do you suppose this seemingly simple statement is so complicated, so infused with subtle meanings and when offered, often sends a mixed message?

I used to be the one who apologized even when I didn't do or say anything that warranted an apology. My reason is easy to explain: I operated under the assumption I was in control of my world, therefore responsible for everything that went wrong; please note: not right, only wrong. My stepson brought the tendency to my attention. Since his astute observation, I am conscious when I start to say it and stop myself...most of the time.

Some apologize when they don't really mean it because it is easier to accept responsibility than to talk through the issue and resolve whatever caused the conflict in the first place. It seems to put the person in a position of control. Many times, it appears to put the other person "in his proper place" in our mind. An apology almost always brings the conversation to an end.

None of these rationalizations come close to understanding the true reason for an apology. We say, "I'm sorry" because we recognize and accept responsibility for causing pain and sometimes harm to a fellow human being. We acknowledge we messed up. We want to make amends for our behavior. We can't change what we said or did, but can admit our part in the interaction was inappropriate and/or wrong. We take responsibility for our actions. A concept our fractious world would do well to practice more than we do.

FEBRUARY 18

Willingness to take chances, to risk moving into unknown territory is scary. Better the devil you know, than the one you haven't met yet. The problem with that approach is we never learn anything new about the world, about our neighbors, about ourselves. We stay stuck in our safe cocoon. As an introvert, I am intimately familiar and altogether comfortable with that attitude. As I have gotten older, I am better and more willing to delve into the unknown than I used to be. It is almost as if I unconsciously decided to throw caution to the wind because I finally realized, I don't give a hoot what anyone thinks of me. As long as I treat people with respect and kindness and don't step on anyone else's rights, I am free to be me. A ten-ton weight came off my shoulders when I adopted this approach to being me with all my faults, idiosyncrasies and eccentricities and living a life that makes sense for me.

But what does it actually mean? A prime example is my absolute terror of flying. I have not been on a plane in twenty-five plus years. I have claustrophobia and the thought of being trapped in a metal tube 30,000 miles above terra firma is more than I am willing to attempt. The other part is trusting pilots I do not know to keep me safe going up and coming down. I admit, it is also a bit of a control issue. I am working to overcome my irrational fear. See I know it is irrational, but I still haven't consented to boarding a metal tube. I am working on it, but have no idea if I will ever be successful letting go of my fear and turning over control.

Because of my unwillingness to get on a plane, I am limiting myself. I am missing adventures and experiences, which would enhance my life and encourage me to grow. Now I just have to figure out how to make myself do what I know I should. Maybe someday...

FEBRUARY 19

I recently discovered the prophets and how influential they have been through the ages. Most people automatically think of ancient religious prophets when they hear the word. They certainly have their place in history and influenced the path civilization meandered down through the millennia. So too the stoics and philosophers. Many of the beliefs we hold dear came from these sources. But have you stopped to consider, there are prophets in our midst? I didn't until I began to study and understand the motivations, messages and meanings of the early wise men and women.

One important caveat to remember: Prophets do not predict the future. Their assignment is to tell us God's truth. To help us understand His divine message.

Have you ever read a book or heard a speech, which profoundly changed your view of some belief you thought was cast in concrete? I have. I am not suggesting all authors and speakers are prophets, but I have come to believe if someone shares something to make me stop, think and question a long-held concept, those words were meant to touch me, if no one else. Does that make the person a prophet? Not necessarily, but as a writer and speaker, I believe if what I say and write affects even one person, my words and the effort to string them together in a sensible manner, were worth all the time and thought used to produce them.

Using this definition, we are all prophets to some degree. How we live our life. How we interact with others. What we say and share with love. All these actions project ways of being, ways of relating to our fellow humans. We can show love and joy. Or we can show distain and disrespect. It is our choice which kind of prophet we want to be.

FEBRUARY 20

Who are your prophets? At the end of a week reading reflections on prophets, this question popped into my mind. It startled me because, like most people in and of the 21st century, I don't think of anyone in those terms. Prophets are from long-ago yesterdays; they do not live in my time and my place. Yet as I suggested in our last reflection, as caring, thinking people, we are all prophets in one way or another.

Examining this question, I realized I have known several prophets who influenced me. At the time, I didn't view them in that light, but they surely were, at least in my personal environment. Looking back, the first was my beloved grandmother, not so much from what she said, but how she related to the world. She really didn't care what others thought of her. She quietly went about her days being kind, helping when she could and always encouraging those around her. And enjoying her evening martini. She passed her way of living to my mom (her choice was scotch), who passed it to me (mine is red wine); I have tried to pass it to my children and grandchildren. Isn't that one of the responsibilities of a prophet? To live a life worth emulating, worth passing on and then making sure they do?

There were two prophets on my first job out of college, Leona and Ben. In their unique ways, these colleagues showed me how to function in the business world. Their reasoning was, "ask for forgiveness rather than permission." In other words, take ownership and run with it. Since I had already learned to admit when I messed up, adopting their approach as well, meant I couldn't blame the world when life spun out of control. I was the one responsible for me, my reactions and my behavior. Powerful lesson for both my professional and personal life.

FEBRUARY 21

Are prophets perfect? Of course not; they are human. But their defining characteristics are the foundation by which we can try to walk a more perfect path: Love God. Love others as God loves us. All other instructions flow from these two. Most faith traditions and spiritual philosophies embrace a similar tenet as the basis for their conduct.

Another defining trait of prophets is they speak truth to those in power and they never give up or back down, no matter what the power structure says about or inflicts upon them. They are stubborn in their beliefs and share them with courage. Some by their behavior. Some proclaim the truth from the pulpit or podium. Some in the written word in essays and books. No matter the communication method, they never stop sharing, sometimes loudly, even very loudly.

Not long ago, I discovered three prophets had come into my life quietly, when I wasn't paying attention. These gentle souls gradually opened my mind, my heart and my soul to understanding what belief in my God really means and how I should live my life to honor Him and Her. All three encouraged me to listen for and pay attention to my Inner Spirit and Her messages. Besides being extraordinarily loving and accepting, they tell me in no uncertain terms when I stray from my appointed, God-given duties and ignore what I know to be true. They are living examples of God's presence in our turbulent, unpredictable world.

One other important trait my friends share with the prophets of old: They never stop proclaiming God's word and how to live with it and by it in their daily life, no matter the pitfalls, potholes and naysayers they encounter on their journey. They make a difference every day sharing love through their actions, with their words and by giving great hugs. Powerful examples of what it means to be a prophet, especially in the fractious 21st century.

I challenge you to take a few minutes to identify the prophets in your life. You might be surprised which faces comes to mind and why. I sure was.

FEBRUARY 22

Just who are the spiritual people? Are they the ones who steadfastly follow the rules, but don't treat others with respect? Are they the ones who embrace everyone with kindness, but don't follow any rule or even seem to recognize there are rules? Maybe they are the ones who love their God, but don't especially like mankind? Or are they the gentle people who know the rules, faithfully follow the ones which show respect for everyone and love their God with their whole mind, heart and soul? In my life, people who view everyone with kindness, respect each one's humanity and treat all with love are the truly spiritual people. They "get" it. They listen and learn from their Inner Spirit and follow Her lead.

As many people do, I used to proclaim I am not religious, but spiritual. Even after finding my way back to the religion of my childhood, I still struggle with trusting any organized faith tradition. Wait, that isn't exactly what I want to say. What I don't trust are the hypocrites who appoint themselves the arbitrator of what is right and acceptable behavior and try to impose their way on me. That isn't exactly it either. I have a problem with any authority figure who puts himself or herself above everyone else, that is "the rules apply to you, but not to me." Still not quite it, but closer.

As you can see, I continue to struggle identifying the "good guys" from the "bad guys," the "saints" from the "sinners." especially since I believe we are all a little bad and a little good; the proportion is just different in each of us.

What I am saying is I have no right to judge anyone. As a friend so colorfully put it, "I can't climb inside anyone's head and know how they really think and feel and what their true motivation is." Honestly, I find it scary enough wandering around my own mind without invading someone else's psyche. That is God's domain. We all need to remember and adhere to that truth, make it our defining way we deal with all humanity, no exceptions.

FEBRUARY 23

The Jewish sages tell us to accept the truth from wherever it comes. Seems straightforward. But is it? How do we decide what is the real truth and what just sounds like it? Maybe we want to accept the explanation because it fits into our preconceived ideas? Maybe we don't want to think something we believe isn't really the way it is or supposed to be? If we accept a concept from a person we believe to be a trusted source, what do we do if the idea turns out to be wrong or the person has an ugly ulterior motive? Who has the wisdom and insight to know the truth? Is there only one truth?

These are all legitimate questions. If you think I have the answers, or even some of them, listen closely and hear me clearly say, "I do not!" Remember I told you in the Introduction, I figure out the answers to one set of questions and immediately another set pops up. To make the lessons challenging, the new questions are always more complex than the previous ones. Can't get ahead in this game.

I started asking "why" when I was a young child; I am still asking why. As the years have gone by, I added "how come," "why not," and this is a biggie for me, "It doesn't make sense." Frequently, I hear someone say something that defies all logic and common sense. It baffles me why and how so many people buy into what is clearly nonsense and often potentially hurtful to a lot of people. Ah, but there is a catch. What makes logical sense to me doesn't necessarily make sense to anyone else. If it seems we are back to square one, you are correct. We are back to the original conundrum: How do we know what is truth and what isn't?

I have decided truth is what encourages sincere thought, causes honest reflection about our current behavior and produces positive change in thinking, functioning and relating to others, the world, ourselves. If a statement creates a seismic shift in understanding, it is truth. If society in general and individuals in particular grow into better human beings, it is truth. This is my criteria. Make sure you develop your checklist. If you don't, you will have nothing to lean on for an answer to: What is truth?

FEBRUARY 24

Once we determine what truth is, then what? We accept it; truth becomes ours. We live it day in and day out, no exceptions. How do we do that? We incorporate it into our belief system; we carry truth in our mind, in our heart, in our inner self. It becomes an influential part of who we are. If we do, we will make good decisions based on verifiable facts available to us in the moment.

Don't misunderstand. I do not believe truth changes. What changes is how we interpret it. Our interpretation may not sync with those loud voices insisting their way is truth. All the noise is distracting and can cloud the Spirit of truth. Sometimes the letter of truth seems to point in a contrary direction. What then? How should we react? What should we think? Do?

My fool proof fallback is to trust my heart. My heart operates solely with love. So I know without a doubt, if I listen to my heart and follow her instructions, I will not be wrong. I may be moving against the prevailing winds, and frequently am, but I firmly believe love always triumphs. I also firmly believe my God stands with me when I apply love to any thought or action. Since God is pure love, I learned I can't go wrong when She has my back.

You won't either.

FEBRUARY 25

You might think believing in magic is a frivolous suggestion. Give me a minute to explain why I believe it is imperative to believe magic exists and should be part of our belief system. Why I know magic sustains us when we are about to give up on everyone and everything, especially ourselves.

There is magic in our everyday world, if we open our eyes and ears and appreciate what is happening all around us. Trees offer cooling shade. Flowers bloom in glorious color. Birds sing with the morning sun. Our furry, feathered and finned friends love us unconditionally, even cats who seem aloof, show love in their own ways. The earth provides sustenance to maintain our bodies. There is magic in every forest, every waterfall, every sunset.

There is magic in an infant's gurgle. A small child's laugh. The giggle of tweens sharing secrets with each other. Even a teenager's grunt lets us know they really do hear us. There is magic in the first kiss and the final one. The loving look in the eyes of a special someone. The genuine smile of a friend. A warm hug from anyone.

If you don't believe in magic, you will miss out on all the wonders around you. Life will be grey instead of vibrant with color and alive with joy. You won't appreciate God's handiwork in all of creation. You won't appreciate the pure love of God, no matter how you know Him and Her. As the writer, Roald Dahl said, "Those who don't believe in magic won't find it."

You won't regret believing in magic.

FEBRUARY 26

Everyone has a safe place; a place where we can just be, without any worries or pretense. We can skip a shower and leave our hair tangled, wear holey underwear and an old, wrinkled t-shirt and it is okay. We can indulge in what I call a "be a bum day," sometimes two in a row, and it is okay. But eventually, even introverted me has to face the outside world. A world I sometimes do not understand, frequently find scary and acknowledge is very unpredictable. Since I have a strong belief system with its hidden meanings and subtle nuances, it provides a firm foundation upon which I face my world, so I am able to venture from the protection of my safe nest.

Is it always easy? Nope, sure isn't. And some days are harder than others. But I know I can't hide forever. No one can. I also know in order to function in society, I need to learn from my mistakes, forgive myself, lean on my hard-earned experiences and pay attention to the wisdom all around me. If I am tuned into messages from the world and all its creatures, I will know the right thing to say, the right way to behave, the appropriate way to respond. If I listen closely, I will hear my Inner Spirit; She won't lead me astray.

FEBRUARY 27

Insight into our belief system, what it is, what it means, how to follow it, will gradually lead us to acceptance. What does that mean? Acceptance is knowing we have done the work; we have dug deeply into what we believe and what we don't. Both views are necessary to develop a solid foundation on which to base our thoughts, our behavior, our interactions with and treatment of our fellow humans, the creatures with which we share our planet and our care for Mother Earth.

If we don't know why we act the way we do, how can we hold ourselves accountable? If we don't develop, accept and practice a firm system of ethics, we will be unmoored from reality. It will be extremely challenging to function in our weird world. Leading a positive, enlightened, loving life is impossible without a map, without guidelines to light our path. They won't prevent pitfalls and potholes, but they will make it easier to climb out, dust ourselves off and try again when we do trip. And we will trip because we are human, with human frailties, preconceived notions and ingrained habits we need to recognize and work to overcome. The change won't happen overnight. This journey we are walking separately and together is a life-long learning, growing process, which will not end until we take our final breath. Remind yourself there will be happy times, joyful moments along the way. Promise yourself you will hang in there. Your reward will be worth it.

FEBRUARY 28

February's theme is belief. We learned what it means. How to define it for ourselves. How to accept our definitions. How to make them work effectively in our lives. How our world is frequently askew and having a firm, well-defined belief system helps us navigate our days and nights, our interactions with others.

When we have a belief system in place, we recognize truth, how important it is to forgive, to let go and let God. We react with love in our hearts so all is right in our world. Few things need fixing because we know what to do, how to behave, Who is in charge. We trust ourselves because we listen to our Inner Spirit for grace and guidance.

Questions to consider:

- Do we accept we need a firm belief system?
- Do our beliefs help or hinder us in our day-to-day life?
- What have I made my own? What do I plan to carry into March? Into the rest of my life?

Gratitude Entry: I am grateful I took the time to identify my beliefs, define them and decide how to follow them. I am grateful I have learned a few things to help me have more positive interactions with my family, my friends, my colleagues, strangers on my path, me.

Reader: Add at least one thing you are grateful for as a result of reading, and contemplating the February reflections.

FEBRUARY 29 (LEAP YEAR)

> God, please help me to go through my day with dignity and treat everyone I encounter with respect. Help me make sure I view everyone with love because we are all Your creations. Give me the words and wisdom to say and do the right thing,

These words are part of my morning prayers; ones I composed for me. They remind me of my commitment to be the best me I can be. They also remind me I can't do it alone. I need Divine guidance to successfully navigate my day, to faithfully follow my belief system. They are a gentle reminder I need to listen to my Inner Spirit, especially in challenging situations. So do you.

MARCH

Hope

"Once you choose hope,
anything is possible."

Christopher Reeve

MARCH 1

Mary Davis tells us, "Courage is getting up one more time." Bravery is first cousin to courage. Many people we call heroes don't think of themselves in those terms, they may use different words, but all say, "I just did what anyone would do." False humility? No, I don't believe so. I have seen ordinary people step up just because it is the right thing to do. They do not want praise; they just want "to help." Mr. Rogers said his mother told him when he was a young child, "Look for the helpers." The helpers show us another way to identify courage and bravery and discover hope.

I live in Houston. An area prone to hurricanes and all the storm-related catastrophes that accompany these nasty storms. When the wind quiets, before the rain stops, the helpers come out. They come by car, truck, boat, on bicycles and horseback. Neighbors sharing food, clothes and comfort; offering a place to sleep and regroup. Boaters ferrying strangers out of dangerous flood waters. Those with electronic know-how organizing people who want to help by identifying those who need help and putting the two together. People donate blood; come from sister cities and other states. Many work alongside the first responders. They don't "have" to do any of these things, but they do anyway. They help their unknown neighbors in times of need.

Ever wonder why. I have decided part of the unconscious reason is these helpers have not given up hope. Hope better days will come. Hope this too shall pass. Hope they can be of help. Hope the weather and the world will right itself. And you know, eventually it does. The helpers go home until the next time they are needed. What a way to live your life.

MARCH 2

Life is not an either-or proposition. We could avoid the world, live only with and for ourselves. But even to an introvert who treasures her alone time, this approach does not sound appealing. It sounds sterile, boring, lonely. Eventually I accept I have to be around others. I need to replenish my stale thoughts and starving soul with loving interaction. We all need people nourishment.

Frequently I have to talk myself into leaving my safe nest. I have to remember to be brave. I have to give myself a positive push to enter the big, scary world. In order to find reasons to be hopeful, I need to leave my comfort zone. I won't find examples to encourage hope if I am not in the world. I don't have to be of the world, but I do have to interact with it.

When I am tuned into the environment, I see and hear hope all around. A pregnant woman. A newborn baby. Young and old holding hands. Puppies. Kittens. Budding trees. The shining sun. Raindrops on flowers. Ripples on the lake. Wind through the leaves. Love on display. These things reassure me God is ever on the job and all is right with the world...if I pay attention, I am reminded.

MARCH 3

Am I blind and deaf to what is happening outside my nest? No. I face reality every day. I am aware of current events. But how I choose to face the real world is up to me. I can believe civilization is going to hell in a handbasket. Everyone is out for themselves. No one cares about anyone else. Or I can believe there is more good than bad in the world. More love, than anger and hate. I can choose to look for the positive instead of always expecting the negative.

Is it easy? No, it is not. I have lived with pain, frustration, disappointment and anger. My personal world has been threatened and come crashing down more than once in my 77 years. I had to train myself to seek out and expect the best of people. I had to find hope instead of giving up on everyone and everything in my world, including me, especially me.

I didn't make the transition alone. I am blessed people come into my world exactly when I need them. Sometimes they only stay long enough to teach a lesson. Sometimes they stay through a season of growth. Some are still with me. Showing through their words and actions how to live with hope instead of despair. That the world and the people in it are more good than not. They continually remind me to expect to find good. To have hope.

If you open your heart, you too will discover the people you need to help you find hope.

MARCH 4

When I read this message from motivational speaker, Zig Zigler, I had a lightbulb moment. "The 3 Cs of life: Choices. Chances. Changes. You must make the choice to take a chance, if you want anything in life to change."

We all have choices every day. They determine how our day will unfold. If I expect a disaster, I will find one. If I expect joy, I will find it. In essence, I choose how my day will go. I work on being a half full kind of woman. It isn't always easy. My personal world is filled with seemingly unsolvable problems. The outside world is always teeming with catastrophes, ugliness and endless whining. Can't ignore either world. But I can choose to look for good in both. When I do, I find it, even in the worst situations.

Taking a chance has never been easy for me. I am cautious by nature. I study my options, sometimes to the point of paralysis. A few years ago, I decided to take small chances. Trying a new food. Introducing myself to a new person. Venturing into a place I've never been. It is getting easier. Most of the time, I enjoy the new food; the new person has an intriguing story to share, the new place is interesting. And I am learning I am not going to go up in a puff of smoke if I take a chance.

Making positive choices and taking measured chances, I have changed. I have grown. Not in big ways, but in small ways, quiet ways. They have improved my life, renewed hope. My days are calmer, more joyful. These changes have encouraged me to willingly leave my safe nest more often.

Try making positive choices. Taking measured chances. See how your life improves. As you quietly change, you will grow closer to the person you are meant to be.

MARCH 5

We have all gone through our personal deserts. Usually more than once. It is a dry place where we can't see hope, don't feel love. Where we want to give up on everything and everyone, especially ourselves. What if we viewed our deserts through different eyes? Instead of seeing an arid void, we see a place to review the choices we make, the people with whom we spend time and decide to tackle each issue separately.

Let's look at some of our deserts. Our closet relationship broke down. Our kids don't listen. Our friends never seem to be available. We lost our job. Our finances are a mess. We just want the world to go away. Leave us to our misery so we can suffer in solitude. Sound familiar? And these are just a few deserts we might enter. At first glance, they all seem unfixable, insurmountable. But are they?

I would never tell you any of these challenges are easy to fix or overcome. They are not. All take time, persistence and the will to take charge and take action. I can't give you a magic formula; what works for me probably won't work for you anyway. I can offer a few general suggestions. Like any project, divide each into manageable pieces; one step at a time needs to become your mantra. List your goals in priority and most important: *Write them down* and *check them off* as you complete each one. When you get discouraged, reviewing your list of accomplishments will give the nudge to keep on keeping on. As you cross each item off, you will find hope. In your world. In your family and friends. In yourself. And with hope, you can conquer most any obstacle.

MARCH 6

When someone close dies: Our spouse. Our child. Our sibling. Our parents. Our grandparents. A cherished friend. It has an effect on us. These losses can send us into a desert of despair, loneliness, anger. Our grief can be overwhelming, even paralyzing. Sometimes it comes immediately. Other times, grief pounces when we least expect it. For some, mourning lasts for years. Others are able to move on more quickly. Some of us are able to work through our feelings by ourselves. Most of us, if we are honest, need help navigating our way through this particular desert. One thing I have learned is each death produces a different reaction. And we always grieve for the change in our life. A change we didn't want, which means a future we won't share.

Over the years, I have written a lot about death and its effect on me, on close friends, on casual acquaintances. How it changes our life, our ability to relate to others, our entire world. Words do not help; they often sound meaningless and empty. I finally realized I cannot understand what the grieving feel or hold in their heart. I simply say, "I have no words to ease your pain." For some reason, these simple words, when said with love, and combined with a heartfelt hug, seem to bring solace to the grieving, if only momentarily.

When my beloved soulmate died, it took five years, two grief support groups and many sessions with a mental health professional to even consider removing my wedding rings. Nine years later, I still "feel" them; when I look at my left hand, I expect to see them. Occasionally, I wear our rings and a gold heart on a gold chain he gave me on our first anniversary. For the most part, I have come out of my desert of loss and grieving. I accept he will always be a part of my her-story and I will always miss him. And that is okay. I have also accepted it is okay for me to move on with my life. He wanted me to be content and fulfilled when he was physically here on earth. Why would I think he wants me to stop living because he has entered his eternal rest. He loves me and wants the best for me. I love him and want to honor his memory by being the best me I can be.

MARCH 7

When our world comes crashing down slowly, quietly, with a dull thud or a spectacular splat to claim our attention, our inner and outer life starts to unravel. Doesn't really matter what causes the collapse, we have a decision to make. Do we indulge in a pity party or do we pick ourselves up and start rebuilding?

I have learned no matter what I decide to do, the best way to put myself back together is to take one step at a time. Identify what happened. Sometimes it is easy. A loved one dies. A relationship cannot be repaired. Our life is uprooted in some way: a job changes, a move to another home, a long-term illness, either ours or a person close to us. These are the biggies. A lot of seemingly inconsequential actions and events can and often do upend our life. These can be harder to identify, but it is necessary so we can adjust our mindset.

After identifying the cause, design a specific plan on how and what is needed to get back on track. These goals will vary depending on the reason and the season. Write the steps down so you don't lose momentum and stop your search. You will stumble, even fall. That is okay as long as you pick yourself up and start again.

Understand and accept this is a slow process. You didn't get into this situation overnight; you are not going to fix it overnight either. One step at a time. One day at a time. One hour at a time. Hold firmly to hope. Hope in yourself. Hope people will help when you ask. Hope your Higher Power will hold your hand, whether you ask or not.

MARCH 8

If we operate using our free will tempered by our code of ethics, we usually make the right decisions for where we are with the knowledge we have at the moment. This does not mean we won't modify, change altogether or even abandon what we decide today. We collect new information. Circumstances change. We view life through a different lens. We have grown past viewpoints which no longer serve us. Whether it is a relationship we have outgrown. A job that no longer satisfies. A lifestyle that doesn't fit who we are today. If we are paying attention, we will know when we have to revisit certain long-held assumptions and decide, once again, what is right for us — today, right now.

A few years ago, I realized I was no longer the person I was when I was a wife; my life had changed in ways I never anticipated. I was so busy doing, I hadn't paid attention to whom I was becoming. Who am I? Have I lost myself? Now what? Scary questions for a woman in her seventies!

Time for an inventory of me.

I am more relaxed. More patient. I see more beauty in the world, more joy. I do a better job accepting and forgiving the foibles in those around me and, just as important, myself. I still crave solitude and desperately need rest and recouperation after interacting outside my nest. The difference is I recognize when my Inner Spirit is telling me to slow down, say no and be kind to me. And I actually follow Her advice...most of the time. Wow! What a change from my previous hurry up, can't stop behavior. I slowly came to understand this one change is responsible for all those that followed.

So don't think you can't change? If a stubborn, hard-headed Irish woman like me can change, you can too. Stop your world for a bit. Take inventory. See how you have grown closer to becoming the person you are meant to be. You will be pleasantly surprised what you discover.

MARCH 9

When you make an internal journey, you are on a search to discover some part of the real you. The reason can be to fine tune your beliefs, find your spiritual anchor, listen for directions from your Inner Being. You are looking for hope. Hope for a reason to get up in the morning. Hope to be able to forgive those who have hurt or disappointed you. Hope to forgive yourself. Hope to recognize joy.

Because we humans are not static beings, we need to touch base with ourselves periodically. Take time to find out who we are in this moment. We need to consult our advisory panel: the me of yesterday, the me of today and the me of the future. Past me has lessons to remind current me how far I have come. The current me needs to be gentle to me. The third member of our advisory panel is tricky to know. She can't see into the future, but can know what she is working to improve, where she wants to go and how she is trying to get there. I view the third member of our panel as the goal we have in mind. It is a powerful motivator for the me we are today.

Check in with your advisory panel. Get used to listening to what she is saying, In what direction she is pointing you. How she is guiding you. Since I realized the wisdom my advisory panel has, I rely on her more and more to help me make the right decisions.

Get acquainted with your advisory panel. You will be amazed how wise she is.

MARCH 10

What we do matters. The actions we take, consciously and unconsciously, determines how we live our day-to-day life. Our interactions with everyone we encounter tells the world who we really are. And if we are paying attention, tells us deep in our being whether we are becoming who we hope to be; who our Inner Spirit is urging us to become. This is a critical reason to allocate quiet time every day. We need to examine our outward behavior and our inner thoughts.

Wait a minute. What am I saying? Am I recognizing I am responsible for my behavior, my thoughts? Me? The one who is busy doing, busy trying to accomplish self-imposed goals. Oh my. Do I really want to dissect everything I think about the people around me, every action I take, every response I make? Yep, I do if I want to grow into the me God wants me to be, I need to review me every day. If I don't devote the time to understand the motivations for my behavior, I will never know if I am heading in the right direction.

Warning: This is not a time to beat up on yourself for whatever you think you could have handled better, more lovingly. Whatever imperfections you discover. It is the time for honest reflection to help you learn how to modify your thinking, your behavior. Decide how to adjust your approach to people and events. How to be a better you.

It doesn't matter what time of the day. In the morning. In the evening. As long as you keep the daily appointment with yourself.

MARCH 11

We have been on an internal pilgrimage the last few days. It is a bit different from a pilgrimage to an unfamiliar location. When I first read about pilgrimages, they were the kind where someone was on a quest. Usually in ancient history or a fairy tale. The kind we are on in the 21st Century is to learn about ourselves. This is a kind of scary not found in history or the pages of a book!

A journey to unfamiliar surroundings creates other opportunities to learn who we are. Studying the land, the architecture, the food and drink, the culture and the people of another place can teach us volumes, if we pay attention. Interacting with those we don't know can show us what kind of person we are. After all, we will never see these people again, so does it matter how we treat them? Yes, it definitely does.

Most of us rarely, if ever, take time to discover who we are now, who we are becoming and if we really like the me of today. Why is that, do you suppose? What are we unconsciously avoiding?

Introspection requires looking at our private thoughts, behaviors and goals honestly, with no buts, excuses or caveats. Most of us find it a challenge to formulate a list of to-dos, let alone study ourselves.

Searching inward with the only goal to know myself is downright intimidating! What if I don't like what I learn? How do I change? Do I want to change? Questions only you can answer.

MARCH 12

Forgiving myself is one of the hardest tasks for me to accept and practice. I am human. I am a perfectionist. I am my own worst critic. I rarely give myself a break when I mess up, especially if my behavior caused discomfort for or harm to another person. If the one harmed or hurt is me, I am convinced I deserved it. I have difficulty practicing the wise advice I offer to others: Be kind to yourself. Nope. Not going to do that. I don't deserve loving consideration.

Does this thought process sound familiar? Why am I able to forgive others, but not myself? When I remind myself, it was a real challenge to learn to forgive others, I shouldn't wonder why it is hard to forgive myself. Two sides of the same coin. Understanding that fact altered my perspective. I started to accept in order to truly forgive others, I have to forgive myself first.

When I treat myself with compassion and understanding, I am better able to treat others the same. Part of loving someone is recognizing they are human and make mistakes. And forgiving their mistakes; in this case, mine. Logically, if I believe the Holy Spirit lives within me, I need to forgive myself. Because She already has.

Forgive yourself. You are worth it.

MARCH 13

When we do something nice or helpful for a fellow creature, two legged or four, we do something for ourselves. What? Say again. Studies have shown, a kind act brings satisfaction and contentment to the giver, as well as the receiver. It has to do with releasing the happy hormones called endorphins present in all animals. What I found interesting is it doesn't seem to matter what the action, large or small, all have the same effect.

Picking up dropped keys. Kicking the soccer ball back. Fetching a cup of coffee. Paying for the groceries of the person behind. Changing a flat tire. Scratching the dog's ears. Rubbing the cat's tummy. Waving at the police officer. Smiling at the stressed mom. Comforting a screaming child. Saying I'm sorry. Forgiving a hurtful word. Ignoring a rude salesperson. Holding the door open. Thanking someone for being themselves.

You never know what your loving gesture may mean to the other person. Your kindness might be the one thing that keeps a person from doing something dangerous, hurtful or even fatal. The ripples in the water.

Practice being kind. Being thoughtful. It is easier than it seems. Reverse roles. React like you wish other people would act toward you. Quietly and inevitably, it will become your modus operandi. You and the world will be better for it.

MARCH 14

I have learned when I notice the beauty in my world, my perspective shifts. The serenity of a walk outside. The predictable sunrise and sunset. Surprise at seeing the full moon during the day. Rain on the grass. The sun peeking out from behind a cloud. The soothing movement of the ocean waves. Stars on a clear night. Animals behaving naturally. Children being carefree. Teens giving their all in any activity. Adults treating each other with respect. All these things bring joy to my day. And give me hope there will be another day, another opportunity to be the best me I can be.

Why? I believe a Higher Power created everyone and everything in the universe. Doesn't matter how you define your Deity or understand the process of creation, someone or something greater than humans made all these wonders happen. And keeps them happening. No matter what the doomsday folks and the naysayers proclaim, we live in a glorious Eden created just for us. That alone is cause for joy. That alone is reason enough to hang on to hope.

We are back to what we "see" is what we find. When we appreciate where we live and what we have rather than moaning about what we wish we had, we are pretty much guaranteed we will find it. I want to appreciate the wonders around me. I want to find joy. I want to see love. So I do.

What do you see?

MARCH 15

Labyrinths have always fascinated me. Surprisingly, the first time I had the opportunity to walk one, I was 74. I was attending a conference on ways to find contentment in the final season of life. The setting was an 1100-acre forested paradise located about a ninety-minute drive northwest of Houston. The camp is serene and peaceful. The air is clear and the stars shine brightly. Just being on the grounds is a joyful experience. I went alone during my first year of living boldly. I met several interesting people, one of whom has become a dear friend.

There is an unpretentious chapel snuggled in a corner of a spacious hall. One of the events was the opportunity to walk a labyrinth. My chance! At the appointed time, I quietly entered the hall. On the stage was a huge canvas version. The chaplain gave a brief history of this form of prayer. The design of a labyrinth is the same no matter how large or small or where it is located.

I didn't know what to expect as I slowly started my journey. As instructed, I stopped at each crossroad, said a silent prayer and moved on. As I progressed along the winding path, my breathing slowed, my attention became focused, my prayers became more heartfelt. I lost track of time. When I reached the end, for several moments, I was rooted to the spot. I didn't want to leave. I was afraid I would lose the exquisite serenity I had discovered. As I became aware of my surroundings, I realized the room was eerily quiet. Apparently, my fellow travelers were experiencing similar feelings. We smiled gently. And quietly left. I have never forgotten the joy of that special moment.

Someday, I hope to walk another labyrinth. I want to assure myself it was real. I didn't dream the experience, the feelings. Whether you are a spiritual person or not, I recommend a walk through a labyrinth. It will change you.

MARCH 16

Since my labyrinth journey, I have slowly recognized a change began that day. I didn't realize until I started writing this book, the experience was the unconscious beginning of my inner growth. There have been thoughtful discussions with diverse people. Attendance at functions where I met fascinating people. Working on interesting projects taught me things I didn't know I needed to learn. All contributed to my gradual growth and inevitable change. As I was listening and absorbing, a transformation was happening, even if I wasn't aware of it. The labyrinth opened my heart in a way I can't describe and couldn't predict.

The Greek word, *metanoia* means a transformative change of heart usually from a spiritual conversion of some sort. The first time I heard the word, I was immediately reminded of the changes, my growth the last few years. Not only of my heart, but my thoughts and eventually, my soul. While I recommend a labyrinth journey to kick start your growth, in reality, anything that profoundly gets your attention and causes you to stop and think about the trajectory of your life, can mean metanoia for you.

A caveat: In order to have a lightbulb moment, you need to be open to growth, which means change. Oops! We humans almost automatically resist change. It is scary. It leads to unknown places. But it also leads to a better me, a more loving me. If everyone was open to personal growth, I firmly believe we would have as President George H.W. Bush wanted, "...a kinder, gentler world." What a marvelous idea.

MARCH 17

Being of Irish heritage, my paternal grandparents immigrated from the Emerald Isle, I am particularly fond of this day. Since my dad's birthday was March 10, we celebrated from the 10th through the 17th. Dad saw no reason to stop the party. What kid wouldn't enjoy that happy observance of the calendar. It was during these days I was given my first taste of Irish coffee and green beer and introduced to the Irish jig, even if the participants were a bit wobbly.

However, it was my paternal Irish grandfather who opened my eyes to one of my favorite traditions from the "old country." He introduced me to the Little People, Leprechauns to outsiders, and how to use them to my advantage. He was full of mischief and enjoyed pulling pranks, especially on mom. When I would mildly protest, he would assure me everything would be okay, "We'll just blame it on the Little People" and off we would go on our latest adventure. Mom was never amused. Full Disclosure: I still use the Little People from time to time.

As I have gotten older, I remember those eight-day birthday celebrations and Little People inspired adventures with fondness. It brings back the joy of childhood with adults who loved and protected me. The carefree time when life was simple and I didn't know stress existed. On this one day of the year, no matter what else may be going on in my world, I focus on my childhood joy. I put aside worry. I escape the ugliness in the world. I find a friend to spend a happy, carefree day playing as children do with hope in my heart, spreading laughter and love. And singing an Irish song or ten. Not limber enough anymore to dance the jig.

Join me as I start the day with Irish coffee and end it with red wine. Gave up green beer some years ago; really never liked the stuff. Please don't tell my grandpa or my dad.

MARCH 18

An affirmation from many twelve step programs reminds us, "God doesn't make junk." The first time I read those words, I was in my cynical phase so my automatic response was, "Except me. There are always exceptions" Talk about low self-esteem; I didn't have any at all. It took a long time, a lot of searching and encouragement before I slowly began to accept I was okay. Not perfect, but okay just as I am. What a freeing discovery.

I learned to like me. I learned I didn't need anyone to tell me I was good at something; I knew when I was. When I was able to help a friend through a difficult time, I knew I was in their life for a reason. I was paying my life lessons forward. I began to take on volunteer projects because I wanted to, not because I felt obligated. I eventually learned the world wouldn't stop spinning if I said, 'No." I still have days and nights when I doubt a decision or regret a harsh word, but after apologizing, I am learning to let it go and move on.

These lessons didn't come easy. I still struggle accepting I am going to make mistakes. All humans do. And I am not making a higher percentage than anyone else. Another freeing discovery. Looking back on all the times I had to stop, take inventory and adjust, I realized making the choice to face my demons head-on was one of the best decisions I ever made. It changed my life, the way I relate to the world and my interactions with the people in it. I finally am able to say and believe, "God doesn't make junk."

Listen closely, I want to tell you something important. Just you being you makes the world a better place. You light up any space you enter.

MARCH 19

Hope grows when we let go of old definitions of who we were yesterday and last year and twenty years ago for ones that reflect who and where we are on our personal path right now, today. Maybe I worried about my hair and my hips and my social life when I was a teenager. Today, I don't give a hoot. Maybe I was anxious about what kind of a parent I was when I had responsibility for the children I was given to nurture and teach and mentor. Was I teaching them by my actions how to be kind people in a world that frequently discounts that incredible behavior? My children have grown into beautiful, kind adults who live life with love in their heart. Maybe I fretted about my work ethic and if I was doing all I could to help my employer succeed. All I have to do is read the glowing recommendations from several managers to know I did more things right than wrong.

Not often, but occasionally I questioned my personal ethics. The way I responded to sticky situations both personally and professionally. With most of my life in the rearview mirror, I have a better perspective on my actions and reactions. Did I make mistakes? Of course I did. But I always admitted them, didn't try to blame them on colleagues or circumstances or overwork. A simple apology and a "Yes. I take full responsibility for the screw-up. How can I fix it?" was my go-to response. And I tried to learn from them so I didn't make the same one again. Had to leave room for new ones!

As we age, we need to take time to evaluate how we define ourselves. Are the definitions accurate for the person we are today? Do we need to update how we see ourselves? My guess would be, yep, sure do. Thank goodness I am not the same naïve teenager I was when I graduated from high school or the overconfident college graduate. I have grown into a somewhat wise septuagenarian. What a relief to finally recognize the change in my outlook, my behavior and my acceptance of the me I am today. Let's celebrate the grown up me and you.

MARCH 20

Spring is here! There is change in the air. It may be only a small change, but it is there. Trees are beginning to show tiny green or white buds. Maybe where you live, some of the buds have started blooming. Early spring flowers are poking their heads up through the barren earth returning color to the landscape. Birds are gathering strings and things and twigs. The grass is beginning to stand tall and green again.

Where I grew up, we started looking for the first robin. When we spotted his red breast, we knew his mate was close by. The bright yellow crocus bravely bloomed even if it wasn't very warm yet.

These signs of nature awakening told us spring was here. Cold weather would soon be gone; warm weather was on its way.

Wherever you live, spring eventually arrives. The long, dreary winter is finally over. Nature is waking up from its annual slumber. Take a stroll outside. Smell the fresh air, Gaze at the clear, blue sky. Notice something beautiful. Let it remind you whatever is preying on your mind and causing pain in your heart will eventually right itself. It may not be easy or quick or painless. But as Mother Nature nurses the earth back to fullness, God will nurse you back to wholeness. Ask your Higher Power for help to heal, to find peace, to find hope. Believe She listens. Know He answers.

Spring is here. Celebrate!

MARCH 21

Sometimes life throws crazy curve balls. Often the event takes me by surprise; I am not prepared. But I look for the positive in the worst situation. It is always there. I may not see it right away, but I keep looking. It takes time to process the event and its consequences. I may have to adjust my thinking of and reaction to the situation and the person or people involved.

Maybe I learned a valuable lesson so won't repeat unacceptable behavior. Sometimes I handled the situation just right, but circumstances beyond my control took over. Perhaps an overly aggressive person stepped in and elbowed me out. I learn to avoid that individual. I am grateful the accident wasn't worse. No one was injured or died. My loved one made it home safely.

People have accused me of being a Pollyanna as if that is a bad way to be. They tell me I am naive to view the struggles of being alive as teachable moments. My response? Stuff happens. Why waste the opportunity to use these inevitable events to my advantage. Because I carry hope in my heart, I am able to see and share something positive in unfortunate circumstances. When I do, it makes me feel better. Funny thing, it helps the people around me feel better too, even if they do think I am a Pollyanna.

MARCH 22

Despair is a complete lack of hope. It is more than giving up. It is dropping out of life. Turning away from reality. Refusing to even acknowledge there might be hope for a better tomorrow. Convinced getting through today is going to be a challenge. Avoiding human interactions. Longing to stay in my safe space. The inability to find one positive anything. Thinking, feeling, talking negative. Can't identify anything for which to be grateful.

When I am in the throes of depression, my world is black. Not grey. Not black and white. Total blackness. Winston Churchill called it his "black dog." I refer to the state as my "black pit." It took many sessions with mental health professionals over the years to be able to even acknowledge there may be a slight chance there is something, anything positive in my world when in my black pit. It is a helpless, scary way to be and attempting to get through an hour, never mind an entire twenty-four-hour day, can seem impossible.

I have finally learned how to pull myself, albeit slowly, out of my black pit. I stop hiding from and denying my mood. While I can identify my feelings, it is not easy for me to admit them and reach out for help. I don't like to ask anyone for anything. I feel I should be able to work my way through these times by myself. A huge, life-changing lesson for me is acknowledging, I can't. No one can.

Depression is the parent of despair. Learn to recognize the mood for what it is: Desperately trying to run away and hide from a problem. It may not be fixable and you may have to learn to live with whatever drove you to the land of darkness, but there is always a way to walk through it. You will come out the other side whole. How? Hold on tight to hope. Know God is within you. When you feel unlovable, know She is always unconditional love. And She will help, if you lean on Her.

MARCH 23

Apologies for leaving you in a dark place yesterday. As I wrote the last few reflections, I have been in my black pit, fighting an on-going battle with depression. Even though I am an expert at keeping the mood under cover, it does permeate my view of the world. After reviewing the essay, I considered deleting it and waiting until the mood lifts to continue. I finally decided if I did eliminate it, I wasn't being honest with my readers; and I would be wasting a teachable moment vis-a-vis March 21.

Most of the topics I discuss in this book, I have experienced or have a family member or close friend who has. Depression is my life-long nemesis. Why should I avoid a difficult subject because I am concerned about the potential consequences? What is the worst that can happen? Readers will put the book down in fear because they don't want to visit there? It hits too close to home. In the pro column, maybe my words will help one person, even just a tiny bit, start to recover from their bout of depression because a stranger admitted she suffers too. Perhaps sharing my demons and dark places will assure that one person, they are not alone, there is help available, they are lovable. They just need to reach out and ask for help.

I do strive to be as honest as possible and being the best me I can be. I have accepted, I will never be perfect. So I keep on keeping on. You should too.

A reassuring note: Because I shared my definition of depression and how it affects me, I feel a bit better today. As if I am slowly starting to climb out of my black pit. Thank you for giving me the gift of your thoughtful attention. Thank you, Inner Spirit, for your unconditional love and encouragement.

MARCH 24

One of my passions is a memoir-writing group I facilitate. We are in our sixth year and have developed a special camaraderie; there is a palpable love, respect and acceptance among the members. We are writing our story in short essays, which we share with the group. Combined with spirited discussions, we have gotten to know each other fairly well. Since I have been using my free time composing reflections for this book, I didn't have anything prepared for our meeting. I decided to read the last two reflections. What happened is an example of the unexpected consequences of a decision...

I told them I was writing a book of reflections and wanted to share a couple with them. I knew I piqued their interest. When I finished reading, there was a few moments of complete silence. All looked a bit stunned. Eventually, someone said, "I never would have guessed someone like you who is so friendly and outgoing suffers from depression." The observation didn't really surprise me. I know I am an expert at hiding "those days."

What did surprise me is who confessed to suffering from depression. The discussion led to how sad it is we keep this struggle inside rather than risk society's dismissing it as the "blues" and instructing us to "get over it." Those of us who live with the disease know you can't just "get over it." If we could, we would. It was a lesson for me to be more willing to take a chance and share my demon with people I trust. I just might find support in places I never would expect. God works in mysterious ways.

MARCH 25

When I shared the surprising acceptance by the writing group with a close friend, who knows about my depression, he said, "Now that you are beginning to open up about your depression, maybe you will finally be able to start healing." Really caught me off guard. Talk about a revelation! After thinking about his observation, I realize he is right.

When we share overwhelming feelings with people we trust, our burden is lightened. It doesn't cure the ailment, nor does it take it away. But when we feel someone understands, we begin to get a glimmer of hope, and eventually even accept, we are not alone; we are not the only one who feels this way. In our saner moments, we know it. But when in the middle of a crisis, emotional or otherwise, we tend to forget our friends want to help by listening with a loving heart.

I promised myself the next time I start to slide into my black pit, I will reach out rather than waiting until I have hit the bottom and depression has completely taken over my life. I know from experience, once I am at the bottom, not much of anything or anyone will help. Why? Because I don't want help. I want to wallow in my black pit until I am ready to come out. More importantly, I don't believe anyone really loves me or wants to help. Talk about self-sabotage. Instead, I will be grateful a friend cares and does love me. Wants to help me be kind to myself. Sincerely wants me to love myself. I am hanging on to the hope I remember my promise to myself the next time I start the slide.

MARCH 26

Thinking about the way I ended yesterday's reflection, a thought popped into my mind (my muse at work): We should all strive to hold out the hand of hope to everyone we encounter. Not just a loved one or close friend or someone who reaches out to us. I hear you thinking, "How is that even possible?" Let's consider the question together.

If we commit to wearing a positive demeanor every time we venture into the world, we will radiate quiet joy. While we may never know, maybe someone who sees our smiling face or hears our cheerful voice, will be uplifted, even for a moment. Or perhaps it will be the one thing they encounter, which alters their view of the world, even for a moment. We might be responsible for someone giving themselves "one more day." What an incredible gift to the world and the best part, we will be spreading hope and won't know its impact. What a heady thought!

Another way we can all spread hope is to respond with an upbeat attitude when someone does come to us searching for a soft shoulder, a quiet moment, a concerned ear, a loving heart. Whatever else you offer, make sure you include a note of hope in your message. I'm not talking about clichéd phrases, but showing genuine concern in your eyes, in your voice and in the look on your face. A gift the recipient will cherish and hold in their heart all the days of their lives. I can't think of a better, more lasting, more loving gift.

MARCH 27

The state flower of Texas is the bluebonnet. It is a lovely white and purplish-blue bloom which grows on a slim stalk. They bloom for about three weeks in late March/early April. Farmers devote fields and fields to these flowers; their brief spring fling is glorious to view. The fresh country air is a balm for the weary psyche. The sight affirms belief the Divine is active in our world.

As a result of sharing my gloomy feelings with a close friend, he spontaneously suggested we take a drive into bluebonnet country the next day. Our calendars were clear; a rarity for both of us. We left the next morning with a light jacket, a bottle of water, umbrellas (just in case) and no plan other than to find bluebonnets. And did we ever, along with fields of other colorful spring wildflowers. We stopped frequently to take pictures of beautiful scenic vistas; some with us standing in the midst of the blue blooms. A pictorial journal of two close friends spending a joyous day together, which I tucked gratefully into my memory box. I will pull out the mental pictures and remember how a friend's simple suggestion was the final yank out of my black pit. His thoughtful gesture reminded me I am okay. I am loved.

An early spring day meandering leisurely on winding country roads is a gentle antidote to lighten the heaviest heart and soothe the most frazzled psyche. I highly recommend it whenever the world is too much with you.

MARCH 28

A Buddhist belief is we are "born again" every morning. We are given a fresh start. We shouldn't worry about the past or fret about the future. Live today with hope, with a can do, why not, no problem attitude. When I first read the sentiment, my immediate thought was, "What a marvelous way to face the day!" My second thought, "It's an impossible goal!" How can anyone, especially always-preparing-for-a-catastrophe me, actually live it.

I thought I had stored the concept in the "nice, but not in my lifetime" file. How wrong I can be. A quiet little voice I call my "I'm not going to let you forget good ideas" conscience, kept nagging me repeatedly saying I should at least consider the idea. Oh well, alright. If it will turn you off, I will think about the concept and how I can apply it to my life.

What does it really mean to "start fresh" every day and live with a "can do" approach anyway? Do I have to ignore or avoid everything mean and ugly and concentrate on the good and kind? In a way, that is what it means. Remember when I told you I can always find something positive in the worst situations (March 21), this is what I am actually doing: Living with hope. Starting fresh. Facing the day with a clean slate. Accepting I can do whatever I set my mind to. So can you.

MARCH 29

Life can and often does, get complicated. Every day does not bring sunshine, sometimes the rain invades. As my dear husband often said, "The sun is going to come up." When I heard him mutter his mantra, I understood it was his way of holding on to hope. Paul was generally an upbeat, positive man, but even he had occasional moments of doubt. His favorite mantra always seemed to shake him out of the doldrums. He would smile his special smile and cheerfully continue his day, respecting the rain while patiently waiting for the sun he knew would come.

Hope opens a new way of thinking and feeling and offers an energized life. Maybe even a restart. Perhaps it is time to move on from an unhappy friendship, an unfulfilling job, a self-defeating attitude. When we carry hope everywhere, we open our life to all the good people, joyful experiences and wonderful opportunities life presents. An open heart brings open hands to nurture, to soothe, to love. A closed heart brings the cold, the mean, the destructive, which leads to loneliness and fear. As the spiritual writer, Mary Davis said, "...what we dwell on, we create; what we imagine, we attract; what we ponder, we empower."

What do you hope to bring into your day-to-day life?

MARCH 30

This month we have been discussing hope. What it is. Where to find it. Why we need it in our life. Since I learned its power, I think of hope as the spark plug of life. Like the spark plug in your car, hope gives us the extra boost to start moving through a challenging situation and do something with whomever and about whatever we meet on our path. When we hold on to hope, we have a reason to get up in the morning and keep putting one foot in front of the other because we believe we will get where we are going...no matter who or what tries to stop us.

Questions to consider:

- Do we accept we need hope in our toolbox?
- How does hope help or hinder us in our day-to-day life?
- What have I made my own? What do I plan to carry into April? Into the rest of my life?

GRATITUDE ENTRY: I am grateful I understand why hope is so important in my life. I will strive to invite hope into my world. I want to encourage positive vibes. I know if I have hope, I naturally generate love all around me. What a glorious way to live.

Reader: Add at least one thing you are grateful for as a result of reading, and contemplating the March reflections.

MARCH 31

As with many of my prayers, I modified a few words discovered when reading to make them my own. When I stumbled on the message, it spoke to me. I wanted to remember it, so I noted the brief phrase. Writers learn to write down an inspiring idea, lest it be lost to an unpredictable memory.

> I practice hope because it is born from love. I choose to see the good, the positive in the world. I acknowledge there is pain, most of which I can't do anything to change or make go away. I hold hope in my heart because I trust God knows all and loves all, so in the end all is right with the world even if I can't see it. Hold on to hope with all your being. It is a shining light in a sometimes-dark world.

APRIL

Prayer

"If the only prayer you said
in your whole life was
Thank You, that would suffice."

Meister Eckhart

APRIL 1

Prayer means different things to different people. It frequently depends on how you were raised. If prayer was important in your childhood family, it is probably important to you as an adult. Maybe your family only went to a house of worship on special holy days: Rosh Hashana, Yom Kippur, Easter, Christmas, during Ramadan. Perhaps grace before meals was only recited at large family gatherings instead of every mealtime. Maybe you only said prayers before bed as a child. Just because you may not have formed prayer habits in your early life, does not mean you can't begin a prayer practice now, today.

If we attended religious services as youngsters, we learned the prayers important to our faith tradition. I find these prayers comforting especially when I'm tired or faced with a frightening situation. They come to mind automatically and bring solace in a time of acute need. They have a firm place in my prayer practice.

I gradually came to believe prayers should be personal. As I progressed on my spiritual journey, I began composing my own prayers; prayers with meaning for me and where I am in life. They are my way of personalizing my conversations with God. They reflect me and what is important in my world.

I believe there is a place for both forms of prayer and God accepts either one when they are offered from the heart.

APRIL 2

What does it mean to pray? Intriguing question with multiple answers. I think of it as a dialogue with God. Some call it a conversation with God. Others believe it is time spent with their Deity. Some people consider meditation a form of praying. However, you define the act of praying, it is a means of communicating with your Higher Power. Recognize communication is a two-way process. Be open to response from your Higher Power in whatever form the response may take.

Recently I stumbled on an anagram. In my haste, I didn't note who came up with it, but it is a good definition of what we are doing when we pray. This is how I define what each letter means:

Petition: Many of our prayers are asking for something for ourselves or someone else. Or maybe to bring peace to the world or for a specific cause.

Release: We are letting go and letting God take control of whatever is troubling us or thanking Him for a joyful experience. Whatever our reason to pray, we are sharing our inner self with our Deity.

Agreement: We accept what is happening in our life as a gift from the Divine. Sometimes it is a gift we enjoy. Other times it is a gift to teach us a painful lesson we didn't know we needed to learn.

Yearn: We are requesting something we desire whether it is relief from a burden, a change in our situation, or help for a friend. We want something so we turn to our God.

When we look at the word in this way, it becomes clear why we pray. Maybe we just don't think of it in these terms. Be assured our Higher Power knows what we are doing and accepts the motivation behind it.

God is always listening with love.

APRIL 3

A friend says the shortest prayer is, "Help!" Can't argue with that. Used the petition many times before I thought of it as a prayer. I now think of "Love you" as a short prayer. "Be safe" is another. Until I began to study prayer and its power, I said a lot of words and phrases I have come to believe are prayers. Prayer is a direct petition to my Higher Power. I believe He and She listen and respond. I would be a fool not to believe in the power of prayer whether I am asking for me or someone else. Too many anecdotal instances in my life prove prayer works.

There is a bit of a glitch: God works in His time, not mine. I believe He answers prayers, just not in my timeframe. For a control freak, that is a challenge to accept. Even harder to accept is He frequently ignores what I want and provides something much better and more satisfying than what I thought I wanted. Took me many years to catch onto His MO. This hardheaded Irish woman can be difficult to convince of anything, especially when I think I want something, pray fervently and then am rewarded with something entirely different! God really does know best.

Clinical studies are being done to scientifically confirm people who believe in and have a strong prayer practice experience milder pain, heal quicker and have less fear of death. And our brain demonstrates this fact clearly by lighting up in various areas of the two hemispheres. Someday scientists may understand the where and the how; I already know the Who and the Why.

APRIL 4

Small everyday things are a form of prayer: preparing dinner; soothing physical and mental hurts; finding misplaced car keys, shoes or homework assignments; holding the door open; stepping in for a colleague at the last minute; helping a confused neighbor with a computer problem; saying please and thank you; sweeping the sidewalk; filling her car with gas; preparing his morning cup of java; a genuine smile; a warm hug. These gestures, when done with no expectation of reward or return, are all mini-prayers. They show kindness and acknowledge the humanity and Godliness in those we encounter, family, friend and stranger.

When I think of my actions as prayers, the days take on a whole new meaning; it is amazing what happens. I am forced to be in the moment, live in the now. When I am present in my life, I don't miss all the little joyful events around me. My mood lifts. It changes my approach to the world, to people, to life. I actually have a reason to get up and venture into the chaos because when all my actions are a prayer, it isn't quite so frustrating out there.

As I gradually got used to thinking of my normal activities as prayers, unexpected benefits appeared. I realized I help because I want to, not because I have to. The warm fuzzies generated for me and thee soothe our souls and calm our frantic mind, even if just in the moment For an introvert, it is a life-changing way to view the world and my place in it.

You might be pleasantly surprised what you learn about yourself if you think of your actions as prayers. I sure was.

APRIL 5

Not everyone prays the same way nor in the same places. I feel my Deity everywhere, so I pray wherever I am. I have never mastered the GPS on my smart phone; when I have used it, I ended up more lost than I was when I opened the app. I say a frantic "help" then a relieved "thank you" for leading me to the location I was searching for and rejoice I only got lost twice. When I see a new baby, a prayer of gratitude is offered for the new parents and the infant. When I make it home safely after a frazzled time in snarled traffic, I quietly vow never to go out at that time again — ever!

I pray sitting in my special space in the study. I pray privately, silently; out loud with others, during church services; in the car while running errands; walking around the block, sitting by the lake. When I am out and about, it is a quick prayer. At home and in church, the prayers are longer and more formal. But no matter where I am or what prayers I say, I feel close to the Divine.

It doesn't matter how or where you pray, God hears you. If you want to hold a dialogue rather than a monologue, you need to listen for the message, feel the encouragement, know the Divine Spirit is within you. Loving you unconditionally.

Prayer should be personal. Make it so.

APRIL 6

Let's get something straight. I am an ordinary woman. I am not a saint. I mess up and disappoint myself every day. I do try to remember God doesn't expect perfection and loves me no matter what. He wants me to be the me He created. My share in this partnership is to keep trying to be the best me I can be. To do that, I need to listen for His encouragement, ask for Her guidance. Pay attention to what is happening around me. Learn how to help the world run a little bit smoother, be a little bit nicer.

Not everyone prays the same. That is as it should be. We are individuals with a unique relationship with our Deity, however we communicate with Him and Her. One way to enhance our prayer practice is to stop during the day and give a moment to God. These mini-breaks help us live in the now. Stop fretting about the past. Worrying about the future. Be in harmony with the Divine for a brief moment. Let our love shine for all to share. Be one with humanity. For just a moment.

Back in January, we explored setting aside time in our morning ritual for prayer. To anchor our day in the positive. Four months later, we should have the practice firmly rooted in our daily life. Do you? If not, why not? Questions only you can answer.

APRIL 7

It is a challenge to hear anything in our noisy, chaotic culture. We all need to talk less. Listen more. I confess to being one of the worst offenders. People tell me I talk too much. Some lovingly. Some in frustration. Difficult as it is for me to admit, they are right. I do. But they also tell me I listen better than most. I give the speaker my full attention. I'm not forming an answer while they are talking. I am listening with my heart. I figured out when I was young, most people just want to be heard. They really don't want advice or directives or a lecture. They just want to have their thoughts and feelings acknowledged, validated. Feel they are understood. What a priceless gift we provide when we listen with love.

If we humans need to learn to listen to each other, all the more reason to learn to listen to our Higher Power. How well do you listen for God's message? The gentle guidance? The whispering of your conscience? The wisdom of your heart? Your Inner Being?

I will stop talking now. I want to give you time to listen with your heart. That is the way you will learn to recognize the messages you need to hear, from a friend, from yourself, from God.

APRIL 8

One of the reasons I always start my day with prayer is because I am rested. I am calm. Haven't had time to build up stress. Depending upon my schedule, the morning ritual may be the only time I devote complete attention to my Higher Power. Talking to Him. Listening for Her guidance. Try as I might to avoid it, sometimes I get caught up in the drama of the world around me.

I get frazzled and frantic. No matter how many mini-moments of brief contact with the Divine, I get lost in the craziness of life.

Admitting my failure to reach out for a soothing touch of comfort via a quick prayer reminds me I am human with human distractions and human failings. It reminds me God loves me anyway as He patiently waits for me to remember She is within me all the time, not just when I turn to Her. When I have a day I don't see and feel the miracles and goodness all around me, I end the day feeling as if something is missing. And it is. How many times did I miss an opportunity to bring a little sunshine into someone's day? How many times did I ignore a kind gesture? Too many! All because I was focused on the craziness instead of the people.

After a brief moment of chastisement, and peeling myself off the ceiling, I ask forgiveness for overlooking how much joy there is in the world. And apologize for not recognizing it.

APRIL 9

For those of you who may be new to prayer or maybe you are searching for a new approach, there is a method you might use to help you get started or improve your prayer practice. It is applicable to all faith traditions and spiritual philosophies. It is a way to structure your prayer plan. It is ACTS.

Adoration: Begin by telling your Higher Power you love Him and accept Her as your guiding light and the inspiration for all you do. Dedicate your day to following your Divine assignments with love. It will remind you Who is in charge...and it isn't you.

Confession: Admit your faults and failings. Consider ways to overcome whatever is tempting you to behave in ways that are disrespectful to others and yourself and don't honor your Deity.

Those behaviors which cause mayhem and mischief and leave a trail of hurt and destruction in your wake.

Thanksgiving: Remind yourself how grateful you are for everything you have in your life instead of complaining about what you don't have. Be specific. It will focus your attention on the positive vibes and help eliminate the negative influences.

Supplication: Ask for what you and those you care about need. Use names and be specific with the requests. Even though God knows what is in your heart, He wants you to explain. It is one way to make sure you know what you are asking for and if you truly want and need it, whatever "it" is.

When I started composing my own prayers, I used this method, I just didn't realize it. The Spirit was inspiring me before I knew She was my Muse for everything I write. I'm a slow learner.

APRIL 10

Another way to develop and help you keep on track with your prayer practice is to decide on a monthly theme. Just as I did when I decided to write this book of reflections. Each month has a theme. It helps me keep focused on my goal. I have the book mapped out in my mind. So too with your prayer practice; it will give you a plan. Don't misunderstand. I'm not suggesting you stop using the ACTS approach, or saying your favorite prayers, or reading sacred scripture or remembering specific people in your daily prayers. Assigning a monthly theme is simply another tool to add discipline to your prayer life.

Assigning a theme to each month will assure you are addressing whatever your particular "big picture" concerns might be. Maybe it is world peace. Mass shootings. Conservation. Justice. Gun violence. The grey wolf. Agribusiness. Family farms. Religious strife. Saving the rain forests. Clean water world-wide. Affordable health care for all. Children's safety. The wild mustang. I could go on, but you get the picture. There are innumerable causes that need our prayerful attention.

Prayer is powerful. What do you think would happen if we all prayed for the good of the world, the health, safety and welfare of humanity? Even my active imagination can't conjecture. What I do know for sure: God is capable of anything and everything. Simply ask Him.

APRIL 11

I can almost hear you muttering to yourself, "This woman is nuts! She has no idea how busy and hectic my life is. There is no extra time for anything. My day is filled. Adding one more obligation will blow my circuits." Yep, I get it. I know the feeling. I fought the suggestion because I just didn't have an extra minute. I was exhausted by the end of the day. I'm not sure when or why I decided to give in to the internal voice challenging me. My thoughts went something like this: What you are doing now isn't working. You are frustrated. Feel overwhelmed. Weary all the time. What have you got to lose? If it doesn't work, you can stop at any time. I just wanted to quiet the nagging voice!

What finally pushed me to add more prayer into my daily life was realizing the "nagging voice" was my Inner Spirit giving me an answer to a petition I didn't know I had been asking. Without conscious thought, weary me was pleading silently for help. When I finally realized the solution was within my control, I accepted the advice. Like I said, I am a hard-headed, slow learner.

APRIL 12

Since I refer to the Spirit, the Holy Spirit and my Inner Voice, perhaps I should tell you who She is and how I came to know Her.

As a Christian, I believe in the Holy Trinity: God, the Father, God, the Son, and God the Holy Spirit. The first two Persons have always been clear in my mind. Although I was taught The Third Person was a gift on my confirmation, She was a little fuzzy. Through a combination of conversations and study, I began to slowly identify Spirit. As I learned about various faith traditions and spiritual philosophies, most referred to a Spirit as integral to their belief system. My curiosity was piqued. I wanted to know Who this Spirit was and what role, if any, she played in my life.

A friend recommended a book, *The Shack*, by Wm. Paul Young. As literature so often does for me, reading this compelling story, I slowly began to understand Who the Spirit is and what role She plays in everyone's life. I eventually realized She is the Muse behind everything I have ever written. When I ask for and accept Her wise advice, my writing efforts are so much better and so much easier to understand with a clearer message, no matter the audience. What a powerful source of inspiration and I just have to ask!

As I called on Her for help writing, my requests soon went beyond written compositions. I now ask for Her guidance in most areas of my life. I don't disregard the Father and the Son, but The Holy Spirit has become a stabilizing force in my life. For some reason, I can relate to Her better; She is very real to me. And I didn't do anything to deserve Her wise advice. I just accepted Her presence within me. The rest is Her precious gift to me.

She is within you too. Get to know your Inner Voice, your Spirit. You will be amazed at what happens in your life. I certainly was.

APRIL 13

One way to make room in your busy day is to create specific spaces for prayer in your schedule. If you block time on your daily calendar, it is more difficult to avoid or ignore "prayer time." The calendar on my phone "yells" at me thirty minutes before an appointment, which is why I enter everything into it. Blasted phone alarm won't let me ignore or "forget" what I want and need to do. We already committed to prayer during our morning ritual. Let's see where else we can insert prayer into our day.

Create a plan. Decide when you usually feel the most frantic and harried. Mid-morning? Mid-afternoon? In the middle of an important professional project, which isn't progressing as you thought it would? During dinner preparations when everyone is restless because of fatigue and an empty tummy? Or maybe after the duties of the day are done, and you are able to sit and say, "ahh," which may not happen until your bedtime routine. Whenever you decide you want and need to devote a few moments to prayer is when you should schedule it.

As encouragement, in the beginning, set a time limit. Hmm...now why would I suggest that? I am borrowing one of the tenets of the twelve step programs: If I know the time commitment isn't open ended, I will be more likely to actually do it. Start with a two-minute prayer. As you get into the habit, you may find yourself extending the time. But if you don't, that is okay. Prayer should be a joyful experience, not a dreaded chore. This is how praying more during my day helped me turn my everyday activities into a prayer. Please try it. You will be amazed at the results.

APRIL 14

There are two types of prayer; both are important and deserve a place in our prayer practice. Discursive prayer is what we do most of the time. We talk to God. We ask for what we think we need. We bring the needs and desires of others to His attention. We tell

Him about our day and our concerns. It is our time to share our life with the Divine.

Contemplative prayer is another way to devote time to our Deity. Instead of telling our Higher Power what we want, how we want it and when to give it to us, we listen quietly for what He and She want us to know. This is not an easy state to enter or be in. But the only way to hear Him and Her is to tune out the world, quiet our thoughts, surrender control. Let go and let God. Some know this method as Centering Prayer, some as Oneness Prayer. (Instructions on Jan. 10.)

After a few months of practicing Centering Prayer, I began to consider it might be a way to help me overcome my self-defeating thoughts, my obsessions about everything I think, say and do and the things I ignore, don't say and regret.

I am still in the process of answering the question: How I do I rewrite the definition of who I am? Some days I am confident I am doing what my God wants me to do. Other times, I am convinced I am messing up everyone and everything I touch. In my kinder moments, I remind myself I am human and God loves me for who I am, faults, idiosyncrasies and all.

Your Divine Power feels the same about you.

APRIL 15

If you practice meditation, you are praying using a slightly different method. Even though I pray in traditional ways, I also practice meditation, just not daily. I learned taking a break or entering into mini-hibernation, invites calm into my day, into my mind. Many years ago, I was introduced to meditation by a wonderful boss who noticed I was frequently frantic and unsettled. He shared his concept of meditation; he called it his mental quiet room. Here is what he told me.

In your mind, create your quiet room. Remember, this is your room so make it a perfect place for you. Where is it located? What do you see when you look out the window? What do you hear? How is your room decorated? Furnished? What items do you have in your room? The more specific you are in setting the scene, the more your room will soothe you.

I have refined my room as my life changed and my needs morphed. My quiet room is in the woods on the edge of an ocean. I want to look out the window and see the sky, listen to the waves roll in and hear the wind in the trees. Both are soothing sounds for me. It is a small room painted in a soft, soothing blue-grey. There are pictures created by my grandchildren; they bring me joy. There is a comfy recliner with a good reading light and a soft blanket draped over the back and a small table to hold a mocha smoothie, a cup of tea, a glass of wine. There is a fireplace for the chilly nights of my soul; the sound of a crackling blaze induces calm. A bookcase dominates the room. It is filled with spy novels, mysteries, biographies and autobiographies, inspirational books and of course, daybooks. I add to my library whenever I read a book that speaks to me, to who I am and who I am striving to be. On the top of the bookcase is a CD player for times I want to listen to soft music.

I mentally retreat to my quiet room whenever the world is too much with me. It is especially appreciated when I am away from my special corner in the study. Whenever I need a moment of solitude in the midst of a crowd, it offers security, solace and serenity.

Build your mental retreat. You will be surprised how taking mini-hibernations will refresh your soul.

APRIL 16

I have suggested several ways to pray and how to add the practice into your day. I have given you places to pray. We have talked about how prayer affects us personally and helps calm our frantic mind, bring our Deity into our consciousness, add serenity to our day. Now let's look at other reasons we pray.

When I tell someone I will pray for them, no matter the reason, I mean it and follow through on my promise. To me, those are not just words. As soon as I am able, I add their name and specific need to my daily list. If it isn't written down, even with the best intentions, I will not remember my commitment. Not an excuse. A fact. I respect my unpredictable memory and do what I need to do to circumvent its quirks.

With a good-bye hug, I whisper Godspeed to family and friends leaving my space, whether to go across the street, across town, or across the sea. I make sure they know I wish them safe travels in God's presence, no matter how far they may wander. It is also a teeny reminder to God this person is special to me and please keep them wrapped in Your love. Just covering all the bases.

I send people off on their journey with a smile, a hug, a cheerful word and a quick prayer to the Divine for their safety and wellbeing. Bon voyage!

APRIL 17

The first step on the path to making adjustments in any behavior is admitting we are powerless over whatever is causing us stress and bringing distress to everyone in our world. When we admit we can't change by ourselves, it gives us permission to ask for help. This is the first part of twelve-step programs for a reason: If we don't admit we can't change on our own, no matter what we do or how hard we try, we will not be successful. Oh, we might stop for a few days, a few weeks, even a few months, but eventually we will return to our crutch.

One of the stumbling blocks to asking for help is the misguided conviction you are a "bad" person, so who will help me. Additional thoughts include: you have no self-control; you are too old and set in your ways; have held on to the habit for much too long; have tried and failed. Hogwash! Anyone can change with the right attitude and the proper support. But first, you have to admit you are powerless over whatever needs to change.

It doesn't matter the habit or behavior; you will not be successful changing without the support of the people in your life. Depending on the particular problem, you may need medical intervention. But at the top of the list is asking for Divine assistance and believing you will receive the grace and grit you need to overcome the problem. As it says in Matthew 11: "Ask and you will receive. Seek and you will find. Knock and the door will be opened to you."

What are you waiting for?

APRIL 18

What do you fear the most? Resist the most? Hide from the most? Perhaps this is the most effective time to seek Divine help. Maybe the best time to pray is when you are broken, vulnerable, at the end of your patience with the world, other people, yourself.

Most of the time, I pray consciously and focus my thoughts. Other times, when I am frustrated, frantic or fearful, my thoughts are jumbled; I am out of sorts with the everyone and everything, especially me. I wonder if even God knows what I am feeling and why I am pleading with Her. This is when I try to calm down by thinking about a quote from the writer, Anne Lamont, "Prayer is our sometimes real selves trying to communicate with the Real, with the Truth, with the Light." When I remember this observation, I am usually able to peel myself off the ceiling and concentrate on whatever is bothering me and focus on what needs attention.

And just who is the "Real," the "Truth" the "Light?" It is my Higher Power, my Deity, my God. She knows me the best; loves me the most; is the best One to guide me; the perfect One to lead me out of the wilderness I have wandered into. And She is always available.

What a gift for all of us!

APRIL 19

Grace is a gift from God. We don't deserve it and can't earn it. God gives it to us because He loves us and wants us to be the best we can be. He knows we need Her guidance. Because She sees our beauty, not our imperfections. It is in our recognition of needing our Higher Power, we are vulnerable, we are open to accepting grace in order to grow.

The key word is *accepting*. Grace comes in different guises and God uses many ways to bestow His gift. I don't believe in coincidence. All people come into our lives and all experiences happen for a reason. I think of it as a God wink. Some call it synchronicity. Others view it as serendipity. Whatever word you use; it means God is actively stepping into our life.

We may meet a person who is inspiring. Who may invite us to participate in a worthy cause from which we gain much more than we give. Someone whose conversations introduce us to a new way of thinking about a complex topic. We may read a quote that causes us to stop and ponder its truth. We may witness an act of kindness, which enlightens us to the importance of everyone, no matter their age, stage or circumstances. Those light bulb moments is the Deity whispering into our heart. Gently giving us our Divine task for the day, maybe even our life.

Be open to accepting God's grace. I promise you will learn more than you expect and grow more than you thought possible.

APRIL 20

I am, or rather used to be, a first-class worrier. Don't misunderstand, I still worry, just not as often, about as many things or for as long. Most of the time, I am able to convince myself whatever I am fretting about, likely won't matter a whit in a year, let alone five or ten years down the road. As the French philosopher Montaigne said, "There were many terrible things in my life, but most of them never happened." At 77, I can absolutely attest to that truism!

I learned how to worry from my mom. If the Olympics had a medal event in worrying, she would have won gold every time. She worried when she didn't have anything specific to worry about. She was always anticipating the next calamity and preparing for the coming catastrophe. The result? She couldn't truly enjoy anything or appreciate the good in life; she was always afraid it would be snatched from her without warning. What a sad way to live.

When I remember Zen Buddhism teaches the way to live life is in the now with openness and curiosity, I can stop ruminating about something that probably will never happen and instead fill my thoughts with possibilities. I am able to live in the present, enjoy now and stop worrying about an unknown future I can't change anyway. If I pledge the day to my Higher Power, I see life with a clear lens. Instead of looking for the negative, I find the positive. Instead of seeing selfish behavior, I encounter thoughtfulness. Every day, I pray for the inner sight to see the good in God's world and remember to recognize and appreciate the wonderous gifts and say think you when they appear.

APRIL 21

Sometimes when given an assignment, I think, "Ok, God, are You speaking to the right person? This is Jan. You know, the woman who messes up all the time and has no idea how to even begin this project! I can't possibly do what You are asking! I don't have the talent or training." It isn't I don't want to do what He asks; I just don't have the confidence I can. With help from a professional mentor early in my career, I discovered all I have to do is start and be willing to ask for help. And you know when I stop looking at how inept I am and just start doing, God helps me accomplish the task. She gives me the tools I need, be it the right person, the right insight or the right words. Funny how that works.

It took me a lot of years, a lot of frustration and a lot of negative self-talk before I finally realized as British philanthropist and abolitionist, Thomas Foxwell Burton said, "With ordinary talent and extraordinary perseverance, all things are attainable."

This book of reflections is confirmation the strategy works.

APRIL 22

Earth Day was first celebrated on April 22, 1970. The rallies, marches and educational programs were the result of people recognizing we only have one planet and we better start respecting its fragile ecosystems if we hope to leave a habitable place for future generations. I will skip the politics and what has happened in the intervening years. Suffice to say, there are still people who champion the cause of healthy air, clean water and land used wisely. Who want to not only preserve our earthy home, but perhaps leave it a little better than we found it.

Native Americans have always had a reverence and respect for Mother Earth. They accept we are responsible for its care just as she cares for us by providing the sustenance we need for life. The following traditional Navajo prayer is one I find especially meaningful particularly on Earth Day.

> As I walk, the universe is walking with me.
> In beauty, it walks before me.
> In beauty, it walks behind me.
> In beauty, it walks below me.
> In beauty, it walks above me.
> Beauty is on every side.
> As I walk, I walk with beauty.

APRIL 23

It is okay to get mad at your Deity. There are times in life when I just don't understand why someone is diagnosed with an incurable disease; loses a loved one; is left without the means to feed their family and provide a decent place to live; is handed a particularly challenging situation to navigate. Or when there is a catastrophic natural weather event: tornado, hurricane, flood, winter storm, crop failure, lighting strike. Or a man-made crisis occurs: a fatal auto accident, a train derailment, a plane crash, a shuttle failure, a company faces bankruptcy. Or war breaks out and it is the ordinary citizen and soldier who suffers the most; not the politicians and people in power who start the conflict and stay safe in their protected cocoons. I turn to my Higher Power for reasons and solutions to these unanswerable questions because my human mind can't figure out a way to prevent them or fix them when they happen. It makes my heart hurt and my soul sad.

So yeah, I get mad at God. I know it is an irrational reaction, but I don't know who else to turn to when my frustration and fear and yes, my anger get the better of me. Human me needs someone to complain to, yell at. And God listens. She understands my very real human need to search for answers. To find solace in times of grief. To have a loving bosom on which to lay my weary head, heart and psyche. So I turn to the most loving Entity there is: God, Adonai, Jesus, Spirit, Allah, Buddha.

APRIL 24

Most of us have a hard time admitting when we are not our best selves. We like to believe we always do the right thing, make the comforting comment, avoid the temptation that leads us astray. The truth is we don't. When we know we should or shouldn't act in a certain way, make a mean comment, push someone aside in our effort to move forward faster, we are aware of our motivation, even if we don't want to admit it. We forget or ignore or tell ourselves this one time isn't going to cause hurt for anyone. We are Grade A, Number One rationalizers when we choose not to be our best selves, regardless of the reason.

Even our mishaps and mistakes can be a prayer. Our higher Power knows we are human. And humans mess up...over and over again. It took me a lot of years and many missteps before I accepted God forgives, even less-than-perfect me. The catch? I need to ask for forgiveness with a contrite heart and a firm promise to learn from whatever I did or didn't do and try not to make the same mistake again. Is it easy? Sometimes yes, sometimes no. Depends on the infraction and its consequences. What I know for sure is when I admit I made a mistake, I feel lighter, freer and know I am back in tune with my Inner Being.

I also know when my outer behavior matches my inner desire, I feel calmer, more serene. I like me again. I know I am being the me God created me to be. The theologian, Richard Rohr, describes the feeling with this observation, "Only when inner and outer authority come together, do we have inner contentment and true spiritual wisdom."

APRIL 25

Spiritual wisdom is gained by many small steps and minor choices made during our daily routine. The Buddhist teacher, Thubten Chodron explains, "Small things matter; paying attention to them makes a difference." The difference impacts our understanding of what is expected of us and how we chose to fulfill our Divine duty. Do we act only for ourselves? Or do we consider those who might also be impacted by our choices and act accordingly? Do we accept responsibility for our behavior? Or do we make excuses and assign blame to others? Over a lifetime, every day decisions add up to who we ultimately become; we draw our own external and internal portrait. Whether we trust and love the person staring at us in the mirror depends on the picture we create.

Our prayer life has a huge influence on these decisions. If we devote quiet time and undivided attention to our Higher Power every day and turn to Her for advice, we will make better decisions and wiser choices. If we listen to our Deity, He will guide us toward the right path and lead us away from dangerous side trips and help us avoid the inevitable potholes in life. Slowly, we will recognize when we are about to go astray and turn toward our God for guidance and support instead of trying to manage on our own.

When we achieve spiritual maturity, it does not mean we will never make another mistake or ugly comment or avoid a prideful attitude, we are always going to be human. And humans make a mess of their life all the time. But we will know what we need to do to make things right with whomever we harmed, with ourselves, with our God. And that is a lesson we all need to look forward to learning and putting into practice.

APRIL 26

When I began to take my daily prayers seriously and put them first on my agenda, I received unexpected benefits. My heart came to attention. My soul started hearing. My mind started believing. My unconscious started accepting. This metamorphosis didn't happen overnight nor did I wake up one morning and suddenly have workable solutions to my world's contentious issues. No, I gradually became aware of the importance of living in the now instead of spending my waking hours living in my head and avoiding people. I became aware of the gentle sounds of the sacred soil on which I stumble through my days. I became present for myself so I could be present to the beauty and magic and awe all around me. More importantly, I learned to listen for and hear God's messages.

I'm not sure when I woke up to the changes happening within me. I just know I slowly began to realize the only one I can control is me and the only actions I am responsible for are mine. Because I accepted this truth, I suffer fewer episodes of depression and days of craving solitude in my safe nest. I became more willing to venture into the chaotic world and interact with unpredictable humans. I have more patience and call upon it easier and with more success. I am calmer, more serene. I started becoming the me God created me to be.

Astonishing gifts because I consciously made time for God in my every day. WOW!

APRIL 27

One day my Inner Muse posed these questions: How well do you use the reflections you read every morning? Do you listen for Divine messages? Do you hear them? Do you put them into practice? Do you grab a message from a homily or sermon and apply it to your life? Do you pay attention to the suggestions your spiritual mentors offer? These nagging questions kept invading my thoughts. Finally weary of hearing them, I took time to answer.

Depending upon the message in the daily reflections and the suggestions from my spiritual mentors, I usually try to incorporate the concepts into my life. Am I always successful? No, I am not. What I have learned is two-fold: If I accept I need to change in a particular area, it is easier for me to alter my behavior. However, if I don't see how or why I need to change, I either drag my feet and procrastinate or ignore the advice altogether. My rationale is I know me better than anyone, except my Inner Being, so I know what needs to change and what can remain as is.

As for a message in a homily or sermon, I pay closer attention than I do to other sources. Usually the priest offers one or two ideas I ponder after I leave the service. Do I always make them my own. No, but I do give them serious consideration. I believe the role of a homily or sermon is to give the congregation concrete examples of acceptable behavior and how to put the lesson into practice. It is our responsibility to listen and decide what we do with the information. God gave us the special gift of free will for a reason: To listen closely when His representative speaks and use our free will honestly and prayerfully to apply the lesson.

When God speaks. I listen. Unlike any human, She always knows what I need. Frequently before I know I need it. God does know best.

APRIL 28

When we have an ongoing relationship with our Deity through a daily prayer practice, we learn to let go and let God lead. We gradually shed our false self and bloom into the real us. We accept who our Creator made us to be. We learn what our Divine mission is. We begin to live our authentic life. We see magic and awe. We find beauty everywhere we look. We witness kindness. We hear the music of our soul. Our heart radiates love. We find true joy and contentment.

When we discover who we are meant to be, it gives our existence meaning. If we are single, we associate with people who help us navigate this crazy world in a safe, sensible way. If we are married or committed to a significant other, our hearts expand to include their well-being and helping them grow into who they are created to be. If we have children, we recognize God shares these treasures for such a short time. He wants us to nurture them, give them a solid moral code by which to live and send them into the world loving their God and fellow humans as God loves us all. As we reach the final third of our life, God still expects us to be the best we can be. She expects us to share our hard-earned wisdom in appropriate ways. All our life, God wants us to see, respect and love the Inner Being of everyone we encounter. Especially ourselves.

APRIL 29

This month we have been discussing prayer. When to set aside time to pray. Where to pray. The different forms of prayer. Who to pray for. What to ask for. What an established prayer practice adds to our life. Once we establish our ritual, our relationship with our Higher Power improves. Our view of ourselves and our place in the world shifts. We begin to access our Inner Spirit for guidance in our daily activity. We begin to meet and appreciate our true self as we become acquainted with who our Creator made us to be. Prayer is a powerful tool for responding to the craziness in our environment. Prayer brings a reliable advisor into our decisions. Prayer brings peace and serenity to our busy lives. Prayer brings us closer to God, our Heavenly Father.

Questions to consider:

- Do we accept we need a consistent prayer practice? Why? Why not?
- How does prayer guide us in our day-to-day life?
- What have I made my own? What do I plan to carry into May? Into the rest of my life?

Gratitude Entry: I am grateful I now know why prayer is important. How it can guide me to be a better me. I learned prayer is a strong antidote to all that is topsy-turvy in my world. I am grateful prayer brings me closer to my true self and to my Deity.

Reader: Add at least one thing you are grateful for as a result of reading, and contemplating the April reflections.

APRIL 30

This is part of my morning prayers. Saying these few words takes a heavy burden from my heart and places everything into God's loving heart. My day starts free and clear of problems and concerns because I place my trust in God's wisdom. I am confident She has my back and walks with me until I lay my weary body down at the end of the day.

Heavenly Father, into your hands, I place my worries, cares, doubts and troubles. Please don't let me take them back. Help me to stop overthinking everything, which causes me to delay doing anything. Help me learn patience and accept You work in Your time, not mine. I place my path, my goals, my decisions into Your loving heart.

With these words, I start my day with confidence, ready to face whatever the world throws at me because I know my Deity is with me every step.

MAY

Feelings

"We open our hearts by
feeling what we feel."

Melody Beattie

MAY 1

"That which is essential is invisible to the naked eye." This wise quote from Fred Rogers, the beloved creator and host of *Mr. Roger's Neighborhood* has a profound message in a few short words. Our emotions are what we feel inside. We may show outward signs in our facial expression or body language, but we *know* them in our heart and soul. If you learn nothing else this month, I pray you learn to accept emotions are never right or wrong; they are appropriate for you in the moment, under the circumstances.

It took me many years to learn to fully embrace my feelings. At a fairly young age, I could identify them. Sometimes I didn't have the right label, but I accepted the feeling. I suspect most children are the same: they feel what they feel and express it with the tools they know. Somewhere along the way, we start concealing our feelings, or explaining them away, or just flat out ignoring them altogether. Unfortunately, many of us were not allowed or encouraged to express them when we were growing up. Or we were told they were not "appropriate" for the occasion. Or we weren't old enough to feel a certain way. No wonder so many people deny their feelings or can't even identify exactly what they are experiencing.

As a young mother, I gradually realized I needed to learn to accept all of my emotions if I was going to understand myself and why I do and say and behave the way I do. I spent a lot of time learning to identify exactly what I was feeling right then, in the moment. I couldn't wait until tomorrow or next week, had to be right now. It was a challenging task I assigned myself, but I knew instinctively if I didn't learn to name my emotions and feelings, I wouldn't be able to operate effectively in my world.

I also realized I couldn't help others cope with their emotions and feelings if I couldn't recognize my own. I would not be able to help my children learn to identify theirs and express them in healthy ways. Another example of putting on your oxygen mask first. So, let's explore these sometimes elusive things we call emotions and feelings.

MAY 2

Emotions and feelings are close first cousins, but are not exactly the same. One usually follows the other. *The American Heritage College Dictionary* defines an emotion as "an intense mental state that arises subjectively rather than through conscious effort." There are several definitions of feelings. The one that defines how I am using the word is an "opinion based more on emotion than reason." To me, you can't have one without the other. A feeling is the direct result of an emotion. Remember: Neither are right or wrong; they just are.

While I will use them interchangeably, they do have slightly different definitions. Why am I telling you this? Words are valuable commodities. In our everyday use of many words, we use them interchangeably. However, if we want to understand why we act and react the way we do, it is necessary to keep actual definitions in mind. For example, frequently someone will say they are angry when they are really frustrated. Two very different emotions with two very different meanings. We may experience both at the same time, but if we act on either one, there are potentially very different consequences.

A big part of understanding ourselves and others is to accurately identify what we and others are experiencing, which gives us guidance on the appropriate response, or in some situations, non-response. Grasping the subtle differences in the words we use can help determine the quality of our relationships.

MAY 3

Giving ourselves permission to feel the emotion allows us to learn from it, so we should embrace the positive ones and release the negative ones. When we accept positive feelings, our inner radiance shines on the outside and gives us a little lift on the inside, if only in the moment. If we practice focusing on the positive emotions, our outlook shifts and so does our reaction to what happens in our environment. We are better able to cope with whatever the unpredictable world and her inhabitants throw at us. We will react in an appropriate manner to stimuli. We will be nicer, more understanding, more loving. What a wonderful gift for us and the people around us just for learning to focus on the positive. Worth a try.

Releasing the old and negative emotions removes the toxins from our heart and our soul. We are better able to forgive our self and others and become unstuck from pain and disillusionment. We can move on. There is a certain freedom in letting go of old resentments, past grievances and personal failures. It gives us the room to learn about ourselves, make deliberate changes in our thinking and behavior and grow into the person we were created to be.

If we give ourselves permission to identify our emotions and feel our feelings, a new world opens up. A friendlier world. A nicer world. Not just for us, but for those around us as well. What an uplifting way to improve our world, if only for a moment.

MAY 4

The first time a friend called me an empath, I wasn't exactly sure what she was telling me. So as I usually do, I researched what an empath is, their characteristics and how they function. It was an eye opening lesson.

The American Heritage College Dictionary defines an empath as "relating to, or characterized by empathy," which means "identification with and understanding of another's situation, feelings and motives." After thinking about those two definitions, I agreed with my friend's appraisal with one addition: I almost always "take on" the feelings of the other person and carry them as my own until their situation is resolved. I recognize the responsibility of my reaction, but even after realizing what I am doing, I find it extremely difficult to step back and let go. My heart hurts when someone I care about is going through a challenging time. Logically, I know I can't change them or their situation, but I can listen with love and help lessen their burden by being available when and how they need me.

As the years have passed, I have gradually accepted my ability to empathize is a special gift from God. She trusts me because I turn to Her for guidance and because I know I can't help others by myself. I need my Inner Spirit to walk this path with me. I can't do it alone. Neither can you, whether you are an empath or not.

MAY 5

Yesterday we talked about how being an empath affects me. You may have wondered if you too are one. I wasn't aware of the designation until my friend introduced it. I just recognized the description. If you think you may fall into this category, but aren't sure, here are a few more characteristics that define an empath.

Sometimes intimate relationships can feel overwhelming. You feel like the walls are closing in and you can't breathe because you haven't set and enforced boundaries and shared your emotional needs with the other person. It is important to gently, but firmly explain you need more alone time, more quiet time than most. You need time to recharge and renew your emotional batteries.

The energy in a room and within others has a profound effect on you, so you have to limit the time you spend in a crowd. You have a strong sense of just "knowing" what people are hiding behind their public mask; another reason you need to limit your time interacting with others. People confide their secrets and tell you their problems, which is a huge energy drain because you tend to take their issues as your own. You are also very adept at detecting lies. Sometimes you are not especially subtle when pointing them out either.

Being an empath can be exhausting, but it is also incredibly rewarding. The joy of listening, advising and watching a person learn and grow because of something you said, an insight you offered, a solution you slowly coaxed out of the person themselves cannot be described. It is a gift from God. Don't know about you, but I for one am not in the habit of turning down gifts from my Higher Power.

MAY 6

Another lesson I have learned through the years: There is a difference between sympathy and compassion. When you feel sympathy, you feel bad for the person. You may be able to identify with whatever the person is experiencing, but you really don't know exactly what they are feeling and how they are dealing with the situation. Remember: We can't crawl inside another's mind and heart, no matter how much we may want to. So be careful what you say to someone who turns to you for emotional support. "I understand" is probably the most banal comment because it is impossible to truly understand what another is experiencing. Better to say, "I'm here for you," ask what they need, listen with love and attention and follow through with your promise.

When you feel compassion, you help carry someone's burden. You step in and "do" without asking. Take over carpool duties. Make a meal or two. Clean the kitchen. Mow the grass. Shovel the snow. Do the laundry. Offer your extra days off. One man shined everyone's shoes and gassed up all the vehicles before the memorial service. A woman stayed with the other kids, fed them, read books and played games with them, supervised nightly baths, answered their questions and listened to their prayers while their sibling was in the hospital. These are but a few ways to show compassion and help a friend "carry" their burden.

Sympathy and compassion. Two emotions we are called on to share many times in our life. Sometimes it is up close and personal. Other times it is from afar. But we can always find a way to respond, if we think about it for a moment and ask for guidance from the family, from the authorities, from our Inner Spirit.

MAY 7

Happy, on the surface, seems to be simple and straightforward. But is it? One of the hardest lessons I had to learn and ultimately accept is happy is an inside job; it doesn't come from outside. Not people. Not things. Not experiences. None of these bring lasting happiness. As the journalist, Ralph Marston, said, "Your happiness will not come to you. It can only come from you." Another way of saying: Happiness is a choice you make, or don't, every day. I can decide to be happy? How do I accomplish that goal?

The Danish people believe it is safe to be happy, They practice Hygge (pronounced *hue-gah*). Roughly translated it means taking mini-moments to look around and see the beauty and magic all around you. Better yet, turn inward and treat yourself with love and respect. If you expect to be happy and allow yourself to be happy, you will. I'm not suggesting life is all sunshine and roses, but if you expect to find the positive, you won't see as much negative. And when you do encounter negativity, it won't affect you as much or for as long. Try it for a week. See what you find. I suspect you will find more happy than you believe.

Sad is a companion to happy. It is not necessarily the other side of the coin. But for me, when I don't feel happy, sad seems to take its place. Not a depression sadness, that is much different. It is a general sadness. I know the world could be so much better, people could treat each other with kindness and wondering why we don't do either. It is a mystery for sure.

Why don't we all choose happy over sad. What a calmer, nicer world we would share.

MAY 8

One way to achieve happiness is to switch perspective. Instead of expecting a disaster, look for what goes right during the day. Be curious about and alert to what is going on around you. Where is the new neighbor from? Who owns the cute little dog? Must tell Sam how much his beautiful flowers enhance the street. Need to be sure to tell Sally how well-behaved her daughter is. Laugh every day. The world is a bizarre place. I had a colleague on my first job who taught me to recognize the absurdity in life. Being able to laugh is a marvelous antidote to taking ourselves too seriously. Pay attention to the good things in your surroundings. See how your happiness meter goes up.

Cultivate a hobby. Gardening. Golf. Tennis. Embroidery. Sewing. Reading. Listening to music. Writing poetry. Crossword puzzles. Whatever sounds like a pleasant way to spend your time and forget the crazy world for a moment or two. It will give you something to focus on when life and its obligations seem to be closing in, blocking out everything. An engrossing hobby will help your immune system, you will sleep better, improve your cognitive ability and give you built-in me time.

Savor the everyday moments. Children giggling. Hot tea on a cold, blustery day. A good book on a lazy summer afternoon. A spontaneous hug. An unexpected text, email or phone call from someone you haven't heard from in a long time. It is the little, every day happenings that make up a life. These are what I remember as my days are winding down. These are the memories that feed my weary soul and bring joy to my heart.

MAY 9

My stepdad, Larry, had a wonderful view of worries. "Stuff all your worries in a box, put the lid on tight, and worry about them the second Tuesday of next week." You must admit, it is a novel approach, if a bit unrealistic. But his point is well taken. Most things we worry about never happen and if they do, the consequences are rarely as drastic as we envision. The author, Melody Beattie, has a "God Box" in which she stores her worries. She turns them over to God for Him to deal with. In other words, let go and let God.

Thinking about these two unusual solutions, perhaps we can each add other uncomfortable feelings to their own God box. Resentment. Jealousy. Envy. Aggravation. Disappointment.

Frustration. I would never suggest these are trivial emotions we should ignore. But we need to find a positive way to face them, deal with them, forgive ourselves, set them aside and move on. If we continue to let them eat at us, we won't be able to live a full life. We need to let them go. If we don't, they will slowly steal our peace of mind, our happiness.

Create your own God box of worries and frustrations. Give yourself a deadline to work through the cause of the feeling and honor your promise to yourself. Once you give them to your Higher Power to resolve, don't snatch them back. I'm a master at that little trick. And it has never given me anything but more of whatever I was trying to get rid of in the first place. I'm better than I used to be, but as I have told you before, I am a slow learner. Sigh...

MAY 10

Detachment helps us let go of our fears, frustrations and frantic responses. To quietly let go of irritating moments and detach from stressful situations, take calming breaths. Remember: 4 – 6 – 8: Slowly inhale positive karma through your nose and count to four; hold for a count of six; exhale negative vibes from your mouth for the count of eight. A psychologist taught me this trick. I use it whenever it seems I just can't deal with whatever is happening for one more second. I take a micro time-out, focus on my breath and intentionally breathe to slow my rapidly beating heart. It worked for me the first time I tried it. Didn't even need to practice.

Take as many calming breaths as needed to be able to objectively face whatever is causing the upset. It will be easier to remember what is happening is but a brief moment in a lifetime of moments. This recognition and acceptance will bring freedom to your mind and peace in your heart. Calming breaths are a surefire way to get in touch with your Inner Spirit, your true source of strength.

What I discovered is the more I take ownership of my feelings, the better I am able to keep them under control and in perspective. It also helps me avoid giving people permission to push my emotional buttons, which means I am better able to react appropriately. What a gift to myself and those with whom I interact.

MAY 11

Emotional distress often leads to physical illness and prolonged stress can lead to permanent health conditions. You need to identify the issue as quickly as possible. This process isn't always easy. It may be simple to determine who or what is at the bottom of the problem but changing or fixing it may not be. The first step is admitting your emotional state is compromising your physical health. Taking an inventory of what is going on in your reality is a must. But is has to be an honest look at the who, what, why, where and when. How you currently deal with the ups, downs and disappointments of life.

Once you take this emotional inventory and determine what needs to change, you may decide it is too much to deal with on your own or you don't know what to do and where to start. There is no shame in admitting you need an objective person to help navigate this rocky road. Whether a trusted friend, a member of the clergy or a mental health professional, ask for help. But remember, the Head of your team is your Higher Power. She is in charge of the process to help you figure out what to do and how to do it. Her guidance is invaluable.

Once you determine the steps to take, make a plan and follow it, being mindful the plan may need to be modified as you move down the path to finding answers and making changes. Don't take responsibility for something you didn't do. but always admit your part in the problem, so you can find a solution. Hear what the objective person is suggesting. Listen for your Deity's encouragement. You probably didn't get into this mess overnight. You are not going to solve it overnight either. If you stick to the process, you will find a solution. Think of how your world will improve once you implement the needed changes.

Godspeed on your quest. Be confident you can do it.

MAY 12

We are going to face negative people, which can bring on negative emotions, leading to negative feelings, most of which are caused by unkind words or thoughtless behavior. Now what? Buddhist teacher, Thubten Chodron, suggests you apply positive antidotes to negative happenings. Her prayer: "May all living beings, no matter whether I like them, dislike them or don't know them, have good health and a peaceful heart and mind."

Whoa. Wait a minute here. I am supposed to wish people good health who make me nuts with their crazy antics, ugly words and hurtful disrespect? And ask for a peaceful heart too? Remember, God, I am not a saint. I am an ordinary woman doing her best to live life in quiet harmony in her world and I am the one who is supposed to overlook and forgive unacceptable behavior? This one took a while to wrap my head and heart around.

After much fuming, fretting, and forgetting, I gradually learned wishing everyone, even disagreeable people, a peaceful heart actually helps me, whether it changes their behavior or not. Consciously whispering that simple mantra forces me to slow down, take a deep breath and remember I can remove myself from the toxic situation and this too shall pass. So can you.

MAY 13

You can and should use your Power from within to apply actionable antidotes to an unstable situation. These include stillness, kindness, gentleness, softness and nurturing. It doesn't matter what caused the bad mood or provoked the outburst, if you keep still and be quiet, it is amazing what usually happens. The person is so stunned, after a moment when your seemingly non-response has registered, they stop shouting. That is when your soft, nurturing side takes over. You kindly wait until the person calms down and gains some control of their voice and emotions. You gently ask what is troubling them? How can you help them put their world back into some sort of order or at least relieve the immediate pain? Be sure to listen carefully to their answers.

The first time a close friend suggested this approach, I thought he had gone completely off the rails. Be quiet? Endure the verbal abuse? Don't shout back? Smile softly? Yikes! But when a situation was rapidly spiraling out of control, out of desperation, I tried it. And blast, if it didn't work as promised. After a few moments, the other person realized I wasn't responding. He looked at me suspiciously, and sarcastically asked, "Giving up? Agreeing with me? You know I'm right." When I still didn't say anything, he was totally puzzled and I knew I had his attention. This is the moment we began to rationally discuss the issue. Within a reasonable amount of time, we were able to resolve our differences. The magic of a calm, quiet, wait-it-out approach was successful. I've used it ever since.

Calm. Quiet. Gentle. Loving. Works every time.

MAY 14

May is devoted to mothers. Birth mothers. Adopted mothers. Stepmothers. Grandmothers. Mothers of our heart. School mothers. Work mothers. Animal mothers. What do mothers everywhere share? Unconditional love for their progeny. They shout with pride for our accomplishments. They cry with our pain. They suffer with our losses. They commiserate with our disappointments. Mother. Mommy. Mom. Mama. Ma. Mo. No matter what you call her, you and your mother have a bond like no other.

I didn't especially like my mom well into my middle adulthood. I loved her, but I feared her more. Mom's approach to child-rearing wasn't the most enlightened. In spite of our differences, I never doubted she loved me and wanted only the best for me; we just didn't agree on what the best was or how to achieve it. Even as a wife and mother myself, I never quite lived up to her impossible standards and unrealistic expectations. The last two years of her life, we spent a lot of time together. She was older. So was I. She had mellowed. I had matured. She was finally willing to discuss our differences. I was ready to listen with my heart. I learned why she did some of the things she did and said some of the things she said. She was able to admit she didn't need to be as hard on me as she had been. I accepted she tried her best with who she was and what she knew and believed to be right. Mom died thirty-five years ago. To my unending surprise, I miss her. I now understand her words of wisdom and sound advice on a lot of life's issues. Do I always agree? No, but the older I get and the longer I am a mother and grandmother, the more I appreciate her. The more I recognize her enormous love for and influence on me. Thank you from my heart, mom.

The moral of my story: Even if you don't have the best relationship with your mother, keep working to improve it. Some day she will be gone and your chance to know her will be gone too. If you are blessed to have a good relationship with your mom, treasure what you share. Be sure to frequently tell her how you feel. You will grow that much closer, that much quicker.

MAY 15

Grief and sorrow are devasting emotions. Whether our spouse, parents, grandparents, a child, a sibling, a close friend, a beloved pet, we will experience death up close and personal. And never accept "it is just an animal and can be replaced." We know better. Our animal friends are an important part of our family. When a human or animal companion passes, it is imperative we face our loss, embrace our grief, learn to accept the person or animal is no longer part of our here and now. We move on when we are ready, not one day or one-hour sooner.

Each loss is different so we mourn differently. No one way is right or wrong, too short or too long. The method and time is exactly what we need it to be to process our devastating loss and let go. Don't ever let anyone tell you otherwise or try to convince you there is something wrong with you because you haven't behaved the way they think you "should." Your way. Your time. Your grief.

I speak from a place of knowing and understanding. I lost people starting at a young age. My paternal grandfather when I was twelve. My dad when I was thirty-five. My maternal grandmother when I was forty-one. My mom a year later. A few years after, two close, long-time women friends died about a year apart; none of us was sixty yet. So when, after a prolonged illness, my beloved husband of thirty-two years passed when I was sixty-eight, I thought I was prepared. Boy, was I wrong! I learned so many things about myself over the next few years. The main lessons: I love him. I will miss him every day and it is okay. Tears are liquid love.

I promised myself if I wasn't able to accept Paul's death, I would seek professional help. At three and a half years, I did. The counselor diagnosed Long-Term-Grief Syndrome and PTSD. She offered tools to guide me through my personal minefield. There were highs and lows, good days and not so good ones. After five years, I decided it was time for me to remove my wedding rings; they had never been off my finger in thirty-seven years. I gently removed them with a prayer and a promise, "I love you and will hold you in my heart forever, my dear, sweet Paul." He is still a part of me and always will be, but now I am able to live my life in the present, rather than yearning for a past that will never be again.

MAY 16

Grief and grieving are separate. Lynda Cheldelin Fell, a founding partner of The International Grief Institute said, "Grief is learning to live with someone in your heart instead of your arms." Grief is a feeling. Some people's grief seems to pass quickly; others may hold on to the emotion for weeks, months, even years. It is necessary to fully embrace grief, look at it, turn it upside down and inside out; it needs to be dealt with. I am not going to give you a time limit; it is different for everyone and every loss. But eventually, grief must be put back in its box in the corner of the closet until needed the next time. Unfortunately, there will be a next time.

Grieving is how we react to the loss. We show grief by our needs, our words, our behavior. Gradually I learned grieving is a process by which we work through the feelings accompanying grief.

Everyone has to find their unique path through the process. It is different for each of us and for every person we lose. We can lean on others when the world and our grieving is overwhelming, but ultimately, this is one journey we have to make alone.

Please remember and embrace: This process and its duration is different for everyone. Don't let anyone tell you it's taking too long or just "get over it." That last comment really annoys me. Doesn't the speaker understand we would "get over it" if we could, if we were ready to, if the devastating pain would go away. But that takes time, our time.

One Entity you *can* lean on, can rely on is your Deity, your Higher Power, your Inner Strength. She is waiting to hold your hand and quietly walk with you while offering Her unconditional love. What a gentle companion on this trail of tears. She will ultimately lead you into the meadow of acceptance.

MAY 17

"Fake it until you make it." A phrase made popular by a 1968 Simon & Garfunkel song titled *Fakin' It.* On first glance, it seems kind of dishonest, pretending to be someone or something you aren't. Especially after the death of someone close, it is a challenge and takes time, sometimes a lot of time to accept the loss and move on. So, if for no other reason than to stop the sincere suggestions and well-intentioned advice, maybe "faking it" while you travel through the minefield of grieving, is a harmless, but effective way to close down the helpful Harriets and Harrys.

It is not easy to move past the pain of your loss; there are no magic spells or happy pills to make it all go away. What worked for me after my husband's passing may not work for you. I can share my experiences and lessons learned, but you have to decide what is best for you. I learned certain distractions helped me heal, if only a little, even if I didn't realize the healing effects until later. I eventually learned to say "yes" when I didn't really want to. I made myself leave my safe nest a couple of times a week, even if I really wanted to hide in the closet Gradually I allowed myself to smile, maybe have a tiny bit of fun. And you know what, the world didn't come crashing down on my head for doing something for me. Didn't happen overnight and I took two steps forward today and one step back tomorrow. But I did move, if only incrementally.

After I moved into a senior independent living community, I slowly, very slowly, came out of psychological hiding and physically ventured outside my safe, enveloping nest. I gradually met new people, both men and women. I agreed to meet for coffee, a glass of wine, eventually a meal. I would stop briefly and actually talk to someone while fetching the mail, picking out books in the library, walking by the lake. Gradually I realized I was beginning to recognize faces and remember names. I actually began to enjoy conversations, being social for a short time. None of my newly acquired friends and acquaintances will ever know they contributed to my metamorphosis from thinking like a "we" to being engaged as "me."

Two or three years ago, I began to acknowledge a woman who was reaching the end of her grieving journey. I was becoming the me I am today, someone who once again enjoys life, looks forward to getting up in the morning and asks my Higher Power what She wants me to do today. I didn't give up on life, on me because the people around me showed they cared in many ways and gave me reasons not to give up. What an incredible gift! Thank you, friends and neighbors.

MAY 18

In the 13th Century, the Sufi mystic, Rumi, said, "The wound is the place where the light enters you." In the 21st Century, the Daily Om said, "A heart that has been broken and seen pain, reveals in it, a crack that allows more light in." Nearly a thousand years separate these two observations, which in essence, have the same message: A broken heart is the conduit to a stronger heart, a kinder heart, a more open and loving heart.

In the process of mending a broken heart from a disappointment, a personal disaster, a death, we grow as we learn life lessons, as we accept loss is a very real part of living a loving life. The message is telling us to embrace the cause of the crack so healing light can shine in the dark corners and teach us valuable lessons. The greater the pain, the greater the growth. I have always had trouble understanding the truth in that result, but so it is. It has happened innumerable times in my 77 years. Hard to ignore or discount what I encountered so many times in my own life.

Once you accept the raw psychological wound is the crack that invites essential growth, it is easier to endure the pain of the process. It is like swallowing nasty-tasting medicine, we do, so we will eventually heal. So too with psychological pain, we take it in, feel all sides of it, then deal with it so we will be able to let it go. Eventually, we will move on down the road of life.

MAY 19

There are times I feel, no I am absolutely certain, I am on a never ending, wild roller coaster ride and can't seem to jump off, no matter what I do or how hard I try. When I am able to stop the craziness for a moment, I am so dizzy, I don't know what is up or which way is forward. Noticing my predicament, a casual acquaintance sarcastically offered, "It is all your imagination." Besides being condescending, it was *such* a big help. Some people just don't understand me. Ever feel like that?

After pondering possible solutions, I decided I needed to let go of unnecessary drama and unneeded dogma. They were pulling me down, preventing me from moving from point A to point B, no matter what my goal. I had to take a breath (or several), study the situation and understand my reaction. I had to calmly decide what was more important: my peace of mind or following outdated rules, which didn't pertain to my life or work for me anymore. After looking through that lens, the solution was obvious: Dissolve the dogma, the drama disappears.

Two unexpected benefits: Whatever I was worrying about faded away. If it did happen, didn't even come close to what I anticipated because when I removed the drama, I could see the solution. Another example of worry not being as awful as predicted by my frenzied imagination. The second benefit: Whatever I was fearing seemed to magically fall away. Dropping my desperate clinging to a belief or behavior no longer relevant in my life, cleared the way for a sensible solution to appear. After expecting the worst, I learned if I let go and let God, the world really wasn't conspiring against me, I just thought it was.

MAY 20

It is okay to feel your anger. It should not be ignored. It can be used as a danger signal something is out of kilter around you or within you. As with all emotions, it is neither right nor wrong, it just is. It needs to be acknowledged and dealt with in a constructive way. It offers a choice with real consequences. You can only internalize anger for so long, eventually, it is going to erupt. It will either cause irreparable damage to a relationship or serious mental and/or physical health issues for you or maybe both.

If you allow your anger to control you, chaos reigns. You cannot think clearly and rationally. You lash out at the ones close by. Usually it is the people you care about the most and are the closest to. As the Mills Brothers' song said, "You always hurt the one you love, the one you should not hurt at all." It could be your significant other, your child, your parents, your sibling, your BFF, your pet, those who, many times, are not the reason for your anger. They are just the nearest available target. The result? Hurt feelings. Resentment. Sulking. Tears. Anger in return. Everyone loses in this scenario.

Getting angry at a stranger, an acquaintance or an inanimate object doesn't solve anything. Frequently, they have no clue what you are ranting about. If they do, many times they can't fix it anyway. And the louder you get and the more you go on about your perceived problem, the less they want to try and help. As my beloved Gram said, "You catch more flies with honey than vinegar."

How do I control my anger? I realized I don't like myself when I take my anger out on anyone, whether they are guilty or not. When I am in a full blown, adult temper tantrum, it is not healthy for my blood pressure, stress level or relationships. It took years of practice and patience to stop shouting, take a deep breath (or five), count to ten (or twenty), calm down and approach the situation rationally. Is it easy? Nope. There are times I just want to give in and shriek. But I finally learned, ranting and raving doesn't solve or fix anything. It just complicates the problem and makes me feel worse. So I acknowledge my anger. Determine what caused it. Decide how to fix it. Apologize, if needed. Learn from the incident, forgive myself, and move on down my path. You can do it too.

MAY 21

There is a difference between regret and guilt. Regret is being sad something happened, frustrated in the way it happened or disappointed it failed to happen at all. Sometimes we didn't have a direct involvement, but if we did, we may feel the need to do penance. If so, we need to accept the penalty with grace and make sure we follow through. If it was something another person did or did not do, it is okay to express our disappointment, then forgive and move along our path. It is over and done.

Guilt is acknowledging we messed up, taking ownership for our actions, our words, our intentions and their consequences. Doing what is necessary to repair the damage we caused. Don't try to pass the buck or make excuses. If guilt isn't faced and dealt with, it is another emotion that can cause serious internal harm and manifest in unacceptable external behavior.

I have thought about these emotions a lot over the years. Why? I am a master at both. I regret saying and doing anything which hurts another person. Even after I apologize and make amends as best I can, I replay the event over and over; I carry the regret for my words and actions. Even if the person forgives me, I have trouble forgiving myself. Long past the statute of limitations, I am still hanging on to my quilt. I am plagued by the idea I have to be perfect at all times. Never make a mistake. Never say a wrong word. Never hurt anyone. Forget I am human. Wait. I'm human? Gosh, I didn't know. I remind myself as many times as necessary. You can too.

MAY 22

The Buddhist teacher, Cuong Lu said, "Suffering is not a problem to be solved. It is a truth to be recognized." When I read the quote, I stopped, shook my head and read it again, then a third time. The words didn't change. They ran around in my head for several days. I was determined to figure out his message.

I know a lot of people who suffer from one ailment or another: some are life-threatening; some are physical, some mental; some are annoyances one can learn to accept and live with. But no matter the severity, suffering is a challenge we all face at one time or another and watch our loved ones tackle too. So how do I reconcile the message of Cuong's quote: It is not a problem, but a truth. Yes. Suffering is real. Some deal with it better than others. But why is it not a problem? I turned to my faithful *American Heritage College Dictionary*, which says suffering is "a source of pain or distress." Gosh, I know that. Not much help.

Suddenly I understood the message: Suffering is what I believe it to be; it can't be defined by anyone but me. It exists, which means it is my truth to identify and decide how I allow it to influence my behavior. I can keep quiet or I can moan and groan. I can choose to wallow in discomfort, live with whatever incapacity or inconvenience it causes or I can get help. There are decisions to be made and help available; be it over-the-counter relief or professional advice.

One of my medical doctors believed there is no reason for anyone to suffer. There is always a remedy to relieve the pain and discomfort, we just have to search for the one that works for the ailment and the person. If you are suffering, start searching. Don't give up until you find relief. You don't have to suffer. Relief is available.

MAY 23

"God whispers to us in our pleasures, speaks in our conscience, but shouts in our pain." This thought-provoking comment from the lay theologian, C.S. Lewis, offers an intriguing look at how our Deity talks to us. After thinking about his message, I decided his observation is spot on.

When life is going as we want it to and feel it should be, we have to make a concerted effort to "hear" when God speaks. We are caught up in the enjoying aspect of whatever our indulgences provide, so we have to listen more closely, because the noise is louder. I believe the reason God "whispers" is He wants us to stop focusing on me, myself and I and listen. Listening can't be an afterthought. We need to make the time to listen and hear the Divine message.

That quiet, usually nagging, voice is our conscience telling us to do something, stop something or notice something. It may be reinforcing what God whispered, which we didn't hear, so our conscious brain says the words in a way more difficult to ignore. It is louder, more insistent. One of the important lessons I have learned about my Higher Power's advice is many times She offers it quietly. She is leading me, not pushing me. But when She really wants me to pay attention, She delivers the message louder, in a more insistent way.

When I am hurting, I just want the pain to stop, especially when it is emotional pain. There is usually medicinal relief for physical pain; emotional pain relief is not as readily accessible. I have to dig deep to ease my psychological suffering, which forces me to try to figure out why I feel as I do and what God may be trying to tell me. I have come far enough on my spiritual journey to have learned to recognize when He is using the proverbial two-by-four to get my attention. I finally acknowledge I can't solve whatever it is on my own.

Your Higher Power has ways of getting your attention too. Learn what they are. Decide how to respond. When you do, you will ultimately find relief.

MAY 24

Every one of us is afraid of something. Spiders. Snakes. Dogs. Heights. Water. Flying. We probably know our fear is irrational, but we are not talking about thinking logically; we are talking about reacting emotionally. I do not like anything creepy crawly. Having two very curious grandsons cured me — sort of — but I still keep a safe distance between me and the icky creatures.

The fear I am working to overcome is flying. I know part of my anxiety stems from not being in control of: the plane, the pilots, the weather, the other passengers. I know I am a control freak, which is making it that much harder to let go of my dread and get on the scary plane. There is an important conference I really want to attend. I am trying desperately to face my unrelenting fear of getting on a giant metal tube and relinquishing the driving to someone else. Combined with my claustrophobia, the fear is winning. I am not sure which is going to triumph: my fear of flying or my desire to attend.

I know this fear is irrational. It is keeping me from enjoying the last season of my life to its fullest. But knowing and doing are very different. Say a prayer for me, Actually, say a lot of prayers. I have no doubt I need Divine intervention if I am to get on that intimidating, flying contraption!

I am sharing this fear because I want you to know I do understand relinquishing any fear is difficult. There is no surefire way to overcome it or magic formula to let go of it. I am trying to practice wise advice from the writer, Melody Beattie, "Do not allow the fear of what if to ruin the joy of what is."

MAY 25

There are a few ways to try to curb fears. I offer them because some may work for you. So far, none have been successful getting me on any durn plane, but I haven't given up hope one will work someday.

I know I need to stop obsessing about the object of my fear. I don't obsess, exactly, more like ignore the topic unless someone brings it up. When flying is mentioned, instead of thinking about the worst, I try to switch my thoughts to a positive outcome. In my case, the joy of attending the conference. I respectfully listen to one rational reason: There are few alternate transportation methods. Why? The conference is on another continent. Definitely have to consider that argument.

My travel companions have promised they will be on either side of me as I board the plane and stay with me throughout the entire flight. I have been assured they will not abandon me should I freak out at any point of the adventure. They are loving friends so I accept they will keep their word. I am trying to visualize getting off the plane at my destination and enjoying the conference events.

Will any of these suggestions actually get me on the plane? I have no idea. But I offer my struggle to encourage you to face your fear with the knowledge you are not alone. Even the most confident people have some fear they are working to overcome.

MAY 26

Jealousy to anger to resentment. What does this destructive cycle bring us? Nothing but pain, disillusionment and discontent. It is easy to say we shouldn't be jealous of someone's seeming good fortune, whether in relationships, career or life in general, but sometimes it seems impossible to avoid it. I wish I could tell you I am never jealous, but I would be, as my late husband used to say "stretching the truth." Fortunately, I have learned to recognize when I experience this self-defeating emotion. I have also learned how to work through the feeling.

I accept the negative emotion doesn't hurt anyone but me. The other person in the equation isn't affected unless I plan and follow through on some form of retaliation. Then we are looking at a different situation, which may require outside intervention. I am talking about a momentary feeling, which attacks my self-confidence and self-worth.

I take an honest look at why I feel jealous. What do I believe I lack? What can I do to overcome my perceived deficiency? Do I really want what the other person has? Most of the time, the answer is no. I am content with what I have. Funny how that happens: When I focus on what I already have instead of wanting what I don't really need, the jealousy disappears as fast it popped up. Self-knowledge is a powerful tool.

MAY 27

How can we protect ourselves from thoughts that hurt? We need to look at them honestly. Decide if and how they may be valid. If we keep replaying them in a constant loop, we will never heal and be able to move on. Solution: Find a way to fix whatever is fixable, even if it means giving up something or someone. If it truly isn't fixable, and some situations are not, learn to accept it and set it aside. We need to clarify our priorities. It's called forgiving oneself and practicing self-love.

Sometimes it isn't easy to clarify our priorities. Too many people and chores and tasks are pulling at us, all demanding our attention RIGHT NOW. When I am faced with this dilemma, I stop my world, list the demands, and decide which one comes first. My General Priority List begins with family first, family by choice second, friends in need next. Everyone and everything else follows. When I review the people and things calling for me to say or do something, it makes it a lot easier when I consult my General Priority List. Note please, this list is Capitalized. Why? As a veteran writer of lists, it is my way of focusing on the most important people in my life before all else. After I ask my Inner Guide for Her advice, it is easy to decide who needs my attention now and in what order.

Most of the time when I use this method, those hurtful thoughts suddenly become less important and are easier to let go. When I focus on others, I don't have the time or emotional energy to think about what someone, including me, said or did that caused my pain. I take my thoughts away from me and turn them to how I can be helpful to someone else. Works every time.

MAY 28

How do we create joyful thoughts when the world is full of pain, discontent and just plain meanness? Be grateful for the good things in our everyday life. Family and friends. Our four-legged companions. Waking up to a new day. The first cup of coffee or tea or smoothie. The blue sky. Thanking friends and acquaintances for being part of our world. Making a new friend. Connecting with old friends. Encouraging those we meet with a smile, a nod, a warm hug. Planning interesting activities by ourselves or with others. Emerging ourselves in nature by taking a walk, sitting in the garden, watching birds play in their aerial domain. Volunteering with a worthy organization; joining an interesting group.

One surefire way to have joyful thoughts is to stay grounded in the moment. Stop ruminating about past failures and fretting about future events. All we have is right now, this moment, so savor every one given, it might be our final one. Keep our minds active. As the saying goes, "A mind is a terrible thing to waste," no matter our age and stage. Learn a new game, a different language, an intriguing recipe. Read an uplifting book. And when finished, share it with a friend.

There is absolutely nothing wrong with devoting an entire day to self-care. In fact, it is essential to take a mental health day now and then. Take a bubble bath. Get a haircut; consider a new hairstyle. Give yourself permission to indulge in retail therapy, whether you buy anything or just browse. Treat yourself to lunch at a restaurant you have wanted to try. Listen to music. Have a glass of wine or a cup of tea. Laugh. Spend the afternoon with a friend you haven't seen in a while. You will create joyful thoughts and warm memories and reinforce a healthy self-esteem.

Joy is what we make it. It is different for everyone. If you don't know what gives you joy, start paying attention to whoever and whatever makes you smile, reminds you of the good things and memorable times in your life and adds peace to your day. Write them down. Soon you will have your own list of joy-makers to call on when you are frazzled and need a gentle reminder. What a joy.

MAY 29

When you open your heart, you will discover joy, peace and love comes from within. If you appreciate what you have and savor the gifts from your Inner Spirit, you will receive more of whatever you need. You will learn sharing yourself in loving ways brings joy and whatever you share will grow exponentially. The more you have, the more you share, the more you receive and the more you appreciate what you are given and the cycle begins again. It took me a long time to learn this lesson, even longer to accept and practice it.

God has given every one of us special talents and abilities. She assigns people for us to nurture, to be there when they reach out and for us to reach for them when they can't. She assigns tasks no one else can complete but us. Don't panic. Our Deity also gives us what we need to perform our Divine duties. We just need to lean on Her and ask for Her guidance before we begin and during our assignments. Our Higher Power is always available for consultation, day and night, twenty-four/seven.

I derive enormous comfort knowing, without a doubt, God has my back and supports me as I go about my day trying to live the life He wants for me. When I begin to falter and fear I am messing up, I remind myself, God doesn't make junk. I nod, smile and keep going.

MAY 30

My prayer in the beginning of May was you would learn to accept your emotions and feelings are appropriate for the moment. We have discussed many situations to help you understand the what and the why. I suggest you keep track of your feelings for a month. This exercise will help you define what represents contentment in your life. It is different for everyone. Don't forget to include how you react to the unexpected. Consider your mindset, the company and the circumstances of all your encounters and expectations. They will tell you something about who you are and what you are searching for.

Questions to consider:

- Do we accept emotions and feelings are neither right nor wrong? Why? Why not?
- How do our emotions and feelings affect us in our day-to-day life? Be specific.
- What have I made my own? What do I plan to carry into June? Into the rest of my life?

GRATITUDE ENTRY: I am grateful I understand emotions and feelings are human reactions to the people and events in life. We all experience them in our own way. Accepting and dealing with them in a positive way and letting go of negative responses is necessary to maintain a healthy perspective on life and our reaction to its stimuli.

Reader: Add at least one thing you are grateful for as a result of reading, and contemplating the May reflections.

MAY 31

Seek inspiration in people, places, things, and events; it is all around, simply pay attention. Be curious about the cause and effect of your emotions and the feelings generated. Remember happiness is momentary. Contentment lasts.

Dear God, please give me the grace to accept my emotions and feelings are normal and healthy. Ignoring them or disrespecting myself for experiencing them is self-destructive. Help me remember, they are gifts from You. When I don't know how to accept an emotional reaction, help me stop, look and decide what I can do myself and what I need to give to You. Help me learn to forgive myself and accept Your forgiveness.

My feelings are mine. Your emotions are yours. They may have the same name, the same definition, but we each react differently and deal with the consequences in our own unique way. There is no right way or wrong way, there is your way, there is my way. Both are valid.

JUNE

Intuition

"Intuition is seeing with the soul."
Dean Koontz

JUNE 1

The American Heritage College Dictionary defines intuition as "the act or faculty of knowing or sensing without the use of rational processes; a perceptive insight; a sense of something not evident or deducible." Most of us, when hearing the word, automatically think of women, but men are also blessed with intuition. But they often don't trust it, so they ignore it. I am asking my male readers to at least give the reflections this month a fair hearing. Think about the messages in the days ahead. You will learn something inherent about the women in your life; maybe about yourself too.

Your intuition always speaks with love and wisdom from your heart. Pay attention; it will never lead you astray. Since the message is actually coming from your guiding Inner Spirit, the One who will never lie to you or send you down the wrong path, it is safe to listen to and follow your intuition. Sometimes the message comes as a lightbulb moment. Other times, you just "know" what to do or say, how to behave in a given situation or with a particular person. It is the right response for you in the moment. It comes exactly when you need the insight and understanding.

If you think about it, you will remember a time when your intuition came to the rescue. Believe with certainty it will happen again. Don't ignore it. Don't evade it. Don't walk away from it. Accept it is your Higher Power guiding you at the precise moment you need Her guidance. What a special gift.

JUNE 2

Perhaps if you think of intuition as a "hunch" or a "gut" feeling, it will be easier to respect it as real and worthy of your attention. You might think of it as something is a little off. You can't quite explain what it is you are experiencing, you just know you need to act in a certain way, say certain words, be a calming presence. That is your intuition working; your Inner Guide directing you to act now, help restore order to chaos, pay attention to a particular person. Or maybe you smile because everything is right with the world, for the moment at least.

According to Buddhist teaching, if you listen to your intuition, you will open your heart, find your truth and live it by your actions. What I think of as a lightbulb moment is our Inner Spirit teaching us a lesson we need to learn. We need to pay close attention to hear Her message, accept what our intuition is telling us and engage in whatever we are being advised to be or do or share. Or stop.

Is this practice always going to be easy? No, it is not. Even though I know it is the truth for me right now, my self-centered ego will frequently reject the knowledge. The traps I fall into the most are when I am enjoying whatever I am engaged in and don't want to stop. Or feel I am caught in a situation I can't find a way to end. What happens when I ignore my lightbulb directive? I always end up regretting the decision. It comes back to bite me because I ignored my truth. As I used to tell my children and have passed along to my grands, "Learn from my mistakes. You need time to make your own!"

JUNE 3

One of the ways to avoid making, as my gram used to say, "mountains out of molehills," is to make sure whatever you are experiencing is real drama, not ego-drama. What is ego-drama? It is believing everything that happens in your life is either because of you, caused by you or should be controlled by you or a combination of all three. Who put you in charge of the world?

Thought that responsibility belonged to our Higher Power, however you know Him and Her. It is a humongous undertaking watching over the world. I don't know about you, but I have enough to do taking care of me and keeping me under control and away from mischief without fretting about the whole world and everyone in it.

Listen to your intuition. It is your heart, your Inner Wisdom speaking to you, guiding you toward good decisions, protecting you from foolish choices. With this reliable, divine driven, built-in backup system, why would you ignore it? It is an integral part of your internal advisory board: the younger you, the current you, the you striving to be the best possible you with all your faults, failings and idiosyncrasies. The you your Deity knows and loves. Listen to Her wise council. Heed His loving warnings. Pay attention to the lightbulb messages. Listening to and heeding your intuition will not lead you astray.

JUNE 4

Rest is so important. Body, soul and psyche need rest and relaxation to be open to hearing and heeding our intuition. If we are weary, it is difficult to focus on the quiet voice whispering to us. Giving us instructions. Suggesting alternatives. Or maybe telling us we are where we need to be and are doing what we need to be doing. Maybe our Inner Guide is telling us we don't need to change a thing. All is as it should be. We know how life is, so we don't expect our body, soul and psyche to always stay in tune, but savor the moment, enjoy the experience for as long as it lasts, even if it turns out to be fleeting.

I am not going to give you a lesson on how to take care of yourself. It is different for each of us. But there are a few standards, which apply to everyone. I don't know about you, but I need to be reminded of them now and then. I am prone to forgetting what Jan needs because I am focused on what everyone else needs. Seven to nine hours of sleep. A balanced diet. Some kind of exercise every day. Allotting quiet time to my Deity. Time for a favorite pastime. How you define these essentials is your choice. Just make sure you follow your personal agenda. Don't skip any item, for even one day.

Over the years, I have discovered, if I ignore these basic needs, I am weary to my bones. I have no energy for anything. It is easier to ignore my intuition and my inner wisdom. When I do, I always regret it because I missed something important I needed to know about myself, my loved ones, my world. In my life, it is easier to slip into my black pit. For your peace of mind and openness to hearing and feeling your intuition at work, make sure to give yourself the essential gift of R&R. You will never regret it. It is time well spent.

JUNE 5

Sit still. Be quiet. Relax. Breathe. I suggested these steps in an earlier reflection. It is time to remind ourselves of their importance in our frantic, crazy, unpredictable days. Let your heart, your soul, your inner voice take over. For most of us, the very thought of sitting quietly, not saying or doing anything is almost impossible to even consider, let alone actually set aside time every day to practice this calming, soothing ritual. Now I am going to suggest something even more radical: As often as you find yourself mentally or physically weary, take a time out. What is this lunatic saying? I am advising you to pay attention to what your mind, body and soul is saying and follow through as often during the day as you need to.

Start with two minutes. Set the timer on your phone. Don't fidget. Just sit. Relax. Clear your overactive mind. You can do it for two minutes. When the timer goes off, go back to whatever task put you down for the count. When you conquer two minutes, move to five minutes, eventually ten whole minutes to do nothing but Be, just Be. Practice this simple, calming exercise as often during the day as you need it. You will be pleasantly surprised and wonder how you managed to go through life without these restorative minutes. It doesn't change what is going on around you. It changes your perspective about what is happening. And sometimes that is all you need to shift from a negative attitude to a positive one. So give yourself the gift of time, especially in the middle of a crazy day.

JUNE 6

Our self-image is how we see ourselves. One valuable lesson I have learned is my view of me, myself and I isn't necessarily the view everyone else has. We all see the world through our own eyes. Goes without saying, my perceptions are different than yours. We each have a history that has colored how we see the world and everyone in it. The people with whom we interact and the experiences we lived through contribute to who we are and how we view our environment and its inhabitants. Hence, others rarely see us as we see ourselves. And we rarely see others as they see themselves. Neither of us knows who the other one really is inside.

What causes this human behavior? Confirmation bias. It interferes with our acceptance of another person as a fellow human being. It is an unconscious, preconceived notion of who a person is and their expected behavior based on some unchangeable fact: red hair, no hair, lots of hair, gender, race, ethnicity, age, culture, religious belief or any other categories you can come up with. This usually unconscious reaction interferes with how we understand others and influences if and how we accept them. In other words, we judge an individual based on something over which they have no control.

I have fallen into this trap. I only realized I was guilty a few years ago. Once I was made aware of this tendency, I made a conscious, deliberate decision to fight my automatic reactions. It is not easy to overcome a lifetime of making unconscious, snap decisions based on a faulty roadmap. It takes concentration and the desire to live what I have been taught by life's lessons: All people are worthy of respect just as they are because God dwells within them. I don't have to like them or spend time with them, but I am required by my Deity to respect them and accept them for who they are: Children of God. The best stamp of approval there is.

JUNE 7

A faulty self-image and a misguided interpretation of other people's character causes all sorts of problems. It controls our behavior, usually in negative ways. It prevents us from growing and improving our little corner of the world. It keeps us from learning people's fascinating stories and discovering how they can teach us to be better. It is a huge roadblock to living life with openness and joy. Having an open mind and an open heart allows new thoughts, ideas and perceptions to enter our awareness and influence our behavior. As Mark Twain said, "An open mind leaves a chance for someone to drop a worthwhile thought in it."

If we only interact with people like us, we can never truly know our world and recognize its wonderous diversity. One of the bosses early in my career believed we all are an expert at something. We have three related purposes: learn what we are good at, share our expertise with those around us and be willing to learn what our neighbor has to offer. He believed if we lived life with that attitude, there would be fewer misunderstandings and the world would be a nicer place. Wise man with only a sixth grade education. Another example of learning from everyone who crosses our path, no matter their background.

People fascinate me. Maybe it is the writer gene, but I want to know what makes people who they are, do what they do and react how and why they do to the many stimuli in our crazy world. One of the most effective ways I can learn those things is to engage with others, accept them for who they are and don't expect them to fit into whatever preconceived box I may have. I also believe it is how our Higher Power expects me to behave.

JUNE 8

Sometimes we do things out of habit rather than intention. This path can and often does lead to friction with others and discord within ourselves. Brushing our teeth. Wearing a coat when it is cold. Holding the door for the person behind. These are all positive habits we don't think about; we just do them. Being afraid of someone because of the color of their skin or the clothes they wear or the religion they practice are only a few of the superficial things by which we habitually judge others. Or maybe we had an uncomfortable or bad experience with someone so we avoid everyone whom we decide is just like "them" without considering the consequences. These are negative and limiting behaviors that keep us from learning and growing and becoming a better person.

I stayed away from the practice of the church of my birth for forty years because of the attitude and actions of a few misguided men. I applied their behavior to everyone who represented my church. The only one ultimately hurt was me. My emotional blindness kept me from enjoying the benefits of the sacred rituals of the church in which I was raised. A prime example of a habit doing harm.

Be careful how you respond to your intuition. Make sure you have all the facts and make sure they are right and true and not something you conjured up in your imagination. Don't blindly make judgements. Acting or reacting without thinking about consequences will often cause harm to everyone involved. Think before you act. Now that is one positive habit to cultivate.

JUNE 9

The Buddhist nun, Pema Chodron advises, "Illusions of permanence" lead us to believe our feelings and situations don't change, can't change, won't change. Believing this about life causes us to "get stuck" and inhibits our growth as a human. Two years after my beloved husband died, I began to realize I was stuck; unable to move from thinking as "we" to living as "me." Unconsciously, I was making decisions as if I were still half of a couple. I was not growing. I was not accepting the fact my soulmate was not physically with me. I was still thinking and behaving as if there were two people for whom I was responsible. I had not only stopped growing but I was in a perpetual state of mourning, which is not emotionally healthy.

This realization led to a thorough evaluation of my choices, the way I was rambling aimlessly through my days rather than living life in all its fullness. As a result of my mental housecleaning, I decided I needed to leave "our" home of twenty-one years and move to "my" space. Was it scary to contemplate leaving the safety of a familiar environment to enter a new chapter of my life?

You bet it was! But I did it anyway. I moved into the independent living area of a continuing care retirement community. It is a totally different atmosphere than I was used to. After six years, I can say with heartfelt certainty, it was one of the best, most fulfilling decisions I have ever made.

Don't misunderstand, I didn't adjust quickly. It was three plus years before I began to think of and call my new apartment "home." I attended two grief support groups, met with a therapist for two years and did a lot of mental homework in an effort to "unstick" myself from sixty plus years of thinking, acting and being. I was blessed to meet several incredibly loving people who walked with me on this part of my journey. I wouldn't be where I am today were it not for their encouragement and support. I treasure their friendship and thank God every day for their presence in my life. All because I realized I was "stuck" and decided to "unstick" myself from an unhealthy way of existing.

You can too.

JUNE 10

Now that I am "unstuck" and living life as fully and joyfully as I can, I cautiously consider potential actions by asking myself, "Will what I am planning to do today matter in five, ten, twenty-five years?" Depending on my answer, I either forge ahead or rethink my decision. If it is a day of fun, I usually go for it. I learned the hard way, the way I learn most life lessons, I need to let the little girl lurking inside take over and play. We always feel rejuvenated when we do. For that, I thank her for the reminder and a few special friends teaching me how to play and, most importantly, not feel guilty when I do.

For different decisions, sometimes I decide the consequences are far-reaching and will benefit future me in some way. Others I discard as unnecessary, destructive, or not worth the hassle, or modify my plan to make the choice beneficial. There are choices I revisit from time to time and end up making a different decision. Why? My life has changed. I have grown. I am better able to accept the consequences. All because I accept illusions of permanence are transitory and inhibit my growth by preventing me from experiencing intriguing people, interesting places and engrossing activities.

Once I unstuck myself from old unsuccessful behavior, I made a conscious decision I was not going to allow myself to get stuck again. I really don't like going backwards. Do you?

JUNE 11

I have claustrophobia. I became aware of the condition when I was on an elevator full of people and it suddenly stopped between floors. I didn't panic, mainly because a woman standing next to me did. I was focused on trying to calm her so wasn't consciously aware of my rapid heartbeat, sweaty palms, nervous stomach and oncoming migraine. It was after the situation was resolved and we were safely off the elevator, I became aware of my physical reaction. Ever since that experience, I refuse to get into an elevator with more than two other people; I will wait for the next one, thank you.

There are other places claustrophobia strikes. It contributes to my terror of flying. I won't sit in the middle of a crowded room. I sit on the edge as close to an exit as possible. I avoid shopping when I know there will be crowds. A mass of people has the potential to bring on an attack. Even sitting in a sacred place, if too many others wander in, I am immediately uncomfortable and start squirming, looking for an unobtrusive way out.

Most of us have something we fear. I refuse to believe these fears are not real. I believe if we "feel" something, it is real for us, even if it isn't for others. My solution is to turn to my Inner Spirit, let my divine intuition take over, and give it to Her to make it all go away. It works more times than not.

Try it. You might be pleasantly surprised how much She soothes the disturbed psyche.

JUNE 12

"Having experiences is called living. Sharing experiences is called loving. Let yourself experience both." Wise advice from author, Melody Beattie. When I read this observation, after some thought, I realized just how true it is. We move from minute to hour doing one thing and another to take care of ourselves, tidy our space, accomplish some task. A personal definition of living: When we share a fleeting experience, spend quality time listening, join someone on their particular journey for even a moment, we are offering ourselves, spreading Divine healing and sharing Divine love. Both experiences help us grow into who we are meant to be, whether we are aware of this result or not.

When we blindly scurry through our day, when we don't take the time to savor our experiences, alone or together, we miss so much. We don't fully appreciate the splendor and richness of our immediate environment. How can we learn and grow if we aren't paying attention, if we are so engrossed in our immediate needs, we miss what the bigger world has to offer? Paying attention is a good way of being in the moment. Some people call the practice mindfulness, others being present. No matter what label you use, stop rushing through your days. Walk slower. Look around. Smell the air. Admire the people, places and creatures you encounter.

You don't have to be "of" world, but you sure miss a lot when you are not fully "in" the world.

Try it. I can almost guarantee, it will change your perspective for the better, which will enhance your life and the life of those around you.

JUNE 13

Maybe you are where to need to be and know where to go and how to get there from where you are. If so, rejoice! Listen to and follow your intuition. Take advantage of this inner knowledge and understanding. Trust it. Sometimes we are sure of our reason for being, where we are meant to be and with whom we are meant to interact. Be careful, though. Make sure you are living in reality and not a fantasy world of wanting and wishful longing. If you see red flags and hear a tiny voice whispering, "Slow down. Take your time. Consider your options," pay attention. Sometimes we want something or someone so much, we fail to heed the warning signs.

How am I so sure of this? Because I have let myself ignore the warnings, even though I heard them, in some cases, even acknowledged them, but still plunged blindly ahead anyway. It may have taken time, even years, but I have always come to regret ignoring the red flags. I wish I could tell you I don't do that anymore, but alas, I can't. I continue to make dumb choices and stumble down dark alleys and get myself into emotional danger zones. I have decided it is part of being human. Letting myself believe I have all the answers and I'm too smart or too well informed to fall into traps. My unrestrained ego gets me into trouble every time. The difference at my age is I am unable to physically do some of the outrageous things I think I want to try so, by default, I keep out of mischief. But I still have trouble not responding to a dare, whether it comes from someone else or from my over certain ego. As the Amish proverb says so eloquently, "You need not call the devil; he'll come without calling."

JUNE 14

Synchronicity. An intriguing concept. *The Merriam Webster Online Dictionary* defines it as, "The coincidental occurrence of events...that seem related but are not explained by conventional mechanisms of causality." The psychologist, Carl Young, used the theory to help patients understand certain phenomena in their life. I was familiar with the concept, but didn't begin to understand its effects until I was in my early 70s.

I don't believe in coincidence, never have. I believe there is a cosmic reason why things happen and people come into our lives at the exact time we need them. Maybe to help us through a rocky time; maybe to show us we are loved and loveable, maybe to help us find our particular path, but rarely do they arrive or occur randomly. Many times we may not understand "why" until years later when the lesson learned becomes evident and the purpose for which we met the person or experienced the event finally becomes clear.

When I decided to move into an independent living retirement community at 71, slowly I met a diverse group of interesting people who posed challenging questions and offered a myriad of opportunities to learn and grow. I gradually began to understand these events happened for a reason and the people were sent to walk with me because I needed their particular presence in my life if I was going to become the me I am today. I couldn't do it alone so my Higher Power sent who and what I needed. Imagine that! Learn to recognize synchronicity. It will enhance the present, improve the future and help you become more you; the person you are destined to be.

JUNE 15

Dreams matter, be they memories from the past or predictions for the future. Studies have shown we dream every night. Many people claim they don't dream, but whether the dream stays in our unconscious or appears in our conscious reality, we all dream. Mine are usually mini-stories with a beginning, middle and a vague end. When I recall them, they almost always have some kind of message. As with other mysterious occurrences, I consider dreams necessary for my mental health. They may not make logical sense, but I can almost always, after pondering the story, figure out the message. Sometimes it is silly, sometimes sensible, sometimes it scares the bejabbers out of me, but all get my attention, if only for a few moments after waking.

From studying psychology and anecdotal examples, I know dreams can organize thoughts, review issues and find solutions to vexing problems the conscious mind is wrestling with. Sometimes the sleeping mind is rearranging non-related bits of this and that in an effort to make sense of what is happening in the awake world. Whatever the message or mood, I pay attention, Through the years, dreams have been my personal crystal ball.

I'm sensitive to the currents in my environment. If an unexpected or unsettling feeling persists, I do my best to determine what may be causing my uneasiness. Uncertainty drives me nuts. Better to know what I'm worrying about than imagine something even worse. Better to pay attention to the dream and prepare for its possible appearance than to be surprised when it happens.

JUNE 16

Visions are close cousins to dreams. The biggest difference is visions occur when we are in a state of wakefulness. Not necessarily wide awake, we might be in what I call the twilight zone between awake and asleep: just waking up or just about to fall asleep. In my case, visions frequently occur just as I am waking from a mid-afternoon nap. Whenever they come, there is a message. Maybe it offers a bit of comfort during a trying time. Or point me in a direction I hadn't considered. Or maybe I "see" a favorite spot I haven't visited in a while calling me to come and surround myself with its curative power.

One afternoon shortly after Paul died, I had fallen into a light sleep while reading with the cat curled on my lap purring softly. Something aroused me. As I came out of that hazy state, I looked up. Paul, bare feet, wearing his usual attire, shorts and t-shirt, was standing in the doorway watching me. He smiled, nodded his head once. And was gone. I believe he was checking on me as he said farewell for now. I am grateful for that final glimpse of him as he was before he got sick. It was a peaceful moment during a difficult time. Almost nine years later, remembering the vision brings comfort, a sense of peace. The assurance I am loved.

Like dreams, visions just happen. Or do they? Can't plan for them. Or can we? As I learn more about how my Higher Power responds to wants and wishes, I am beginning to think our unconscious asks our Inner Spirit for a bit of reassurance when we need a reminder we are not alone in this life. God, the universe and Mother Nature are all in our corner if we just learn to lean on them. They offer a vision as reinforcement they are always walking with us as we stumble down our path. A comforting thought.

JUNE 17

Mysticism and meditation are frequently confused and sometimes considered synonymous. Both practices can be traced back centuries and are found in many Eastern and Western traditions. Depending upon your particular spiritual beliefs, you may be familiar with one more than the other. There are similarities, but each has unique characteristics.

Britannica.com defines mysticism: "the practice of religious...experiences during alternate states of consciousness, together with whatever ideologies, ethics, rites...may be related to them..." The web site defines meditation as a "private devotion or mental exercise encompassing various techniques of concentration, contemplation, and abstraction ..."

Mysticism is passive yet practical, transcendent and spiritual, and opens us to Divine unity, sacredness and timelessness. Meditation is regarded as conducive to heightened self-awareness, spiritual enlightenment and physical and mental health. Both require a relaxed presence with no expectations for any particular outcome. One major difference is mysticism requires gently letting go of all thoughts and outside distractions. Meditation invites gentle thoughts and ruminations. Mysticism is time in silence devoted to the Deity. Meditation is quiet time focused on discovering answers. Both are worthy of your consideration as a way to calm the inner turmoil we all experience. If practiced regularly, they have the potential to bring personal peace to your mind, heart and soul.

I practice both. They each offer unique ways to slow down my frantic thoughts, help me discover answers to vexing issues and remind me I am not alone. There is a Higher Force waiting, willing and wanting to walk with me. I need only issue the invitation.

JUNE 18

When I was in college, I met a woman in her early seventies. This was at a time when being over sixty-five was considered old and only fit for sitting in a rocking chair and knitting baby blankets. What an enlightening story she shared. A few years earlier, on his deathbed, her husband made her promise to return to college and get the degree she interrupted to marry him and raise their children. They had a good marriage and a good life, but he wanted to make sure she didn't stop living after he died. She mourned for a couple of years, got bored doing nothing worthwhile and decided to follow his advice. She enrolled in an archeology program because she was curious about people and their cultures. She had just returned from a semester working in the jungle of some far off country. She was alive and vibrant. Said she felt light-years younger and even if her arthritis caused a pain now and then, she didn't let it interfere with her incredible adventure. All because she remembered her husband's advice, listened to her Inner Guide and said, I'm going to follow my dream," and then did.

Sometimes our Inner Guide seems to be pushing us farther and faster than we think we are ready to go. What to do? Ask yourself, "What is the worst thing that could happen?" Get lost? Make a mistake? Look foolish? If the potential outcome isn't going to cause harm to you or anyone else, go for it.

Nothing is cast in concrete. You can always modify or abandon the plan. So go! Do! What are you waiting for? You might meet someone interesting or learn something new or find yourself on an exciting adventure. Or maybe, you will just have good, old fashioned fun. What an unexpected treat.

JUNE 19

My definition of a "lightbulb moment" is suddenly understanding how or why someone, something or a particular event impacted my life. It may have happened just now, yesterday, a month ago, ten years ago or in an earlier stage of my life. The timing isn't especially important, but for whatever reason, the message stuck with me, even if I didn't understand its importance at the time. The farther I am on my path, (translation: the older I get) the more these lightbulb moments inspire me. I may not be able to remember what I had for lunch yesterday or the author of a book I read last month, but my crazy memory stores bits and pieces it intuitively knows I will need at a later time and appreciate then...

I have learned to recognize this seemingly sudden ability to finally understand what I was supposed to learn when the person came into my life or I read something or the event occurred. My Inner Guide held on to the message until She knew I was ready to hear it, make it my own, share it with others. None of us are wise until we have lived life, until we have reached a certain age, until we have taken the time to analyze the results of our choices, our actions, our behavior. Until we are able to comprehend the lessons we learned were messages from our Higher Power preparing us to follow His direction and complete our Divine duties. God, our memory and our mind work together in mysterious ways.

JUNE 20

Through the year, I have been pointing to various quiet places inside ourselves and ways to find safe spaces outside our inner world. I have offered reasons why they are important to recognize and utilize. So why am I revisiting the subject? I had a lightbulb moment today I want to share with you. Yes, even at 77, I am still looking, listening and learning.

This truth I discovered for sure today: At this age, I am much better at paying attention than when I was younger. Lots of reasons. In earlier stages: I was busy being a wife and mother, an employee and a domestic goddess; listening with my heart; trying to do the best I could and learning "good enough" is sometimes acceptable. Didn't have much time for "just being me" and "taking care of me." What changed? My children left home. My husband moved on to his eternal reward, My job went away. I realized chasing dust bunnies wasn't important anymore; I moved into a new chapter of my her-story. And recently, I started writing this book of reflections, which is teaching me more about myself than I expected.

So, where am I? Where are we? We will discuss this question tomorrow.

JUNE 21

Today is the Summer Solstice. It symbolizes changes and new beginnings. It is the perfect day to stop, take a break and a breath and review our spiritual and emotional progress. Where are we on our personal path? Each of us is in a different place because we are living our particular story. However, if we have been paying attention to the messages in these daily reflections, we do share at least a few similarities.

We have created our special space for meditation, reflection, reading, relaxing, and quiet time devoted to conversations with our Deity and patiently listening for Her advice. We have been introduced to ways to be present with our Higher Power, with other humans, with ourselves. How we do these things is personal, we do them "our" way. We have learned how we live our story and why we do and say what we do is a matter of choice — our choice. We acknowledge the world and her people can be scary and unpredictable, but it is okay because we have accepted we live in a complicated world, but we don't have to be of that world. We know people can be nice, they can be naughty, and they can be both kind and arbitrary, but we are all children of God deserving of respect.

My answer: we have come a long way on our pilgrimage. I look forward to the rest of the journey with you. As Martin Luther King, Jr. said, "Faith is taking the first step even when you can't see the whole staircase." We have quietly taken several steps. Good for us.

JUNE 22

Until recently, I never gave much thought to comfort beyond a soft sweater, a cozy blanket and favorite childhood foods. One day, I received a lovely note from a friend thanking me for spontaneously spending an afternoon with her. We used to get together frequently and talk about whatever. Her note reminded me of those precious hours and how I felt when we were together. This led to thoughts of other friends who have a similar effect. How did I intuitively know I was safe with certain people? Why did I always feel comfortable in their presence? I realized time is the most valuable commodity we have. When shared, it becomes an unconscious gift we offer each other. Our time together gives us a safe, neutral place to open our hearts, share our intimate thoughts and work on any vexing issues keeping us from moving along our personal path to healing lingering hurts and growing into who we are ultimately meant to be.

These thoughts also led me to consider why I sometimes seem to instantly "click" with a particular person. Why we feel as if we have known each other all our lives. Buddhism teaches we have lived previous lives, so when we meet someone in our current one we feel we "know," it is because our "souls connect in a meaningful way" so we respond with immediate acceptance. The writer, Shakti Gawain explains, "The Higher Power of my universe is guiding my life through my intuition." Some religious philosophies tell us our Deity sends us the people we need at the exact time we need them. These views each have merit. Besides, it helps me understand a phenomenon I have experienced several times in my life with an eclectic group of men and women, young and old. I can't explain it, I just accept it as the gift it is.

JUNE 23

Make sure what you are experiencing is real drama and not ego-drama. In other words, stop and think a minute before you jump to the conclusion the sky is falling and since it is all your fault, it is your responsibility to "fix" it. Sound familiar? I can relate because this reaction used to be my default whenever a disaster or catastrophe hit me or anyone even remotely close to me. I still struggle with this usually irrational response, but I am getting better. How?

I finally accepted it is okay to shut down emotionally for a bit to regroup my emotions, get my feelings kind of in control. However, I can't lose sight of the reality, I must eventually put myself back together and interact with the world again. It is the only way I will learn and grow and have a chance to make amends or change my attitude and make a difference. Is it easy? No, it isn't. But as my beloved Gram taught me, "Anything worthwhile is worth working for" even if I must let go of a long-held belief or grudge or annoyance.

Now that I have accepted I need to make a change, how do I do it? For a thought to become a habit, I need to be aware there is an issue, check; have a firm desire to change, check; be dedicated to making it happen, got that covered; decide on a plan, working on it. One last thing, I need to remember to be kind to myself as I make the change. I didn't get into this predicament overnight, not going to remove myself overnight. But as I have learned, whenever I ask my Inner Guide for help, She always responds, so I sincerely say, "Help!"

JUNE 24

When our head is shouting, it is really hard to hear what our heart is saying. Hence, the need to turn off the noise for a while to give our mind a chance to ponder the best way to approach an exasperated friend or troubling issue. It is the best way to listen with our intuition and hear with our heart so we can answer with love. As Carl Jung said, "Your vision will become clear only when you look into your heart. Who looks outside, dreams; who looks inside, awakens."

Don't misunderstand, there is nothing wrong with dreams. Dreams are one of the marvelous ways new ideas are born, which frequently result in beneficial outcomes. But those dreams are always followed with a lot of trial and error, starts and stops. When you slow down and wait for guidance and recognize lightbulb moments, your creativity ignites and you awaken to the unique person you are meant to be. But first, you have to be quiet and listen.

I find it interesting in so many situations, we know we should slow down, stop talking, listen and pay attention. Yet it is one of the hardest lessons to learn and put into practice. Regrettably, I rarely remember to use it until I am ready to explode, or worse, implode. Both of which are destructive; the former to others, the latter to me. Fortunately, at this stage of my life, I usually remember it sooner rather than later, but my stubbornness does take over sometimes. After all, I know best. Right? Sure I do as I sheepishly apologize and hope to repair the damage I caused with my thoughtless behavior.

I promise to keep working to stop the shouting in my head so I can listen to the whispers from my heart. I truly do want my operating system to be based on love. What about you?

JUNE 25

When someone hurts us, our initial reaction may be to hurt back. What if we sent loving thoughts instead? Offered a heartfelt hug? What do you suppose the response would be? How would it change the atmosphere? Let's look at this revolutionary response.

Someone hurts me with an unkind word, a thoughtless gesture, an inappropriate response. Doesn't matter whether the offense was intentional or not. It pushed one of my hot buttons or I was having a challenging day and it affected me more than it normally would. Instead of immediately snapping back with similar behavior, I stop, take a calming breath and try to put myself in their place, for just a moment. I know I can't crawl inside anyone's head, so have no way of knowing what they are thinking and feeling or what kind of day they are having. But instead of formulating a biting remark, what if I sent silent waves of love and understanding their way? What if I smiled? What if I reached out and touched their hand softly? If nothing else, I suspect, it would startle the person into silence long enough to realize their behavior was unkind. It might actually stop the spinning world for a nanosecond, long enough for both of us to pull ourselves together and move beyond the perceived hurt. Might even open the door to a meaningful dialogue and ultimately bring us closer. If it doesn't in the moment, it might lay the groundwork for the next encounter to be friendlier and more cordial.

What an intriguing way to address a situation that could very easily get out of hand and derail a friendship or destroy a mutually beneficial relationship or just mess up an otherwise wonderful day. Worth a try, don't you think?

JUNE 26

Hello! This is the crazy cousin whose words you have been reading for the last six months. Now I am asking us to do something different: focus on our strengths instead of fretting about our perceived weaknesses. Maybe we're not as messed up and off the rails as we think we are. Where do we start? What do we see?

The place to start is to determine what we want from life, how we want to relate to others, to the world, to ourselves. This is what crazy cousin has been helping you learn for six months. Stop. Breathe. Listen to our Inner Spirit. Pay attention to what our heart is whispering. Can we honestly tell ourselves we like what we see in the mirror? If not, what can we do to change our opinion? Be nicer to the nosy neighbor? The challenging colleague? The impatient child? The needy significant other?

Okay, how do we put our good intentions into practice? How about start by being nicer to ourselves. Recognizing we are human, subject to as Hamlet said, "...the slings and arrows of outrageous fortune..." and accept we are going to mess up. I firmly believe acknowledging and accepting our weaknesses is actually our most important strength. The first step to changing anything is to accept we need to change. Can't do that if we don't know what change is needed.

JUNE 27

We have examined our conscience and our behavior to figure out what we want, should and need to change. Now prioritize the items. What do I need to fix first? What is causing the most upset in my day, my relationships, my life? Focus on one task at a time. Remember, our minds cannot do more than one thing at a time, no matter how many times we try to disable, disown or deny that fact.

The first item on my list is to cease and desist over committing my time. It seems no matter how many times I tell myself to say NO and stick to it, I fall back into autopilot and answer before thinking if I have the time and desire to take on another project. I believe it was programmed into my psyche early in life, others' needs and wants are more important than mine. Ah, excuse me, Jan. You are important too. If you ignore your needs, you will not be able to effectively help anyone else. Why do I so easily forget, or perhaps ignore, this basic fact?

I have identified what I want to change. Next step: develop a plan and a process to change my automatic yes response. Instead of answering immediately, I will ask for time to check my schedule. While reviewing the calendar and do-to list, I will ask myself if I really want to take on another project, especially this particular one. If I can't answer with an open heart and a full commitment, I am going to regretfully say no. No reason is needed. A firm no is all that is required. A ten ton weight is lifted.

This approach is going to take practice. I know because I had to implement it a couple of years ago when my life was completely out of control because of an overwhelming number of

174

commitments. I wavered and wobbled but, surprisingly, eventually stuck to my promise to myself. As a consequence, I am able to concentrate on accomplishing my dreams instead of always working on someone else's. It is the reason I am able to devote time to this book of reflections.

God works in mysterious ways especially if we pay attention and give Her our cooperation.

JUNE 28

Trust your intuition; it is your Inner Voice. Your truth. If it tells you to say, "No," listen. If it leads to new experiences, believe they are what you are supposed to be doing at this moment in time. If you feel you should stop, rest, relax and take care of you, engage in whatever ways refresh you for however long it takes. Remember, you are your own best friend. Treat yourself as you do your other BFF.

If you are dealing with uncertainty, self-care allows you to accept what you can do,. Let go and turn over what you can't control, develop a back-up plan and live each day fully, with enthusiasm so you can spread your particular brand of joy. You will radiate love in a world that desperately needs it.

Self-care is a precious gift we give ourselves. When we invite our Inner Guide to share our daily experiences, we are nourished spiritually and grow in wisdom. Self-care opens our mind to clear thinking, our soul to prayerful acceptance and our heart to unconditional love. It gives us permission to be who our Deity created us to be and the desire to passionately fulfill our Divine tasks.

What a marvelous payoff for self-care: Being who we are meant to be and accomplishing what we are meant to do.

JUNE 29

We have learned to rely on our Spirit, our intuition, our personal navigation system. She is our Inner Guide, always on call, ready to aide us in our crazy, chaotic life and in our quiet, unsure moments. The innocent child buried deep inside our psyche, knows this. Somehow we adults lost Her or forgot about Her or decided to ignore Her. But She stayed with us. She was just buried in everyday minutia, mindless busyness and the cacophony of worldly noise. This month we started on the path to recall the Holy Spirit's power and wisdom; Her unfailing and unconditional love. She has been waiting patiently for us to summon Her. All we need to do is be silent and open our heart to tap into Her sacred sight to recognize the beauty and awe in the world.

Questions to consider:

- Do we accept we need to call on our intuition, our Inner Guide? Why? Why not?
- How does the Holy Spirit help us in our day-to-day life?
- What have I made my own? What do I plan to carry into July? Into the rest of my life?

Gratitude Entry: I am grateful when I feel I am going in circles or stuck in place, I can call on my Inner Spirit to help me know the right answer to my dilemma. All I have to do is Stop, Breathe. Ask. Listen. Wait. Be patient, My intuition, my spiritual Light will guide me in the right direction. When it is the right time for me to know, I only need to stop spinning and She will respond.

Reader: Add at least one thing you are grateful for as a result of reading, and contemplating the June reflections.

JUNE 30

While writing the reflections for June, I stumbled on a poem by Henry Van Dyke, which sums up my understanding of thoughts. It seems fitting to end the month with his explanation of thoughts since they are both the treasure and the trash in my life.

> I hold it true that thoughts are things;
> They're endowed with bodies and breath and wings;
> And that we send them forth to fill
> The earth with good results, or ill.

The words of Mary Davis speak to me. They carry a lovingly gentle message. I added this short poem to my daily prayers because I need to continually remind myself to be nice to me too.

> Be gentle to yourself.
> Listen to your inner voice.
> Trust that grace is here.
> Don't hurry the healing.

I have learned if I trust what I know to be true and keep my heart open, my Inner Power will be there when I need Her. Most of the time, I don't even have to summon Her, She is always waiting.

JULY

Time

"Teach us to use wisely
All the time we have."

Proverbs 90:12

JULY 1

Time is the most precious commodity we have. We are giving a part of ourselves we will never get back. I never thought of time in that way until a dear friend thanked me for the unexpected gift of an afternoon of my undivided attention. I stared at her in stunned disbelief. Then thanked her for giving me an insight into how I should spend my time. I had been living as if I had all the time in the world with this 90-year-old friend. Her soft words made me realize how wrong I was. Everyone's time is limited. She had spent more of hers than she had left. I promised myself I would spend more of mine with a loved one who keeps me rooted in reality and loves me just the way I am. No expectations. No preconditions. Just because I am me.

Another truth came rushing in. Joy comes from savoring each moment in the sacred now. Not wasting precious seconds worrying and fretting about things over which we have no control. Focus on what is happening right now and with whom we are sharing this minute. It was a powerful lesson I have tried to remember since that moment of clarity. I try to focus on Melody Beattie's sage advice, "Cherish each moment." After all, it really is all that matters.

JULY 2

We are mid-way through the year. It is either day 183 in a regular year or day 184 in a leap year. Time to stop momentarily and recap what we have learned and how we have grown. The lessons are going to be different for each of us depending upon where we were when we started this pilgrimage in January. Our history is different. Our life is different. Our need is different. Therefore, what I have learned and where I am today is not the same as what you have learned and where you are today. The one thing we do share is the completion of half a year and read the same words each day.

I am not the same person I was when I started writing these reflections. I have discovered buried emotions, hidden regrets and unrecognized joys. I have gradually realized this daybook has become my examination of conscience on why I do certain things, think in certain ways and react to certain people in the way I do, being more or less loving than my Deity expects of me. It has helped me focus on behavior I want to change, modify or abandon altogether. It has opened my heart to new ways of living my allotted time and sharing my unlimited love. I am surprised how much I have learned when my original goal was to offer whatever wisdom I have accumulated as I close in on my ninth decade. I continue to astonish myself with the insights I have or rather, my muse points out to me as I type these words.

I am grateful to have the privilege of your attention as I explore the inner me so I can offer humble guidance to you, my companion, on this pilgrimage to discover acceptance, peace and love. Please stay with me on the path we are sharing as we walk toward our ultimate individual reward.

JULY 3

Most faith traditions have a day of the week, some have special times in each day, set aside to worship the Supreme Being. Since time is precious, it is right and proper, we devote some of ours to our Deity. The worship service I attend is a weekend celebration of the holy Mass. I also devote time every morning to daily prayer, which is my private time with God. As my day unfolds, I say quick prayers or have a word or two with Her to ask for help, to say thanks for something, to gratefully relinquish a situation over which I have no control. Before I start typing anything, I ask for inspiration and guidance to use the right words for the message I am composing. These are a few of the ways I use my God-focused time. Are you satisfied with how God-focused you are in your life?

When I was young, I was taught to keep Sunday for God. In truth, I had absolutely no idea what that meant. We usually attended Mass, after which we had brunch. In my family, during the rest of the day, there was no one way to spend the time. As a young wife and mother, my duties never stopped, even on the Sabbath. In my professional life, usually there were domestic chores that couldn't be completed in one day so both Saturday and Sunday were needed. Now that I am more or less retired, I am able to spend most weekends doing what I want, when I want, with whom I want and for as long as I want. I consider it one of the special perks of being "a certain age." I believe God approves.

Most faith traditions suggest the Sabbath should be a day of rest. Rest your body. Refocus your mind. Recharge your heart. However, you chose to do spend your Sabbath, make sure to devote time to your Deity. It is a marvelous way to remember all you have is because of His and Her unconditional love.

JULY 4

Independence Day. The birthday of the USA. It is a day to remember who we are as a country and for what we stand as individuals. It is the commemoration of the day we declared we have a different destiny from our cousins across the pond; we have the inalienable right to pursue our purpose as me, as you and as the collective we.

The curious thing about destiny is it's a point in time. It is now. Life is made of all the "nows" as individuals and as a nation. It is not a particular destination; it is the many stops along the way and how we act and react at each one. All the meaningful moments we experience in our "now" help us, lead us, push us down our personal path. Destiny is the culmination of the "nows" in their entirety.

As the historian, David McCullough said, "How can we know who we are and where we are going if we don't know anything about where we have come from and what we have been through, the courage shown, the costs paid, to be where we are?" On Independence Day, ponder this profound question for our country and for yourself. I am convinced you will have a better understanding of and appreciation for destiny and its implications.

JULY 5

Many years ago, when I was a volunteer teacher, a nun gave me a rainbow banner that read, "Today is the beginning of the rest of your life." The message was new to me; I didn't appreciate it until many years later. The banner disappeared in one of my many moves, but its sentiment was planted in my memory. I don't remember the nun's name but I see her kind face clearly as she handed the gift to me. She wore a knowing smile with a twinkle in her eye. I was in my mid-twenties; she was probably in her late forties or early fifties. She had been around long enough to begin to grasp the meaning in the words. She was a wise woman who introduced me to a way of living. Too bad it took me so long to make it mine.

I finally realized a few years ago, if I don't live my life now, if I keep waiting for some distant future, I will miss the magic and awe of today. I will overlook the joy of watching my grandsons grow into loving, kind, thoughtful young men. The beauty of a marvelous sunrise and a magnificent sunset. I won't enjoy whatever I am engaged in today, right now. So instead of waiting for tomorrow, I am living today and not fretting over yesterday. I am enjoying the journey, not worrying about the destination. I am learning to love the me I am today and be grateful for the special people in my life. When I accepted right now is all I have, I stopped wasting time fretting over inconsequential trivia and unimportant stuff. I do my best to be the me I was created to be and use my minutes offering hugs and sharing love. It is a much more satisfying way to spend my allotted time on earth.

Give it a try. You will discover untapped joys because you are living in the sacred now, not the distant past or the unknown future.

JULY 6

The only reality is this moment. The choices you make now; the steps you take today. But don't neglect the experiences of the past. Value them as the important teachers they are. Don't dwell on them, but don't discount them until you make their lessons part of you. Pull them out. Examine them. Take the positive. Discard the negative. Then relegate them to history where they rightfully belong.

No, I am not contradicting myself. Life is a progression. We are not the same person today as were yesterday, nor will we be the same one tomorrow. We are made up of all the experiences and lessons and encounters from the day we were born. From our first breath to the last one and all the breaths in between.

Life is divided into four parts: the first twenty-five percent is learning how to function in the world. Figuring out acceptable behavior. Discovering reading, writing, arithmetic. How to be *in* the world, but not *of* the world. The next twenty-five percent is gradually growing into who we are created to be. Discovering our

Divine duties and learning how to do them. The third twenty-five percent is sharing our knowledge. Passing on good manners in word and action. The final twenty-five percent is aging gracefully. Remembering just because we have a pain doesn't mean we should be one. Continuing to learn and grow. To never stop viewing life with awe and wonder.

Life is made up of all your experiences, your choices, your failures and your triumphs. Each one is integral to the person you are created to be. Look at the scenery. Engage with people. Learn new information and gather ideas to consider. Love with your mind, heart and soul. Your destination will be a glorious finale to a life well lived if you stay in the sacred now.

JULY 7

In the song *The Circle of Life* by Elton John and Tim Rice from the movie *The Lion King*, this verse stayed with me:

> Some of us fall by the wayside
> And some of us soar to the stars
> And some of us sail through our troubles
> And some have to live with the scars...

No life is perfect. I believe each of us experience all of these fates in a life well-lived. Everyone walks through good times as well as the not so good ones. There is a cycle of life from birth to death and stages within each. We are babies, then toddlers. Children and adolescents. We move into young adulthood. Some become parents with associated responsibilities. We stumble through mid-life sharing lessons learned. We reach our final years and prepare to embrace death and the hereafter.

At each *AGE*, we should pay **A**ttention because we are given **G**race and **E**mpowered to use it for good. As we move through these slices of time, we can see and appreciate our inner beauty. While we acknowledge our imperfections, we don't let them cripple us or prevent us from being our best self. We show our faith and let our love shine forth. Our interior discipline encourages us to practice our spiritual values so we are the loving light of Divine healing in a fractious world. Our Creator gave us special talents to help His flora, fauna and fellows. When we meet our Deity face to face, we each can then humbly say, "I used my time to leave your world and her creatures just a bit better than I found them." Amen.

JULY 8

Over the years, every so often, I ask myself, "Why am I here, in this place, at this particular time?" Six years ago, I didn't have a clue how to answer. I moved from the House of We because I knew I needed to leave in order to find the House of Me. I had absolutely no idea how I was going to do that. What I would do. Who I would meet. What, if anything, I would accomplish. Eventually, I put my broken heart back together. I accepted the scars are permanent reminders I am strong and resilient. I touched my soul. I discovered me and gave myself permission to see, feel, live and love again. My time is devoted to doing what I view as my divine duties, which are productive, never irrelevant, usually meaningful.

I discovered my life wasn't over, it had just changed directions. I am focused on how I can be a whole me and help others be whole, happy and fulfilled. Was it easy? No, it was not. Made a few unwise choices; took a few dead end roads, but eventually, I stumbled on the correct path and met the right people who would hold my hand and help me find my way. I accepted it is okay to ask for help. I don't have to go it alone. God is with me and makes sure I have the human help I need when I need it. I just have to recognize and accept it. She will do the same for you. Just ask. You will discover the best way to use your limited, precious time, talent and treasure. And, I promise, you will learn about you as you do.

JULY 9

Buddha means "I am awake." When I stumbled on this definition my curious mind immediately asked: awake to whom and to what? Upon reflection, I concluded it is another way of telling me I need to be fully in the moment with my mind, my heart and my tongue. Wait a minute. With my tongue? You betcha. Our tongues get us into more trouble than many of our actions. Words are powerful; They can heal. They can hurt. They can incite turmoil. They can restore calm. They can sow hate. They can sow love. What do you want to leave in the wake of your words?

Buddhism teaches not only time but attention and intention is crucial to what we do and say and how we respond. This spiritual philosophy teaches us to ask these questions before we act or react: Is it true? Is it kind? Is it necessary? It is the right time to say it? Combined with being awake, alive and aware, our speech and behavior should invite cooperation, compromise and compassion.

There is a particular woman in four generations of my family who was always calm in any crisis. Her ability to remain cool, calm and composed during the worst situation was passed through the genes. The curious thing about all of us, we are able to sustain this serenity for as long as the crisis needs us. When it is over, we fall apart. We are absolutely no good for anyone or anything for sometimes hours, weeks, months depending upon the severity of the catastrophe. I have no explanation nor do I make any excuses. God uses us and when we are no longer needed, She steps in and gives us permission to turn it over and fall apart. We are there when needed. To me, that is all that counts.

JULY 10

An important lesson I learned the hard way, when I rush, I make mistakes. Which means I have to apologize for the delay and redo the project. So rushing doesn't speed up the process, it actually slows it down. I haven't saved anything, but did end up causing a potential misunderstanding and adding unnecessary time to a project. Both outcomes cause stress for me and many times, the people around me. Self-defeating behavior for sure!

There is a saying in the theater: "There are no small parts, only small actors." Holds true for all professional work and domestic chores. There is honor and value in all tasks, no matter how grand or menial they may be. An unexpected result of focusing on whatever the job at hand is we leave our energy in whatever we do. When a colleague made this astute observation as I was castigating myself for, once again, messing up and delaying our progress, I stopped in mid-sentence and asked what she meant. Her response? If we focus on whatever we are engaged in, we inject the finished product with a little part of us. If we do the job to the best of our ability, we leave positive energy. If we mumble and grumble and complain, we leave negative energy. And whichever energy we leave spreads to those in its space. Which energy do you want to share?

When I am patient and remember to factor in Divine timing, I am able to honor my commitments. If I do the best I can with the time, the knowledge and the training I have, I am able to accept my efforts are sufficient. At the end of the day, if I can look in the mirror and honestly say: "I did my best and spent my time wisely,"

I know my day was a success. That is all anyone can ask of and expect from me, especially me.

JULY 11

"Some days it's simply about getting through the day...and knowing if everything is not going right...you are still going to be okay." This wise saying from the Soulful Penguin should be part of everyone's list of mantras to pull out when it has been "one of those days." We all have them. Silly me thought those days would fade away when my children were grown and on their own and I retired from my professional life. Amazing how wrong one person can be. I may not have as many as I used to, but I still have days when I just want to reach sundown without doing damage to me or anyone around me or mess up one of the many projects in process.

There are days I am convinced the universe has it in for me. Everything I touch goes blooey and I am convinced the world, or at least my little piece of it, is going to hell in a handbasket and taking me with it. Nothing I did or didn't do. It just seems the fates are conspiring to test my patience and persistence. As I see it, the only solution is to stop my world, put my feet up and hide in a good novel where I know everything will turn out just as it should by the last page. Wishful thinking? Sure. But if it prevents me from wasting my limited time in frustration and prevents me from doing or saying anything dumb or hurtful, I will indulge myself in a little self-care. The world and the people in it will benefit and so will I. God approves.

JULY 12

One day when I was mindlessly surfing the Internet, I stumbled on a short item instructing me to make a "didn't do" list. Huh? The idea is simple: If you want to unclutter your life and your space, list all the small tasks that have piled up because you didn't take time to dispose of them when they popped up or just didn't want to do them at the time. Hmmm...guess that means I should go through the neat pile of notes on the corner of my desk. It took about thirty minutes to read, consider, complete and cross off every single one of those tasks. My desk looked so much better. Who knew. Simply tackling small tasks, I didn't want to do made me feel better when I finished them. I found when I postpone less urgent tasks and return to them later, they either solved themselves or were no longer an issue.

Discovering the positive result, I made a list of more important chores I knew needed to be done, but had been putting off because I "didn't have time." Turns out, I spent more time battling my nagging conscience than it took to make the appointments, write the thank you note, and sort and recycle the mail order catalogues. And I felt so much lighter when I finished.

The emotional clutter took longer to resolve but the relief was palpable even while I was still working to clear up misunderstandings, make-up for overlooked promises and reorder my priorities. Gradually, I was able to let go of my embarrassment and guilt for not living up to the me I know I can be. I discovered it is amazing the time we waste not doing what we know we will ultimately have to face. A valuable lesson in the damage procrastination can cause for me and everyone around me.

JULY 13

We all have time limitations. Doesn't matter what age or stage we are in, there are only twenty-four hours in a day and seven days in a week. As much as I sometimes wish for twenty-six hour days and eight day weeks, ain't happenin'. One of the traps I fall into is what Mary Davis calls "a concentration coma." When I saw that term, I immediately identified with it. When I am working on a project, I get so caught up, I lose track of time, which causes all sorts of unintended consequences. My back hurts. My leg cramps. I ignore meals. I am late for appointments. My days are upended. My sleep pattern is disrupted. And worst of all, I disappoint the people in my life more often than I care to admit.

I understand the concept of work-life balance and even agree with its premise. My problem is I have trouble implementing and sticking with it. Am I a workaholic? In some ways, I suppose I am. I never considered it might be a bad way to be, but then I never gave myself the time to think about it either. As I have gotten older, I have noticed my body doesn't take kindly to being ignored, nor does my psyche. Both have gotten more insistent with each added candle on the cake. I am slowly beginning to listen to my wise Inner Guide when She quietly tugs at me to slow down, take a break, be nice to Jan; she really does deserve loving kindness. And a day off now and then. Revolutionary thinking. But so on point. If I don't take care of me, no one else will. With that revelation, I do believe I will take a break. See you next time.

JULY 14

A few minutes ago, I returned from having tea with a close friend. We hadn't spent time together in several weeks. For one reason and another, we lost sight of the importance of being in each other's company. When we sat down in her cozy apartment, I commented how precious time is and what a gift we were giving each other by devoting some of our fast diminishing minutes to "be" together. Becky smiled and nodded in agreement. We caught up on our comings and goings and, as a bonus, "solved" all the problems in our world over a cup of green tea as we enjoyed watching the antics of her feline companion, Angus, being a cat.

Walking back to my nest, I pondered how grateful I am she is a part of my life. How, no matter what we are doing, we enjoy our time together. We find meaning in each moment. Neither of us wastes time in a soulless virtual world, when we can spend time in the same room. We can hug. We can laugh. We can share our lives in a more meaningful way than via social media. What we see and touch is right and real and can never be replaced by a voice in a speaker and a face in a box.

Don't get me wrong. Social media was a life-saver during the long season of COVID, but now that the disease has been more or less tamed, we can once again be in the same room without being fearful. We can see the whole face. Savor the sweet smile. Share a warm hug. One of life's simple joys that cannot be replicated. Call a friend. Set up a date. Meet for coffee. A cup of tea. A glass of wine. A beer. Enjoy the sacred now with a friend and grow closer. What a special gift for both of you.

JULY 15

I walk slowly. It drives the people with and around me nuts. Why do I stroll along life's path as if I have all the time in the world? I want to really see, hear and savor the space I am in. The clouds. The leaves. The ducks. I want to take time to interact with the people and critters I encounter, if only for a moment. It is one way I live in the sacred now. I use my precious, limited time to appreciate the wonder and awe of God's world. I am able to listen carefully to the person I am with and the people I meet. I am present to and in my life.

Moving slowly and thoughtfully gives me the time and opportunity to enjoy whatever my allotted minutes in life. I am not rushing through my day. I am not rushing through my earthly life, the only one I'm given... I am not wasting my time with frantic activity. I am giving myself permission to just "be," to appreciate God's amazing creation. As I move leisurely and deliberately, I am telling the Creator "thank you" for His wonderous gifts.

Try walking slowly for the next week. See if it doesn't change your perspective for the better. And bring a smile to your face while adding pleasure to your days.

JULY 16

Proverbs tells us to "Cherish each state of life for who it brings, what it teaches, how we grow." (20:30) Over the years, I have learned it sometimes takes a painful time to make us change our ways. When my first marriage crumbled, I was crushed. I truly believed I had made a life-long commitment to love and cherish "until death do us part." In spite of trying my best, I made a lot of mistakes as he did. We learned we didn't want the same things in life. But the most devastating for me was to learn, we didn't really like each other; we were never friends. Out of this loss, came a much more discriminating woman who discovered she related to the world in a more accepting way, a more loving way. In time, I met a wonderful man who embraced me and my daughters. Together, we created a blended family for our four children and we both regained our faith in the marriage vow. It was a joyful thirty-two-year adventure.

The worst loss of my life was when my soulmate died. He is still and always will be, the love of my life. His death wasn't a surprise but it caught me off guard nonetheless. I wasn't prepared for or ready to face the crazy, chaotic world by myself. Or was I? Since Paul's passing, I have learned I am a survivor. I am tougher and stronger than I ever thought possible, even after being a single mom raising two teenagers, which surely tested my mettle. I learned my world is bigger and broader than I knew and I fit in comfortably, even with my scars and cracks. I have met men and women who showed me how to open up and enlarge my perspective. I learned I have a lot to offer my little corner of the world. I learned God has a plan for my life.

Trust in the dark days. They are almost always a time of learning, growing, changing even if we don't know it or can't see or feel it in the moment. Have faith you are in good hands because your Inner Spirit is with you, leading you, holding you, loving you. You will emerge like a beautiful butterfly from its cocoon to face your world with confidence and calm. Trust your Deity loves you as you are and has a plan and a purpose for your life.

Be sure to say, "Thanks!"

JULY 17

The world has dark days too. Floods. Tornados. Hurricanes. Snow storms. Earthquakes. Epidemics. Pandemics. Mass shootings. Wars. Violence. We seem to be living in a time of upheaval. Climate change. Evil. Hatred. Man's inhumanity to man. Is our world headed for extinction because of unpredictable acts of nature? Unrestrained human behavior?

As a student of history, I believe we are in a predictable cycle of change. In my life, when change is happening, my personal world is turned upside down. Filled with uncertainty, with seemingly unanswerable questions. Sometimes I am fearful. Occasionally I am rewarded with surprises. Until I come out on the other side, I usually don't realize I am in the midst of a metamorphosis. So too, I believe our world, our country is experiencing a fundamental shift in perspective. We are struggling to find answers, which means we are questioning basic truths. Is this a bad thing? Not necessarily. As long as we keep the good of all people front and center in mind and seek solutions with love as the motivation, we will come out of the current time better than when we started the scary journey. I also frequently remind myself my Deity is in charge. She loves you, me, everyone with passion and mercy. Our Supreme Creator works in mysterious ways, but always with love. We only need to have and keep faith. If we do, everything will be alright for you, for me, for everyone.

JULY 18

Grit. It is an old fashioned, funny-sounding word. Its meaning is simple, but offers food for thought and action. According to *The American Heritage College Dictionary*, grit is an "indomitable spirit, pluck," which is "resourceful courage and daring in the face of difficulties." When I say someone has grit, I mean they have passion and perseverance and never give up on a dream. They are relentless in pursuit of their goal. They are willing to admit they don't have all the answers and are unafraid to ask for help. They cultivate mentors and teachers and people willing to offer guidance and encouragement. When I encounter a young person with grit, I listen to their dream and if I can help in a practical way, I do. If I don't know much (or anything) about their goal, I help them find people who do while I cheer them on from the sidelines.

Even though I was discouraged by my parents, especially mom, who insisted supporting myself as a writer was a very impractical goal, in my heart, I never gave up the dream. In a very eclectic career, I always managed to find at least one task that required a way with words. The closest official title was copywriter, but through the years, I contributed to newsletters, created marketing collateral and wrote policies and procedures and job descriptions. Not exactly my ultimate goal, but it kept my dream alive.

My grit and determination led me to finding my voice in my seventies and following my dream. My retirement time is spent writing two newsletter columns, a private journal, essays for a memoir and a book of reflections. Even more gratifying, people are reading my words and I am facilitating others in their quest to tell their story. Who says you are too old to realize your dream? Not me. I am living proof if you are passionate about your dream, chase after it with grit, just a wee bit of stubbornness and stumble on a little luck along the way, you will capture it.

JULY 19

When I think about the seasons, spring and fall come immediately to mind; they are my favorite times of the year. Spring is new life. Trees come awake from winter slumber. Flowers bloom in the warm sunshine. The weather is moderate; walking outside and sitting by the lake are pleasures to be treasured before the relenting heat of summer. It is time to plan what projects to begin. Fall is a bountiful time to celebrate earth's harvests. Surrounded by family and loved ones, Thanksgiving reminds us how much we owe Mother Earth for giving us food for our body and our kin for giving us love for our soul. If we are alone, there are multiple opportunities to share our time serving the less fortunate in our community. Fall is a time to reflect on the year; decide what we should finish before a harsh winter sets in. Nature's seasons with their time for action and time for rest.

Life has seasons too. Childhood when we grow and learn which behavior is acceptable and which isn't. Adolescence is a time to gently pull away from parents; to begin to discover who we are. Adulthood is the time to mature into who we were created to be while on the road to becoming our best selves. Our senior years are a time to rest and reflect on a life well-lived. Ponder how we want to spend the twilight of our mortal time. Life with its time for noise and time for quiet.

Both nature and life are filled with ups, downs, triumphs and disappointments. One thing I know for sure, they are gifts to be savored and appreciated one day at a time. Since I only have today, I refuse to waste it on hatred and fear and recriminations. I chose to celebrate it with joy and kindness and love. What choice will you make?

JULY 20

Don't worry about getting old. Be sorry about thinking old. I can't do anything about my age, so why should I lament the number? Many people don't make it into their seventies, including my parents, so I am grateful. So far, I haven't reached an age that has been challenging to accept. I keep adding candles on the cake with a smile and a thank you. Takes the pressure off the possibility of burning down the house or melting the icing.

It is hard to be grumpy and mad at the world when you remember life and reality is absurd at best. So why should we take our life and times so seriously. I am convinced our Creator has a sense of humor. Why else would He create man and woman if He didn't. We are funny creatures whose mood and outlook can change instantaneously. How can we not laugh at the absurdity in the world since we humans cause it.

Learn to energize yourself: Smile. Laugh. Chuckle. Giggle. Belly laugh. Move. Dance. Listen to music. Watch kids play. Relive a favorite childhood activity. Take a walk. See nature in action. Watch the squirrels chase each other, Listen to the birds communicate. Enjoy the sound of water moving. You will never be this age again. Enjoy it while you are where you are.

JULY 21

Is there a secret to aging gracefully? If there is, it is different for each of us because we are unique individuals. But after pondering the question, I have come up with a few ideas that seem to apply to most of us. I am not going into detail about any of them. I want you to decide how to apply them to you and your particular situation. These are suggestions learned while on my journey.

At a certain age, we should be willing to let go of unrealistic fears. As I told you earlier, mine is flying. I'm working on finding the courage to walk onto the scary silver tube that goes swoosh through the air. Will I actually board the plane? Won't know until I start the walk down the gangway (gangplank?), but at least I am willing to face my irrational fear. If I am able to conquer my fear of flying, I will definitely be challenging myself and moving out of my comfort zone while giving up a huge negative in my life.

Because of a couple of incredible girlfriends, I am learning to let my little girl out to play. They are teaching me the wonders of being a free spirit, if only for a few hours at a time. It is a start to taming the worry and letting the past go. It is opening my life to a new way to face the world with excitement and find joy in the everyday treasures life has to offer...

As we move along our personal path, change happens; it is inevitable. Pay attention to your thoughts, your surroundings and the people with whom you interact. You will age, maybe with an occasional quiet thud or a resounding bang, but you will age. It is your choice how you do it and if you have fun while you are.

JULY 22

It is raining out. Actually, it is pouring. What we in Texas call, a real gully washer. The lightning and thunder is fierce. The sky is a deep dark black. Seems like it should be the middle of a starless winter night instead of a mid-morning summer day. I am not fond of these kinds of storms, find them unnerving. Kind of like my grand puppy, Coco. She hides trembling in fear in her safe spot on a soft bed with high sides under a desk. There are times I wish her safe spot was big enough for two. Instead of trembling in my socks and slippers thinking the worst, I am going to describe the joy to be found on a rainy day in Houston.

Because I don't like to be using anything plugged into an electric outlet, I am unable to work on my computer during such a storm. I am writing this reflection in an app on my tablet, which is connected to Wi Fi. This means I am forced (sigh) to sit in my comfy recliner. If the electricity stays on, I will listen to soothing music to counteract the noise of the thunder. Today, since I am writing, I listen to the rhythm of the beating rain. This storm reminds me of heavy metal rather than smooth jazz. I watch the water swirling around the drain outside and send a quick prayer it will keep up with the deluge.

As with most of these fierce Houston storms, the worst is over in a relatively short time. As the rain slows and the noise quiets, I hear the birds start to tentatively tweet their sweet song. I rejoice when the clouds part and the sun shyly peeks out. I am grateful for the welcome drink of water breaking the months-long drought and revitalizing the thirsty grass and drooping flowers. I am reminded once again if you look and listen, even on a miserable rainy day, you will see and hear the wonder and awe of Mother Nature and the Creator's handiwork. What a priceless gift.

JULY 23

The first time someone told me to "be present for myself," I had no idea what she was talking about. I was young. Naive. Just starting my life's journey. Had no clear view of what was on the path ahead.

My generation of women were taught to put everyone else's needs first; to finish domestic chores and attend to professional responsibilities before we even thought about taking time for ourselves. By the time everything was completed and everyone was settled in, we were too tired to do anything but fall into bed so we could do it all again the next day. I'm worn out just typing the normal to-do list of most women.

Now that I have trod a few miles, climbed a few hills, made a mountain of mistakes, met a lot of fascinating people, I have learned a thing or three. I think I finally have a little understanding of what it means to be present for myself. When I entered my eighth decade, I decided I would start by devoting the in-between times to me. What exactly does that mean, you ask?

I view the in-between times as those few minutes standing in line at the ATM, the market, the cleaners, the pharmacy, waiting for the car to be serviced or the doctor to arrive in the exam room. Most of the time, it may be only five or ten minutes, twenty at most. Instead of whining about the wait, I read a few emails, play a quick game on my phone, color an electronic picture, or plan my fantasy get-away. Sometimes I daydream; my particular favorite way to spend the in-between time. I usually don't do anything productive; It is my time to be present for me and what I want and that is what matters. Try it. You will be amazed how much your outlook improves with this one little adjustment in your attitude about your in-between time. I sure was.

JULY 24

Honor your body-mind-heart-soul connection. They function as one entity. Pay attention to the whisperings from your body before they do harm to the other essential parts of you. When I ignore my body's needs, restorative rest, healthy movement, nutritional fuel, and human interaction, first my mind, then my body is affected, usually in not-so-good-for-me ways. My mind starts nagging to eat better, walk more, go to bed earlier, take time to rest, relax and recharge, and don't isolate from the important people in my life.

My usual MO is to ignore the first stirrings something is not quite right; I am not functioning at peak performance. Eventually, my body takes over. My head aches. My knees and hips start hurting. I am more tired when I get up in the morning than when I went to bed the night before. If I still ignore the warning signs, my body rebels and lays me low with a nasty head cold, excruciating pain somewhere in my body, the irritable bowel syndrome (IBS) springs into action. I am plagued with ailments I can't ignore any longer. When I am forced to address the physical problem, I realize whatever I have been neglecting is also affecting my relationships, my thinking, and the quality of my writing projects, which frequently sends me into the black pit and often interferes with my spiritual practices.

Opps! I have done it again. Brought on emotional and physical discomfort because I didn't pay attention to the whisperings of my body. My Inner Guide is forced to use a two-by-four to get me to stop and take care of myself. I have definitely disturbed my body-mind-heart-soul connection. Depending upon the problem and how long I have ignored the warning signs, it may take only a day or two to right the ship. Other times, it may be a week or a month to get back to the me I am created to be. In the meantime,

I suffer needlessly and have probably caused some issue with someone I ordinarily wouldn't' think of hurting.

I wish I could tell you I have overcome this destructive tendency, but I can't. I am aware of the issue and strive every day to pay closer attention. But I am human, I miss the mark. But I am not giving into this particular quirk. I am learning to ask for help from my Inner Source of comfort; she won't let me continue to harm myself.

JULY 25

Rituals stop time and connect us with everyone who has gone before us and will come after us. My mom began many of our family rituals; I added or modified some to reflect the changes in my life and times. My daughters have done the same. But when I watch and reflect on how and what we do during the special times, they all come from the base my mother and, to a lesser extent, my grandmother established when I was young. Stockings, reindeer food and fried turkey at Christmas. Hunting for eggs and wearing new clothes to church on Easter. Don't forget cracking an egg on the bald head of the oldest man. Wearing crazy costumes on Halloween and baking pumpkin bread and coffee cake with my grandsons at Thanksgiving. A special dinner to celebrate birthdays, exceptional report cards, professional promotions and other momentous events. All these rituals are moments in time to cherish and commit to memory for our later years.

Your rituals are different than mine, but all are an important part of who our families are and what we share with and pass on to our children and grandchildren. In my family, frequently there are people who join our celebrations because we have become family by choice. My grandmother, my mother and I all hold firm to the belief no one should be alone on a special day if they are in our circle of friends. Open hearts. Open doors. I learned by watching the two previous matriarchs in action. Valuable life lesson I have tried to pass to my children.

JULY 26

"Remain open to the new and unknown. Begin with a question mark and embark on a journey of discovery." This comment from Rick Rubin, an American record producer, succinctly sums up what we have been doing since the beginning of the year. We are asking questions and seeking answers about a myriad of topics. We are discovering all kinds of great and wonderful things about ourselves, our family and friends, our corner of the world. We are learning change is okay if we know why we are making the shift as we begin a clearer way of seeing, hearing and acting. We don't have to continue to be tired or frustrated, stay in denial about our feelings, our needs, our desires. We can search for solutions and ask for help. Our moment in time can be spent in confusion or in growth. It is entirely up to us.

Franciscan theologian, Richard Rohr, tells us "This moment is perfect." It is perfect to make it what we need and want. With a little forethought and planning, we can create our perfect day and spend it with whomever we choose. We do not have to stay stuck in a personal or professional rut. Change is not easy, but it is cleansing and chases away the blues, the boogie man out of the closet and the monster from under the bed. To begin the process of becoming who we are created to be and complete our Divine tasks, we just need to start with one step, loving ourselves. The rest will follow.

JULY 27

According to the writer, Mary Davis, "I have all the time I need for all I need to do." She calls it "Angel time." When I first read her comment about time, I wasn't sure I agreed with her. I never seem to have enough time to do what I need to do, what I want to do and definitely time for me is on the bottom of the priority list. I wish there were more hours in the day and days in the week. Alas, all I have is what everyone else is allotted: twenty-four hour days and seven day weeks.

Upon further reflection, I realized Mary is right. I do have all the time I need if I use it wisely on the important people in my life. If I don't scatter my attention and lose sight of my mission: to live life with love and authenticity. If I measure all my tasks against that criteria, my projects are finished when due and the people I care about are taken care of in the manner I would like for them to be. As the Hindu monk, yogi and guru, Paramahamsa Yogananda instructs, "Be calmly active and actively calm." In other words, stay calm and all will be well. Wise advice on the way to get everything accomplished on a to-do list without ignoring loved ones or myself.

I believe I will add both quotes to my morning prayers, "I have all the time I need for all I need to do" and "Be calmly active and actively calm" to remind myself of both until they become a part of my thinking and my life. Maybe you should too.

JULY 28

Sometimes I have a bit of trouble with the Divine's timing. I finally have to admit God's timing is not necessarily my timing. I had back surgery just before I started composing the reflections for this month. The surgeon warned me, the incision would need six weeks to heal, the rest of my body would take at least three months and it could be as long as two years before I was fully functional. I heard the words, but deep in my mind, didn't believe them. Boy, was I in for a rude awakening!

After six weeks, the incision was mostly healed. My energy and my stamina, nowhere near normal. After two hours of doing anything, I was wiped out and needed to rest. Even after sitting with my feet up for an hour or two, most of the time my desire to be productive had fled. I didn't start again. I stayed stopped. When I voiced my frustrations, the doctors, my family and friends all kindly reminded me I am not as young as I once was and older bodies take longer to heal. So, on top of having no energy and less stamina, I had to face I was getting old. Me! Old! What a jolt to my sense of self.

The following quote from Ecclesiasts (3:1-8) is a beautiful way to view time. It helped me reconcile my human frailty with divine reality:

> For everything there is a season, and a time for every matter under heaven: a time to be born, and a time to die; a time to plant, and a time to pluck up what is planted; a time to kill, and a time to heal; a time to break down, and a time to build up; a time to weep, and a time to laugh; a time to mourn, and a time to dance; a time to throw away stones, and a time to gather stones together; a time to embrace, and a time to refrain from embracing; a time to seek, and a time to lose; a time to keep, and a time to throw away; a time to tear, and a time to sew; a time to keep silence, and a time to speak; a time to love, and a time to hate; a time for war, and a time for peace.

There is time for everything under the sun and beneath the moon and through our days.

JULY 29

There is no other you in the universe. You are unique just because you exist. Don't let fear of the future or fear of failure keep you from finding meaning, joy and love in every moment in time. Trust all your scattered pieces will come together in a cohesive you, no matter how messy your life may seem. Greet each day with excitement about who you might meet, what you might accomplish, what interesting idea or concept you might learn, how you might change the world. How you will grow.

Open your eyes to the beauty all around. Hear the sounds of life in the air. Don't waste a precious moment believing you are not worthy to know who you know, to have what you have, to contribute your skills to keeping the world from tilting off its axis. If you didn't exist, your special abilities would be missed. Your divine tasks would remain undone for all eternity.

The book wouldn't be written. The symphony wouldn't be heard. The bridge wouldn't be built. Your special smile wouldn't brighten someone's day. Your laugh wouldn't enliven the gathering. The world, the universe would be missing one wonderful, giving, loving person. Nothing would be the same without you. And always remember, God created you to be you and doesn't make junk or unnecessary people.

JULY 30

This month, we have been looking at and discussing time. What it is. How to use it. How fleeting it seems, especially the farther we are on our personal path. Our concept of time is definitely colored by where we are in life. Our choices. Our challenges. Our triumphs. Our failures. Lessons learned. How it impacts our lives, our loved ones, our world. We learned our Higher Power has a different time clock and operates in a different time zone than we do. We also learned time is precious so we shouldn't take it for granted or waste a second of what has been allotted to us. We vow to use time wisely. We are grateful we have all the time we need to accomplish what we are assigned.

Questions to consider:

- Do we understand our time is precious and finite? Yes? No? Why?
- Why is it critical to set time aside for ourselves?
- What have I made my own? What do I plan to carry into August? Into the rest of my life?

Gratitude Entry: I am grateful time is my friend as long as I use it wisely and calmly and don't waste it. I am grateful I took time for me and spent time loving others. As long as I give myself and those I care about the proper portion of time, I will find joy and contentment in my days.

Reader: Add at least one thing you are grateful for as a result of reading and contemplating the July reflections.

JULY 31

I have spent a big slice of my life wrestling with the concept of time. I am finally beginning to understand what matters is how I *use* time; not how *much* I have. Have I made a difference in someone's day? Put a smile on someone's face? Time is precious. Time is fleeting. Once it is gone, it can only be recaptured in memories. So help me make sure I use my moments wisely so when I remember them, they will be happy scenes filled with happy people. If I go to bed at the end of the day knowing I spent the hours being the best me I can be, then my time has been spent wisely, no matter what I did or did not accomplish. Thank you to everyone who helped me spend my time in loving ways creating wonderful memories to enjoy at the end of whatever my time on earth might be.

I am adding these affirmations based on using my time wisely:

- I won't fret about yesterday.
- I won't worry about tomorrow.
- I will stay in the sacred now.
- I have all the time I need.
- I will be present with loved ones.
- I will take time for fun.
- I will eat right and exercise.
- I will sleep deeply and peacefully.
- I will take "me time" to rest, relax and recharge.
- I will take time with my Deity.

AUGUST

Relationships

"Be a lamp, a lifeboat or a ladder.
Help someone's soul heal."

Rumi

AUGUST 1

If we don't expect people to be perfect, we won't be surprised or frustrated when they aren't. This is one of the most difficult lessons I needed to learn in life, especially about myself. As an introvert, I prefer my own company to being with most people. However, as John Dunne reminds us, "No man [or woman] is an island." No introvert is either. We need to heal the fear and frustration we feel when someone disappoints us or deceives us or leaves us. It isn't our responsibility or our fault. It is the other person's choice either by decision, divorce or death.

We are all finely tuned instruments who can and do get out of tune sometimes. Our body, mind, heart and soul are supposed to work together smoothly and seamlessly. We all know that is not real life. It is not my life anyway. My body feels achy. My mind is preoccupied. My heart is hurting. My soul is confused. Any one or all of the above causes my circuits to misfire, which means I am out of tune and not sending or receiving messages on the right frequency. The human frequency. The love frequency.

What to do when someone, especially me, isn't on their best behavior? Stop. Breathe. Count to ten or twenty. Say a silent prayer. Momentarily step back from the situation, if only in my mind. If necessary, remove myself from the unsettling environment altogether. Find my center. Give myself a mental tune-up so I am operating appropriately for the particular situation; my world will function smoothly and be in sync once more. I will be sending and receiving with love, the universal language, the language we all instinctively crave.

AUGUST 2

Journalist and author, Carole Radziwill says, "The very best relationship has a gardener and a flower. The gardener nurtures and the flower blooms." Some days we are the gardener. Other days we are the flower. That is how a stable relationship works. Each person is being, giving and doing their best without keeping score. The roles move back and forth depending upon who needs what at any given moment. Is it easy? It sure isn't. But if we acknowledge sometimes one needs more understanding, more patience than the other, our relationships will be stronger and more stable. We know this. The challenge is remembering and embracing it day in and day out.

One secret I learned to help me remember is letting myself be vulnerable. This can be a scary choice. Being vulnerable means being who I am, liking who I am and accepting who I am. If I can't be open and honest with myself, I will be unable to form close, loving relationships with anyone else. We all know the people who can hurt us the most and cut the deepest are the people we are closest to, the ones who know us the best, the ones to whom we open our hearts. I have learned if I am unwilling to be vulnerable, the relationship will not progress beyond the casual stage. To have close, loving friendships, I need to let people see me and all my fears, phobias and vulnerabilities.

Being attentive and responsive to body language helps too. To me, a good, fail-safe option in tense times with special people is a genuine, heart-felt hug. As the writer, Ann Hood says, "I have learned that there is more power in a good, strong hug than in a thousand meaningful words." My response: Amen, sister, amen!

AUGUST 3

The legendary actress, Audrey Hepburn, survived a harsh childhood, coming of age during the brutal World War II years. During the war, her family moved frequently. In Brussels, she witnessed the transport of Jewish neighbors. It is rumored she and her family risked imprisonment or worse assisting the Dutch underground. Audrey suffered from malnutrition and nearly died. In spite of everything she experienced and witnessed, she firmly believed in the promise of kindness. Hepburn said, "To plant a garden is to believe in tomorrow."

When I read the quote, I realized there are different kinds of gardens: flower and fruit, strong communities, ethnic groups living alongside each other in peace and harmony nourished by quiet good deeds. No matter the garden, in order to mature, all need sun, rain, food, attention and love. To mature, each has to respect the space of the other so the individual can grow into who and what they are created to be. Separately they are unique; together they are stronger and resilient. Gardens, whether they be family, church, school, community, city, country thrive in a close, nurturing environment. When all the parts come together to form a unified space, it is indeed a glorious sight.

We can each plant a garden of love and acceptance in our world. If we all did, what a beautiful planet this would be. How peaceful and serene. The universe approves. The Supreme Being applauds.

AUGUST 4

In the practice of yoga, *Namaste* means *I bow to you.* In certain faith traditions and spiritual philosophies, it means, "The Divine Light within me honors the Divine Light within you." When used in some South Asian countries, it is a special sign of respect reserved for elders, teachers and other people worthy of honor. No matter the context, it is a beautiful message using a simple gesture. To me, it is a silent prayer; I use it when I'm not sure a hug is appropriate or acceptable. It was especially helpful and significant when we were slowly coming out of COVID isolation and many were unsure about physical contact. I use it sometimes during the Sign of Peace in my worship service. Many are more comfortable with a quick bow and *Namaste* instead of a handshake. I am almost always rewarded with a startled smile and a slight nod.

I have come to believe the more ways we find to acknowledge and say to each other, "I respect you, I care about you, I honor you as a child of the Divine," the better the world will be. The fewer misunderstandings and hurt feelings, the less stress and strife, the more kind and loving our society will become. If one word coupled with a simple bow can relieve the world of even a smidgeon of its current pandering, posturing and pain, think how much we will all benefit.

My challenge for you: Instead of a handshake or a hug, or worse, no acknowledgement at all, try saying *Namaste* with your arms crossed over your chest and a soft smile while bowing slightly from the waste. Make it one of the ways you greet people. I believe you will be pleased and pleasantly surprised by the reactions you get.

AUGUST 5

His Holiness the Dali Lama instructs us to "Just be kind." A simple but oh so profound statement, it took me by surprise. Is that all it takes to find serenity in mind, heart and soul? Hmmm... After I read his comment, I thought about the previous few days and how it seemed Murphy's Law was in full force: "If it could go wrong, it would and did."

I was busy trying to finish one newsletter, which was already three weeks late. A colleague asked how I was doing editing articles for another newsletter due for publication in three weeks; I realized I hadn't even opened the documents yet. I was in a tortuously slow recovery from back surgery. My energy and stamina was non-existent. What did I do? Took a self-care day. I was kind to myself, which in turn led me to be kind to others. Funny how that works. When I was kind to Jan, it spread to those around me.

Being kind to Jan didn't get the tasks done any faster or smoother, but my attitude shifted. I wasn't in frantic mode. Tackled one task at a time. By the end of the next day, the first newsletter was ready to publish and all the articles for the other one had been edited and submitted. And I still had all my hair and my nerves were not too frazzled. I was able to relax and enjoy a lovely evening with a close friend. All because I took a break and was kind to me. Made me wonder if being consciously kind to others would work the same magic.

AUGUST 6

Let's continue our discussion of kindness. Seems like a simple concept, but it is one that is learned and needs to be practiced. The kinder you are, the more kindness you generate in and around you. Many years ago, a young person commented I was a very kind. I hadn't really given it much thought; it is how I interact with people. During our conversation, I realized I had learned to be kind and thoughtful watching how my parents and grandparents treated friends and acquaintances. There was always room at the table or a sofa bed for the night. The loving adults in my life often "adopted" the person without family, the one who traveled a lot and hadn't time to develop sustaining friendships. There were no strangers in my environment, just people we hadn't yet gotten to know and love. Because my elders were kind, I grew up behaving the same. It was all I knew. As a consequence, I passed it to my children who in turn are passing it to the next generation.

But how do we become kind? One simple piece of advice sums it up for me, "Walk a mile in another's moccasins" before you respond in actions or words. Pay attention. Practice awareness of other people and their particular plight. You will be less likely to snap and snarl or make assumptions that may be incorrect. Can't make a wise decision or a positive choice if you're unclear in your own thinking. Observe, listen and learn before you do or say anything. I am not saying you won't make a mistake or trying to tell you every one is honest and aboveboard, but if we give people a chance, the benefit of the doubt, most are good and kind themselves. The ones who aren't will soon show their stripes. At that point, you have three choices: continue to be kind, ask if you can help by listening or walk away. The important thing is to make a sincere effort, don't judge and do send out vibes of love. And remember *Namaste*. Works almost every time.

AUGUST 7

St. Benedict of Nursia said, "...listen with the ear of the heart." This suggestion works hand-in-hand with kindness. If we listen carefully, with our full attention, we will be less likely to misinterpret what is being shared. If we are preoccupied with forming a response, looking out the window or playing with the cat, we are unable to focus on the message. Another stumbling block is being dishonest when sharing our thoughts and feelings. If we can't trust the information we are hearing, the conversation is not going to be fruitful or meaningful on any level.

We can be superficially kind: hold the door open, pay for the order of the person next in line, say Gesundheit when someone sneezes, which are all positive behaviors. But to be kind from the soul, we need to be willing to be honest and open sharing our thoughts, feelings and history. We need to be willing to open ourselves to the other person. Share our fears, faults and fundamental beliefs. By allowing someone "in," we let them "see" the real us, who we are when no one is looking, how we know ourselves... Scary thoughts, but one sure way to form close, lasting, loving relationships. First caveat: Each person has to be willing to be vulnerable. One-sided doesn't work. Second caveat: Have confidence the person is worthy of knowing your innermost thoughts and feelings. If both these criteria are present, opening up and being vulnerable leads to the most amazing closeness and deepest love between two people, no matter the relationship.

AUGUST 8

We are all interdependent, no matter who we think we are or where we might live. We need each other to function. To accomplish our Divine duties. A graphic example is our phone. You know the hand-held mini-computer we rely on for so many things. Being on time for appointments and meetings. Contact information for family, friends and colleagues. Grocery list. To-do list. Time. Weather. Directions so we don't drive in circles. Now think about all the people it took to put that phone into our hands. The miners who dig up the raw material so the engineers can design and manufacture the device. The programmers who create the apps so the device will perform as we expect it to. The rail workers and truck drivers who deliver the phone to the distributors who get it to the sales associates from whom we purchase it. I may be overlooking someone in the supply chain, but all these people work together to make sure we can check our horoscope, contact family and friends and order lunch.

This example is a reminder of the importance of everyone and the necessity of their contributions. We need each other. Family history, fancy title, salary earned, none of that is important. No one is more needed or critical to success than anyone else.

Maybe if we remembered this immutable fact, we wouldn't be so quick to judge or complain when we have to wait a few minutes or the package doesn't arrive when promised or the car ahead isn't moving with the traffic or the kids forget to tell you they promised six dozen homemade cookies for the party today.

Take a breath. Count to ten. Smile as you decide how to react to whomever is slowing you down or causing you stress. Shift your perception. See the person as a spiritual being longing for the same things you are: sustenance, shelter, security, acceptance and love. A different mental picture elicits a different reaction. And helps create a kinder world, one thought at a time, one person at a time.

AUGUST 9

When you accept people as they are, rather than as you wish they were, you accept the whole person; the failings, false smiles and seemingly forked tongue. Only then can you expect the other person to accept imperfect you. Mother Teresa said, "If you judge people, you don't have time to love them." Wise words, but just how do I apply it to two women who make me cringe when I see them walking toward me? One drives me batty with her incessant chatter about everything and nothing. The body language and look on the face of the other proclaims loudly, she doesn't like me any more than I like her. Avoiding these women is not an option; we live in the same building in our community. What do these challenging relationships teach me? Studies show what we react to negatively in another is precisely what we don't like in ourselves. Gulp. Now what?

I did some soul searching to find what it is that drives my dislike and resentment. What is it that makes me scream silently when I see them? Maybe I talk too much sometimes? Maybe I bore people with my obsession about various projects? Maybe my voice sounds screechy to others? Maybe I unconsciously give off the vibe I am more important than certain people? Maybe I'm jealous of her acceptance by the community? Hmmm...must give these questions serious consideration before I put nasty, negative labels on the other women. Another example of cleaning up and clearing out my mental house before I "see" other people in a less than charitable way.

AUGUST 10

Compassion for others begins with simple actions: make a fresh pot of coffee when you pour the last cup; let the person with only three items go ahead in the check-out line; allow the car to turn onto the busy street in front of you; don't rush for the closest parking spot. At home, replace the toilet paper roll; put your dirty dishes in the dishwasher; discard the empty juice carton; keep your music and TV programs at a reasonable volume. All of these actions take only a few minutes and just require being thoughtful about how your actions affect those around you.

Being compassionate is a skill honed by paying attention and stepping in when the world has turned its collective back. Some people seem to know this instinctively. Others have to learn how to show compassion and its close cousin kindness. The best way to teach it is to practice it in all our interactions. Not because we want thanks, but because it is the right way to be. It is a gentle way to make someone's world a bit better, a little easier, if only for a moment.

According to *The American Heritage College Dictionary*, the definition of compassion is: "Deep awareness of the suffering of another, coupled with the wish to relieve it." On the surface, the examples I gave don't exactly fall into this precise definition. But if we look a little closer, maybe they do. We have no way of knowing what another person is feeling or experiencing. Maybe our seemingly insignificant acts of kindness actually bring a small smile, a bit of peace, a sigh of contentment to an otherwise unsettling day. Perhaps someone received a scary medical diagnosis. Maybe a loved one died recently. They are late for work because their child got up in a bad mood and it took extra time to start the day and get out of the house. Maybe the person needs a hug and our virtual hug of compassion reminded them there is kindness in the world. Remember the ripples in the water, you never know who they touch and how it will affect someone's day.

AUGUST 11

As the English actress, Helen Barry said, "Surround yourself with the people who bring out the best in you, not the stress in you." As much as possible, be around people who reflect who you are or would like to be. The ones whose motivation matches or exceeds yours. You will energize each other and generate positive vibes to share with the world. Spend time with people who help you know your mind, your heart, your soul. Help you grow. Help you know love.

I recognize we don't always get to pick who inhabits our space. We are born into a family whose members may not reflect the best, but we can learn what not to be, how not to treat others from observing them. Same with educational and professional colleagues. I have learned from every boss and coworker; some quietly showed how to behave, others were masters at shouting how not to act. All valuable lessons. Thank you, everyone.

Beware. Don't let others define who you are. That is your job perhaps with help from a life coach or spiritual mentor. But don't give your power to anyone: Parents. Spouse. Significant other. Children. Friends. Bosses. You will have many titles and wear many hats throughout your life, but the most important one is Child of the Divine Creator who gifted you with a free will. She sends people to guide, assist and inform, but it is up to you alone to define who you are, what you believe, and the principles by which you interact with others and live your life. Do not give that responsibility and privilege to anyone. If you share yourself with your Higher Power and listen quietly and patiently for Her counsel, you will be the you He created you to be. If you ask, the answers will come.

AUGUST 12

The differences in a relationship are just as important, maybe more so, than the similarities. If everyone thought the same, behaved the same, it would not only be a boring existence but we would never learn anything new or benefit from someone's hard-earned wisdom. Our differences show each of us facets in both of us. How we learn to relate to one another in a particular partnership, which is really what relationships are, is based on how we "see" each other. Not everyone is the same, nor do we think the same. Thank goodness! It is those differences which encourage us to learn and grow and appreciate the "other" present in everyone.

Sometimes we need to end a relationship. Maybe we are moving in a different direction or have outgrown each other. Or communication has broken down. Perhaps the relationship has become toxic for whatever reason. There is nothing wrong about saying goodbye. The most important part of the ending is *how* we say farewell. Saying goodbye with appreciation for what we shared, what we learned, how we have grown because of our association lets us walk away with good feelings and take the happy memories with us on the next leg of our journey. It is the final gift we offer to someone who has made a difference on our pilgrimage. Say farewell with love. As Maya Angelou said, "At the end of the day people won't remember what you said or did, they will remember how you made them feel."

AUGUST 13

Don't let thoughtless, mean and negative comments about you steal your happiness. Even if they appear to be well-intentioned, don't let other people's opinion affect how you feel about yourself. It is okay to think about the observation, take what is positive, consider the negative, then let the comment go. It is one way to learn and grow, but only one. Don't dwell on the comment. The only opinions which count are God's and yours. The others are merely background noise. As Mother Teresa said, "...in the end, it is between you and God. It was never between you and them anyway," Don't feel guilty about being happy. Whatever you do, don't make excuses. Don't let the outside world claim your joy. You deserve this marvelous gift from the Divine Giver.

Sounds like good advice. And it is. The glitch, for me at least, is remembering it at the moment a comment is made or an observation offered. Especially by someone whom I love or respect or admire. Hard to keep those in perspective, give them their due, then let the remark or opinion go. On the outside, I may laugh, or shrug or even cry, but inside I rarely forget the message particularly the negative and not-so-nice ones. Most women believe the negative and discount the positive. I am better than I used to be, but those biting statements still sting and stay longer than I would like. I replay them during my dark days in the black pit. I am convinced of my inadequacy in everything, even being the me I believe I should be and usually am. Self-defeating thoughts, no doubt. At least, I recognize what I am doing. The first step in changing any habit or habitual reaction. The second step? Turning it over to my Inner Spirit with confidence she will handle it much better than I can.

AUGUST 14

We are social beings created to rely on each other. To be there when the world comes rushing in or crashing down. From earliest times, all animals form tribes, herds, flocks to help and protect the individuals within the group. Family. Colony. Country. Sorority. Fraternity. Unions. Church. School. Corporation. There are numerous ways we come together because one can only do so much. Working together, we can accomplish the impossible. Discover fire. Invent the light bulb. Build a motor vehicle. Establish the Internet. These are but a few of the marvelous things we rely on that men and women, working together, gave to the world.

There is nothing wrong with being independent. Confident. Walking to the beat of our own music. Willing to take calculated risks. This is often how we learn. Why we grow. Just don't take it to the extreme. Don't believe you are able to function 100% of the time without anyone. I have learned the lesson many times because it is hard for me to ask for help of any kind. But too often, when I don't ask, I trip over my independent streak and fall flat on my silly pride.

We all need people. Even introverts like me need help from time to time. I need encouragement I made the right decision. I'm on the right path. I need to be needed. To be able to help someone even with a small task brings joy and contentment. I crave physical contact. Hugs. An arm around the waist. Cuddling. A soft touch on the shoulder. They all silently tell me someone cares.

They reinforce I am loved. They remind me my Deity is everywhere, working silently, keeping the universe operating.

AUGUST 15

Sharing imperfect, me gives you permission to share imperfect you, which teaches both of us good enough is alright. Good is...enough. I have struggled with perfection most of my life. Perfect daughter. Perfect student. Perfect friend. Perfect spouse. Perfect parent. Perfect step-parent. Perfect grandparent. Perfect employee. Perfect boss. Perfect me. What have I learned? Striving for perfection is exhausting. It is self-sabotage at the highest level. Since deep down I know I can't achieve it, many times I have to convince myself to keep trying. Talk myself into believing good is enough. Accept sometimes nothing gets done. I am unhappy with myself because I view my perceived failures as proof I am unworthy. Talk about a vicious circle of self-destruction.

The actor Michael J. Fox said, "I am careful not to confuse excellence with perfection. Excellence I can reach for; perfection is God's business." Ever since I stumbled on his wise statement, my perception of perfection has changed. I have always tried to do my best whatever I am doing, saying, showing. Somewhere along the way, I decided doing my best meant I had to be perfect and everything I produce must be perfect too. Set the trap myself. It is devastating when I realize my work product hasn't turned out exactly as I planned or it was late or criticized by someone. I compound my mistake when I expect the people around me to meet my standards of perfection. Talk about an efficient way to push people away, expect them to work as hard as I do, devote as many hours to projects, give up as much free time. Watch them walk out the door without a backward glance after a sharp, insightful observation about my expectations. The truth often hurts. Ouch!

AUGUST 16

As the writer, Melody Beattie, said so succinctly, "Know when it is time to pick up, pack up and leave." Many relationships end for various reasons. Dad or mom receives a promotion in another city. We graduate from high school. We change jobs or move away for a new opportunity. We change neighborhoods. We marry and gradually drift away from our single friends. We may have the best intentions to stay in touch, not let our new circumstances change our relationship, but eventually our life, their life takes priority and we lose touch. It happens to all of us. When a loved one passes to their eternal reward, the relationship changes from actual arms in a loving hug to holding love in our hearts until we meet again in the afterlife.

Whether you are the one moving on or the one staying put, the result is the same: life changes. However, you react to whomever is gone, all of these partings can be a challenge to navigate, but they are a part of life. We never really lose them. They stay in our memory. The interactions we shared remain part of our history. Each individual taught us valuable lessons and helped lead us to where we are today. They are one of the reasons we are who we have become. Be grateful they were and continue to be a part of your unique story. But don't stay stuck. Know when to let go and say farewell so you can move on to your next chapter. Saying good-bye is an essential part of life. It is accepting your role in God's script for you.

AUGUST 17

One of my favorite Girls Scout songs is as true today as it was all those years ago when we sang it at the end of every meeting,

"Make new friends, but keep the old. Some are silver. Others are gold." Old friends we keep in our unfolding story, especially the ones made in childhood and adolescence, know our saga from the beginning chapter. We don't have to explain anything about who we are and where we came from. They know. We lived it side-by-side. We share precious memories of how we were then and the path we took to get to where we are today. New friends add fresh ingredients to our daily adventure; they help us see around the next bend and over the new mountain. We learn. We grow. We make new memories while living in the sacred now.

Friends are precious gifts to be appreciated, cherished and loved for who they are and who they encourage us to be. Be sure to tell them how they fit into your life, what they mean to you, how they enhance your journey. One of my morning prayers is devoted to the special people in my life. Part of my prayer says, "Help me recognize ways to show them how much I appreciate them...Help me find the words to tell them what is in my heart."

Reach out today. Say thank you for being you, for being in my life, for staying in my life. You make me a better person. This simple gesture and these heartfelt words will strengthen your bond.

AUGUST 18

Pastor and community organizer, Leroy Barber, said, "Human flourishing requires that we establish, mend and maintain relationships with other people." So true. But it is also true boundaries are necessary for healthy relationships no matter the connection. Parents. Siblings. Family. Friends. Partners. Spouses. Children. Professional colleagues. Strangers. While humans need others, we also need our personal space. Each culture has its own definition. But no matter what our society favors, our personal distance is unique for each of us.

As an introvert, I need not only more alone time, but more area around me. When someone encroaches on my physical space, I am uncomfortable. I step back, usually without realizing I am moving. One of the reasons I won't enter an elevator with more than a couple of people? Not enough personal space available. Other people don't seem to mind being crowded. They willingly squeeze together in a church pew. Sit close on public transit. Enter a club, pub or room teeming with people. The mere thought of any of those encounters makes me shudder and shrink. Even though I am a hugger, I am very careful to make sure the person I want to hug is okay with the embrace. I respect people's inherent need for space. I expect others to do the same for me.

There are other boundaries perhaps more important than the physical. The emotional. The psychological. Some people are very private. They guard their thoughts and feelings. They do not share them willingly or easily. It takes me a long time to trust before I share confidences with anyone, even those to whom I feel an almost instant connection. I have to believe they will guard my secrets just as I will theirs. There are individuals in my world who have no idea of who I am, how I think, what I hold in my heart. They may think they do but they only see and know what I allow. And that is as it should be. We are all entitled to keep our hearts, emotions and thoughts safe if and until we are ready to share them. Please don't let anyone try to convince you, cajole you or threaten you to open up until the time is right for you. Remember, it is okay to never be ready with some people, no matter the societal relationship.

AUGUST 19

We have all kinds of people in our personal corner of the world. We feel a different connection with each of them. A friend asked three challenging questions, which made me rethink my relationships: Who invigorates me? Who drains me? With whom do I choose to share my emotional energy?

The first question was the easiest. I am blessed to have several people who enhance my life. They encourage me when I am down. Give me a gentle kick in the posterior when I need a nudge to get moving. They try to help me see and accept my wonderfulness, even though I doubt its existence. Whenever I spend time with these friends, I leave feeling so much better about myself, my contributions, my world in general. Everyone should have at least one friend like this in their life.

The second question caused me to consider carefully. I finally realized, many times I feel depleted after a conversation because of the way I was feeling. If I was down or tired or my feet hurt, I didn't have the patience or the love I needed. Imagine my chagrin when I realized it was more me than the other person when I found our encounters draining. I'm not saying these people don't drive me nuts, because they do, but I now understand why better than I did before. I have a reason to dig deeper to find patience when it is in short supply and love when it is hiding.

With whom do I choose to share my limited emotional energy? Some are close friends. Some casual acquaintances. All offer a psychological shot in my attitude. Positive people with an optimistic outlook even when life is topsy-turvy and out of balance always make my day brighter and improve my attitude. Someone who really listens and hears what I am not saying as clearly as what I am makes a real difference in my understanding of why stuff happens. And those people who smile and cheerfully greet the day. When I started paying attention to these characteristics, I began to see more people with them. Funny how that works. When we encourage each other, listen to our stories and show unconditional love, it is amazing what one encounters during an ordinary day.

AUGUST 20

Buddhism teaches to love means to be there. But what does that mean? In the same room? Sitting close to them? Holding their hand? Looking into their eyes. Sensing their spirit? Yes. All of the above. But how do we do that? To be there for anyone, be they child, adult, family, friend or stranger, we need to ask do you want to be helped, heard or hugged? All three? Respond accordingly.

If the person wants help with a specific task, it is necessary to ask the right questions and listen carefully in order to determine what they need done. If you are unable to help, find someone who can. I have discovered through the years, if I engage the person in the process of doing whatever, it means much more than if I do it myself. We learn about each other working as a team. They increase their self-confidence because they learned how to do something new. Always a positive outcome.

Most people just want to be listened to. Really heard. Acknowledged. They know a situation needs to be improved and want assurance they can overcome whatever obstacles seem to be in the way. Many times I can't fix whatever is wrong or make the problem disappear, but I can listen with a loving heart. I can make sure I pay attention. I can gently offer suggestions or advice or send someone who can help. Remember, we all want to know we matter. The best way we can offer that assurance is to listen and hear heart-to-heart. Works every time.

When I realize I can't fix, change or make "it" go away, I can always give a hug full of love because I know it isn't only me hugging them. It is my Inner Spirit hugging their Inner Spirit sharing unconditional Divine Love.

AUGUST 21

Birds of a feather are friends who see the world through the same lens we do. We are comfortable and safe in our familiar bubble. We can relax and just be and not worry about how we will be perceived or whether we will be accepted into the group. Ahh...pour me a glass of wine.

However, it is important to also interact with people who don't view the world the same as we do. Whether it is religion, politics, how to raise children or how to use words effectively, we learn and grow when we are exposed to new ideas, different ways of thinking and new ways to do things. The only way to experience life in all its magnificent diversity is to invite people with varying views into our corner of the world, join us for a libation, an honest sharing of our thoughts, concerns and ideas...

If I avoid all men because of the bad behavior of a few, I miss out meeting the ones who are smart, fun, accepting and loving. I would not be receiving the incredible insight of my wise male editor if I was afraid of how he might interpret my words or the comments he might make about my ideas. It is his insight making these reflections appropriate for women *and* men. Early on, I asked him if some of my thoughts are too "girly." Linden said, 'Yes. Some are. But I read them because they help me understand the females in my life a little better." With that perspective, we all win, men and women. I congratulated myself once again for my choice of editor.

Keep in mind, we have power over ourselves. Don't relinquish yours to anyone. Listen. Learn. Grow. But never give up who you are or what you believe. Add new ideas if they speak to you, discard ones no longer serving you, but hold tight the ones you hold dear. Adopting the attitude, "Take me as I am or watch me as I go" is not false self or ego or selfish, it is protecting yourself from toxic relationships. It is self-care of the highest form.

AUGUST 22

Everyone and everything is connected. Next door. Down the block. Across the country. Around the world. When one succeeds, we all succeed. When one fails, we fail together. When one hurts, we all feel the pain. Many ancient worship services used the circle to represent the whole tribe because it symbolizes connectedness. The Abrahamic faiths all have specific words to describe the connectedness of all beings. Judaism refers to *halakah,* which means "the way" in Hebrew. Christians call the connection the Mystical Body of Christ. Islam uses the Arabic word *tawhid,* which translates to "the oneness of God." They all believe the Spirit of the Divine is present in everyone.

No matter our particular understanding and acceptance of or disdain for a Divine Presence, it is important to honor and respect how our thoughts, words and actions ripple out and cause change. It is up to each of us whether the change will help or harm. Will we bring a measure of sanity or add more dissension? Will we be the grownup in the room or the demanding toddler? Will we respond thoughtfully or speak irrationally? When we remember common courtesy is a small gesture but adds so much to our world, it is worth much more than casual attention. It is our choice which vibe we send around our circle and out to the world. Because we are all connected, the power of forgiveness becomes evident. It is an act of love, which brings inner peace and outer harmony. And civilization benefits no matter the name of the country or the faith tradition or spiritual philosophy followed.

AUGUST 23

Behind every public face is a private self, a searching soul, a longing heart who desires connection, acceptance and love. Sounds simple, but in reality, it is one of life's most difficult challenges to create and maintain this kind of relationship. Be it a family member, a friend, or a casual acquaintance, it takes paying attention, really hearing and spending time together. When we cooperate in a project or celebrate a victory, we learn about each other in many ways. Some lessons are small, they are good organizers; some lessons are bigger, they really listen; other messages may change a life or circumstances.

Friendships are fragile. They need to be nurtured, When we open up, find a connection, we see the "real" them, they see the "real" us. The façade is down, The invitation is issued, the challenge accepted. The work begins. Yes, it is work to maintain a rapport of any kind. If we don't understand this basic fact, our relationships will remain shallow, on the surface. If this is what you want, so be it. But if you want to relate to someone on a deeper level, open up. Don't let the little, unimportant stuff get in the way. Be kind. Be loving. Be there. Your life will be full and satisfying because, to paraphrase the Hallmark slogan, "You care enough to offer the very best." Your time. Your attention. Your love.

AUGUST 24

There are all kinds of potential friends in my world: good people; too good to be true people; broken people; iffy people; lonely people; quirky people. The list goes on but you get my point. How do I determine which people should or should not be a part of my inner circle? I admit, this can be tricky sometimes. If I share feelings, faults and fears cautiously when I first meet someone, I will gradually learn who is right to let into my life and who isn't. This is not to say who is good and who is bad, but it is the best way to decide with whom I want to spend my limited time. I want friends who are proud to know me, scared to lose me, who fight for and with me. Ones who appreciate and respect me. Care for and love me for who I am, not who they think I am or wish I were.

As Pastor Rick Warren says, "People don't need you to be perfect. They need you to be real." How do I do that? I open up. I come out from behind my façade. They show me them. I show them me. Scary? You bet!

How do I respond when I have let someone into my life and, inevitably, I learn they are human. They make mistakes, disappoint me, disappear when I need them. Now what? These are the times I lean on the strength of our bond. I give them a second or even a third chance. I don't give up on my friend. I remember their inherent dignity as a person supersedes any real or perceived offense. I forgive. I honor their Indwelling Spirit. I never take the people in my life for granted. I thank God every day they are part of my life. I never know when it might be the final time I am blessed to be in their presence.

AUGUST 25

As the philosopher, C.S. Lewis said, "We meet no ordinary people in our lives," so stretch your willingness to engage with people you don't know. Each person we meet touches us. We have an impact on and learn from each other. Our world changes because of all our interactions, good, bad and in-between. Make an effort to get to know everyone who belongs to the same group. Parent Teacher Organization... Church. Social and professional clubs. Driving range. Sports events. Servers in a favorite restaurant. They won't all become friends, but you will energize your time and spread a little love. I used to tell my kids and my grandchildren at the beginning of the school year: Make a new friend every day and pretty soon, you will know everyone's name. Good way to be, no matter our age and stage in life.

Introducing yourself in any gathering is a marvelous way to amend your way of viewing "the others" with wariness. It is a way of avoiding labeling someone because you haven't met and don't know the person inside, the one yearning to be acknowledged. This idea comes from an introvert who has learned the benefits of stretching my self-imposed boundaries. I have met fascinating people and heard amazing adventures, just because I smiled and said hello. If I can do it, so can you. Besides, I am convinced if we view everyone we meet as unique individuals with a story to tell and lessons to teach, it would be a better world. Kinder. Gentler. More interesting. More loving.

AUGUST 26

Proverbs 17:17 says, "Friends love through all kinds of weather, and families stick together in all kinds of trouble." The foundation for all relationships is trust and loyalty. Without these touchstones, nothing is possible, nothing works, nothing gets done, nothing improves. We can't be there in the way needed if we can't trust what the person is telling us. I explained the fallout from lying and leaving out the essence of the issue to my children in two ways: If you tell a lie, the consequences will be much stiffer than if you tell the truth from the beginning. You may still receive a reprimand, but the consequences will be much harsher if you lie. The second promise was I would be with them to hell and back, no matter what, but make sure you tell me your part in the incident so I have all the information, not just the parts that make you look good. This was especially important with issues in school or scuffles in the neighborhood and, now they are older, in the workplace. They remember the message when it really matters. I remember my promise.

We need to always have the best interest of our family and friends in the forefront of our response and stand with them in good times and the not so good ones. It is easy to celebrate when positive things happen: a good report card, a promotion and raise at work, an engagement, a new baby, winning the lottery. It is our response when the not so good things occur, which shows our character and who we are. Death. Divorce. Downsizing. Disagreements. Scary medical diagnosis. Those times in everyone's life when sadness and fear invade and we need our family and friends close by in love and solidarity. We probably can't change one thing about the event, but we can listen with our heart and *be* there if, when and how they may need us. Trust and loyalty wrapped up as love in action.

AUGUST 27

The most important person in your life to be honest with is your Higher Power. You cannot hide from Him; She knows you better than you know yourself. There is no point in pretending otherwise. The second most important person to be honest with is yourself. If you can't look in the mirror and respect the person staring back, you are not being the person you are meant to be. You are not the authentic you. Lying to yourself is disrespectful and causes harm to you and those around you and always catches up with you eventually.

How can you reach out and act in love if you can't and don't love yourself because you are not completely truthful about and with the real you. You can't. Your intentions, your behavior, your life will be based on a lie. Your integrity will be a sham. Your purpose for existence will be built on air instead of a solid foundation of truth. The years I spent disliking and disrespecting me, I was fooling the outside world, and worse, I didn't like the person I saw in the mirror every morning. I started avoiding any serious review of my intentions, my behavior, my real life. What a lousy, unfulfilling way to live.

When I learned to like me for the child of the Divine I am, my perceptions about me and the people in my world slowly shifted. My relationship with God grew closer. My purpose became clearer. My interactions, especially with those in my inner circle, became authentic, accepting and more loving. All because I acknowledged and accepted imperfect me and recognized the Inner Spirit guiding me.

AUGUST 28

Be careful. Don't fall into the trap of relying on just one person to be everything in your life, meet all your needs. It is unfair and draining to be the one person to carry the burden for another's happiness and safety. Whether you are single, married, have a significant other, one special friend or a small group of close cohorts, make sure you are not needy and clinging. Nothing pushes someone away faster than being unable to breathe, physically or emotionally. Feeling penned in and cut off from their world. Be conscious of their need for space and alone time, don't demand what you think you need and deserve and pout, or worse, when you don't get it.

But remember to celebrate the time you do spend together. It can be exhilarating doing even mundane chores with someone special; weekly grocery shopping, cleaning the garage, folding laundry. You learn about each other, how you function as a team, how you view nature, how you react when you win and when you lose. It gives you a foundation on which to build for times when the world is mean and ugly and confusing and we need the comfort of the familiar and safe. But in a healthy relationship, each party should have interests, projects and hobbies away from the other person. When you come back together, you have different experiences and fresh thoughts and ideas to share.

Spending time away from family, friends, an intimate partner makes us appreciate each other and helps make the time spent together that much more special and meaningful. There is an old cliché that says, "Absence makes the heart grow fonder." I believe it states an obvious truth about any loving relationship.

AUGUST 29

A word of caution: Be careful not to confuse prominent with significant. Prominent people have their name in lights and make a splash on the front page of the paper or go viral on the Internet. Just because they make a lot of noise, use up a lot of ink or generate a million clicks, doesn't mean they are worthy of attention. Some may have wisdom to pass along or facts to share, but be very discerning of the ones who demand your time, talent or treasure. Use discretion and common sense before writing a check, sharing their views or adopting their way of life.

Significant people are the ones who quietly go about making a difference in the world in some way. It is the man who is always available for a fatherless boy. Or the woman who feeds and bathes her terminally ill neighbor's children. Or the business colleague who unobtrusively mentors the youngest member of the staff. What about the teen-ager who helps an elderly friend by mowing the lawn, shoveling snow, collecting the mail, walking the dog with no expectation of payment. Or the couple who opens their home and hearth to people visiting for a funeral who can't afford commercial accommodations. These are the significant people who deserve our appreciation and recognition.

Make sure to choose friends and associates carefully. Just because this month we have been discussing the importance of sharing love with all, doesn't mean you have to, or should, invite them into your circle or adopt their way of thinking or approach to life. Our Higher Power instructs us to respect their humanity and acknowledge the Indwelling Spirit. Nothing more, Nothing less. Big difference.

AUGUST 30

This month we have been dissecting relationships. What they are. How each influences our behavior and changes our life and the lives of those around us. How complicated they sometimes seem, but in reality, all we need to do is show love and they become simplicity itself. Our understanding of relationships is defined by our stage in life. Lessons we know we need and those we aren't aware we do. We learned our Higher Power expects us to recognize the humanity in everyone. We learned relationships are precious so we shouldn't take them for granted. We choose to love and respect all with whom we interact. We are grateful for the people in our life, present, past and yet to meet.

Questions to consider:

- Do we understand our relationships are precious and unique? Yes? No? Why? Why not?
- Why is it critical to express our appreciation for family, friends, casual acquaintances?
- What have I made my own? What do I plan to carry into September? Into the rest of my life?

Gratitude Entry: I am grateful for family, family by choice, friends and friends I haven't met yet. I am grateful for the humanity in everyone and accept the Spirit dwells within all of us. I understand we all want the same things in life: sustenance, shelter, security and love. I am grateful for the special people in my life. I know I am blessed.

Reader: Add at least one thing you are grateful for as a result of reading, and contemplating the August reflections.

AUGUST 31

Sometimes I get frustrated when someone says about a particular group, "We are a family." A company. A church. A community. Come on. We aren't family. Not really. And we are not if we define family as only blood kin, by marriage, by invitation. What if we define family as fellow human beings who love, bleed, mourn, hurt, celebrate, laugh, cry. Ah, when I use that definition, it changes my perception of who is a member of my clan, my tribe, my family. When I share the true me warts and all, open my heart, be vulnerable, it changes both of us in profound ways. As Jimmy Carter, our 39th President, said, "The bond of our common humanity is stronger than the divisiveness of our fears and prejudices."

From my morning prayers, an Islamic perspective:
"May Allah bless you with people who have pure intentions for you, May he bless you with people who have genuine love and care for you, May he bless you with people who pray for you. Ameen."

SEPTEMBER

Senses

"The five senses are
the ministers of the soul."

Leonardo da Vinci

SEPTEMBER 1

Most of us are blessed with five senses: taste, smell, touch, sight, hearing plus a sixth: breath and a seventh, knowing. Our senses are open and react to colors, textures, shapes and forms. Most of us don't pay much attention to any of them except on rare occasions. I am as guilty as everyone else. We get caught up in our daily doings and take our environment for granted. Have you ever wondered what our world would be like if we didn't have our five senses? If we couldn't see our loved ones, or smell a carnation, or touch the silky, soft skin of an infant, or hear the soaring sensation of a symphony, or taste the first sip of morning coffee or breakfast tea? Our world would be colorless, tasteless, boring and lifeless.

What if we didn't have books to read, films to watch, paintings and sculptures to study? How would we learn about past civilizations, other cultures, the vast universe, the healing effects of various wild plants? How would we know and appreciate the essence of living animals and plants and learn their lessons? How would we leave boredom behind and find excitement in a riveting read?

When we truly appreciate our five senses, acknowledge our sixth, breathing, the seventh one kicks in: We intuitively know certain truths, understand some of the what, the how and the why. We appreciate our physical world. Humans are sensual beings. When we take the time to notice and delight in our sensuality, our spirit soars and our soul is refreshed. We grow closer to our breath, our essence, our Inner Spirit, our Creator.

SEPTEMBER 2

Energy is the life force we know, we feel, we sense. It flows through everyone and everything. It is our essence. Energy provides power to operate, whether an animal, a seed or a machine. In Chinese this force is known as Chi; in India it is called Prana. Other names include: élan, joie de vivre, brio, psychè, soul. Whatever you call it, this life force, this energy is what makes all the diverse parts of the universe work and move and grow. It is what defines each component, makes an object what it is and humans who we are.

According to science, energy cannot be destroyed but it is transformed and can be transferred. Calmness. Peacefulness. Joy. Only a breath away. Waiting to be changed and conveyed as love in action. From me to you, you to me and to everyone around us. Some faith traditions and spiritual philosophies view the Inner Source, the Inner Guide as a spirit, as the wind, our very breath. Zen Buddhist teacher, Vanessa Zuisel Goddard suggests we, ", sit very quiet, quieter still and follow your breath — say you can, say you will. For there is no anchor so sturdy as this, just follow your breath and you won't go amiss." Our breath. Our life force.

When viewed this way, for me, the wind in the trees becomes the breath of the Divine. Her life force working in, around and for all of creation. The leaves and the grass and the flowers sway gently to give honor to the Creator. Animals respond. They bark, They howl. They whinny. They growl. They moo. They screech. They meow. They honk. They create the beautiful noise of the universe. Stir in laughing. Crying. Humming. Singing. Shouting. Whispering. And the symphony is complete. Listen to the wind. Hear God's voice. Say Amen.

SEPTEMBER 3

Don't grasp and try to control. Release and receive. Be flexible as the wind, as the breath of energy. When you are flexible, you will bend rather than break. Accept the reality life changes, people change, circumstances change. You don't have to give up your beliefs, your integrity to learn to overflow with kindness and love. Being flexible means fewer disagreements and misunderstandings, more positive energy with which to power our inner and outer worlds.

Psychiatrist, Judith Orloff, M.D. calls people who give off negative energy and drain us physically and mentally, "emotional vampires." There are lots of reasons why this happens. When it does, take a time out. Think about why you are reacting as you are. Ask and answer honestly: Can you help the other person or is someone else better suited to step in so you can move away? I am not suggesting it will be easy, but maybe both of you would benefit by turning the situation over to someone new.

Maybe you feel drained because you once battled the same demon or a similar one and you are wisely unwilling to risk going back there. That is okay. Don't feel guilty. It is called self-care. Knowing your triggers and avoiding them. Lovingly wish the person God-speed and walk away.

SEPTEMBER 4

Do you ever stand back and observe yourself? To take a moment to really see what you are doing? How you are interacting within yourself, with your companion, with the world? During an especially deep conversation with a close friend, I realized I wasn't responding in the way I really wanted. In the way of love. In that brief moment, I actually saw me for who I was and didn't like my behavior, my words, me. Wow! Talk about an eye-opening experience.

After some heartfelt thought, I recognized my Inner Guide had gently nudged me to momentarily step away from me and observe. I discovered the power in truly seeing me as I can be in an intense encounter. What a revelation! I wish I could tell you the insights gained propelled me to use my newfound power all the time. Alas, it did not, but I usually remember the tactic as I catch myself starting to talk and act irrationally during an important conversation. Pausing for a moment usually helps me regain my composure, begin to think calmly and speak rationally.

Why is this method so effective? Scientists have learned observation alters the behavior, appearance and energy of an object. If it works with amoebas, photons and cells, it follows it will work with humans. Try it. Take note of what you see. What you learn. I bet it will surprise you. It sure did me.

SEPTEMBER 5

Think of your breath as another sense. Use it to find your calm and regain your balance. When my thoughts, especially the irrational ones, try to take over my mind, I consciously use my breath to rein them in and get the unruly ones under control. The marvelous thing about this approach is my breath is always available. I can use this technique without anyone knowing. It is a silent device to help me scurry back to my internal, private paradise. Regain my equilibrium, find my center. Be a nicer person to me and to everyone around me. And I can use it no matter where I am, who is with me or what I am doing

Give it a try as you read this reflection. Breathe in calm, four beats; breathe out stress, four beats. Breathe in kindness, four beats; breathe out love, four beats. Do this as many times as needed. Not only will you let go of stress, you will find your calming center and spread joy, Bet you feel better already. I am breathing rhythmically while typing this reflection. My heartbeat is slowly returning to normal and my fingers are locating the right keys more easily. In the quiet of my study, I am the only one who knows what a glorious gift I am offering to you, to me and to everyone around us. You are welcome, world.

SEPTEMBER 6

What we give away grows exponentially so we have more to share. We receive in abundance when we have no expectation of getting anything in return. It is a conundrum for sure but it is the circle of life and joy in action. Some call it visualization. Some think of it as meditation. I think of it as having positive thoughts instead of harboring negative feelings. We have discussed this before. One person can't do much to change the big world, but we can influence a wee bit of it if we use our breath to spread positive vibes in our corner of it.

Look at it this way. We all breathe anyway, Why not use it for something besides keeping us alive. Let's get double bang for this invaluable buck. Now there is a novel idea. I breathe. You breathe. Combined with the furred, feathered and finned critters plus all the trees and plants and grasses, that is a lot of breath circulating. Since the other fauna and flora exist without thinking about how and why, maybe we humans need to be the mindful ones asking the Supreme Creator to use our collective breath to clean the atmosphere, perhaps give it a few more productive eons before we unintentionally destroy it from overuse and ignorance and neglect. Maybe we can start our own quiet campaign to leave our planet just a bit better than we found it. By breathing in and out with purpose. Offering our breath to the world.

SEPTEMBER 7

You. Me. We are all made of many different roles. Woman. Man. Wife. Husband. Parent. Sibling. Professional person. Inner child. Outer adult. Reliable friend. Each of these roles is an iteration of the whole person, which makes each of us unique. We spend much of our earthly life reconciling all our disparate roles. Sometimes it is easy. More often than not in our busy world, it is a challenge. A challenge to keep the warring roles in balance, calm, rational. You know that life / person / parent / work dynamic we hear about all the time and seems impossible to achieve. Now and again, maybe, but rarely day in and day out.

One role may be in competition or even conflict with another. Woman / Wife. Man / Husband. Parent / Professional. I am sure you can relate and remember more than several incidents when faced with this dilemma. It is not always easy to make the choice and be comfortable it was the right one right now. After much fretting, fussing and guilt, I finally realized the best way to decide which role needs more attention is really very simple. My solution to this particular dilemma is to stop, take a moment, listen to my heart. Love always leads me to the right decision. When I give my heart the reins, I give my Inner Wisdom control. She never lets me go astray. Love knows the answer instinctively. Why fight it? Let go and let love.

SEPTEMBER 8

Tap into your energy, your life force when you feel drained. Tired. Discouraged. Out of steam. Can't take one more step. Fix one more meal. Finish one more monthly report. Listen to one more complaint. See one more grumpy or sad face. Hear another whiney voice. As I think of it: When the world is too much with me.

We all have those moments, sometimes days when it seems as if the universe is out to stymie anything and everything we try to accomplish. When we just want to give in and give up. Sound familiar? Those thoughts and feelings plague me too. What to do? Stop. Breathe. Call up the fire which burns within you, The life force that keeps on keepin' on. The quiet voice whispering, "You are okay. You are enough just as you are. Give it one more try. One more day." Let hope rule. Have faith there is good in the world. Remember, deep down, people are kind.

Take a breath. Take another one and another until you feel your energy kicking in, your life force stepping up. Accept you are valued. You are loved. Smile softly. Go on with your day. Safe in the knowledge you are enough and the world is a better place because you are in it. And believe it.

SEPTEMBER 9

Connect with your body to identify where you store stress so you can learn to relax and let go of the inner turmoil and be all you can be. Find your center. Determine how to get there. Take a walk. A bubble bath. Exercise. Listen to music. Have a cup of tea. Indulge in a glass of wine or a measure of scotch. Watch the cat chase the sunbeam. Listen to the birds sing. Daydream. Meditate. Pray. Sit silently. Discover what brings you to your center so when you are out of balance, you have a surefire method to regain your physical and mental equilibrium.

The method I use depends on what is causing the stress. Sometimes I stop what I am doing. Shut down the laptop. Lose myself in a novel; engage with my Kindle friends. Leave my literal world and escape into my literary one. Sometimes I stare out the window and let my mind wander into nicer places. Other times, I just sit quietly until I decide what I need. Find what works for you. Write them down. When you need to find your center, all you will need to do is look at your list for inspiration. Little to no thought required. Give yourself the gift of self-care. You deserve it. You are worth taking time for you.

SEPTEMBER 10

Hearing is listed as one of the five primary senses. Speaking is not. Two ears. One mouth. Ever wonder why? Obvious answer: Listen more. Talk less. A real challenge for many of us. People tell me I am a good listener. It is a skill I consciously practice. In order to "be there" for someone, I need to understand their message. I can't do that if I am preparing a response before they are finished talking or I let my mind wander. But even I don't always listen as carefully as I should. Oh, I could offer a host of reasons: fatigue, preoccupied, out of sorts mentally or physically, but the bottom line is when I don't hear, I am not being the person I think I am and strive to be. I am not being a truly caring friend listening with my heart.

The art of listening is a gift to be cultivated and nurtured. Look at the other person. Focus on what they are not saying as much as what they are saying. Nod occasionally; it is a visible signal you are paying attention. When it is time for you to speak, repeat one or two words or phrases you perceive sum up their message. Watch their non-verbal responses. Think a few moments before you respond. Use appropriate words. Be aware of your tone of voice. All of these elements are part of being an effective listener. Working together, listening and speaking create meaningful conversations and is a useful way to share information.

Onelast comment. Light-hearted conversations and funny observations about nothing and everything generate laughter and joy. They are marvelous ways to bring people together. Create common ground. Build a solid foundation. When the inevitable serious subjects come up, you will be glad you shared a chuckle or two or ten with a few belly laughs thrown in for good measure.

SEPTEMBER 11

September 11, 2001. A day that redefined America's vison of safety and who we believe we are as a county, a culture, a people. It is one of those days we all remember where we were, who we were with and what we were doing when we heard the news of the plane crashes and watched the towers tumbling. None of us who were alive that day will ever forget, but for many who were on-site or lost family or friends, the trauma will never leave them.

9/11 changed us forever in many ways. We can't unsee or un-feel the images. So what did America do? What Americans always do in time of tragedy and trauma. We came together, We did what needed to be done in whatever ways we were able. Pulling people to safety. Searching for victims. Comforting the survivors. Giving blood. Passing out water. Quietly weeping. Praying privately.

In honor of those who lost their lives, we decided to devote this date going forward to doing good deeds and helping others. We declared a *National Day of Service* to help heal hurts by sharing our time, talents and treasure with understanding, compassion and inclusion.

Please find a way to make a difference in someone's life, if only for today. Prepare a meal for a lonely single; better yet, invite them to join you. Visit an elderly neighbor and listen as they tell their unique story. Sweep the sidewalks on your block. Volunteer to help in one of the many community acts of service every city plans. Whatever your act, do it with kindness and love. It is the best way to honor those who perished that fateful day. As a bonus, you will feel good about yourself; think of it as self-care of the highest form.

SEPTEMBER 12

Is your speech a weapon of mass destruction or a gift of serenity? Should your actions be imitated or ignored? Strong words, I know, but how we use words, our tone of voice and our actions and reactions have serious consequences. We are all teachers and mentors, saints and sinners, whether we realize it or not. Our actions are on display and our words are heard by everyone in, near and around our space. Usually, we think only children and maybe teens are paying attention, but adults are observing us too.

We all need to be aware of how our words and behavior affects our world. I learn from children and young people all the time. Friends and colleagues are great teachers of both positive and negative responses to stimuli. We are sponges even if we don't realize we are absorbing the waves in the atmosphere around us. I have walked into many a space and instantly felt either positive or negative vibes. Unconsciously, I decide whether I want to stay and schmooze or feel the strong urge to escape as quickly as possible. I probably couldn't say exactly why, I just knew. The seventh sense kicking in. The closer you pay attention to your surroundings and its atmosphere, the better and more appropriately you will respond to the people and activity within. The more you will learn about your world, the people with whom you interact and yourself. Those valuable life lessons we all need, and require a reminder of from time to time.

SEPTEMBER 13

Sense pleasures are gifts we give ourselves, for no particular reason, just because. Be sure to feel with all five senses. These experiences feed your body, enlighten your mind. Speak to your heart, soothe your soul. Pay attention. Look around. Really see, hear, smell, taste, touch your world.

The blue sky and green grass. The shape and structure of buildings and bridges. Water moving. Birds singing. Stars on a clear night. Children screeching. Adults laughing. Cold lemonade made with just picked lemons with an orange added for pop. Fresh blueberry, apple or peach cobbler. Coffee, vanilla or mint chocolate chip ice cream. One luscious piece of dark chocolate. The smell of newly mowed grass. An infant after a bath. Sleeping on sheets dried outside in the spring breeze. Your significant other's loving smile and gentle touch. A child's exuberant hug. A well written book by a first-time author. A soaring symphony. A beautiful painting by a talented friend. A tranquil walk in the park, the woods, the forest. A refreshing dip in the pool, the lake, the ocean. Stomping in puddles after a rain. Sliding down a snowy hill. A quiet hour or day to indulge in whatever your body needs, your mind requires, your heart requests, your soul yearns for.

The sights, sounds and smells of nature and our environment have restorative powers to calm the most restless among us. Delight in the sensory overload all around you on our wonderous, glorious planet. Give yourself the sensual pleasures available, you just need to take time to notice. Remember to shout thank you.

SEPTEMBER 14

Understand your personal space. How you feel when you walk in the door. Whether it is one room, a small first or final apartment, a spacious loft or a four thousand square foot house, what do you want in your space? Want to look at, touch, smell? Your living space, your nest, your home reflects who you are and what speaks to you. It is cozy PJs and a favorite pair of comfy slippers.

Do you want peace, quiet, organized, lived-in tranquility or to be energized and stimulated in controlled chaos? It sounds confusing, but it really comes down to what inspires you, wraps its arms around you and says, "You are Home! Take off your shoes. Relax. Be yourself."

More important than furniture, wall color, window and floor covering, is how you personalize your sanctuary. The accessories. The artwork. The pillows and throws. The special things that generate fond memories. Gifts from family and friends. Reminders of travel adventures. Family pictures. Unusual collections. As organizational guru, Marie Kondo says, "...what brings you joy." This is how you personalize any size space and turn it into your home.

A gentle warning: Creating and curating your home is not a one and done project. It is a life-long process. It takes time to decide and find what is right for you. I have continued to right-size since I moved into my retirement space. A while back, I realized my color choices coordinate nicely even though I have been creating and curating my home since I was eighteen. For the mathematically challenged, that will be sixty years on my next birthday. Because I have chosen and kept what has meaning for me, it all works together, no matter what objects I place next to each other or in which room. It also says, "Welcome. Come in. Sit a spell." to everyone who enters.

SEPTEMBER 15

Color influences our mood. It calms or stimulates. It creates a hands-off or an inviting atmosphere. It is revealing. Color can affect our heart rate, blood pressure and respiration. Its impact can be in-your-face or subtle and understated. Use of color is a powerful form of self-expression. Anecdotally, I have noticed the colors people wear and use to decorate their spaces usually reflect their "real" self. Scientific studies have shown color affects our behavior and people's perception of us. Entire books have been written on the subject of color. I am going to focus on simple definitions of the common primary and secondary colors. I'll leave the analyzing to the experts.

The primary colors are red, yellow and blue. The secondary colors are green, orange and purple. All other colors are made from combining two or more of these colors. There are various shades, hues and tints in each color family. Most of us have a favorite one, maybe two. Look at the clothes you wear most often and the colors in your home. Most likely, you will see a dominant color or color family and one contrasting color. These are your favorites. We instinctively choose the ones we like, emotionally flatter us and we feel comfortable in and around. I have seen color combinations that would give me a headache and bring on nightmares if I had to live with them, but they speak to the person who uses them. That is why there are so many from which to choose. Tomorrow we will look at what the various colors mean.

SEPTEMBER 16

Let's continue our look at color; what it means and how it makes us feel.

Red is a bold, powerful color with both positive and negative connotations. It represents love and danger, passion and anger, vitality and violence. It takes a confident person to use red. It is not a subtle color, although some of the hues and shades in the family are: pink, rose, rust.

Yellow is a cheerful, optimistic color that inspires joy and happiness. It is hard to be sad in a room painted a sunny yellow. The gold shades suggest wealth and royalty. Yellow suggests optimism, hope and creativity. Too much can sometimes be over stimulating.

Blue is a cool, calm color that soothes and creates serenity. It suggests loyalty, trust and openness. It is associated with healing. It is the color of life-giving and life-sustaining water. Our psyche rests when we gaze at the blue sky. Blue is my favorite color; it makes my eyes sparkle and pop. I feel safe and serene when surrounded by blue, which is why it is the dominant color in my nest and my closet.

Green reminds us of nature, spring, renewal, growth. It conveys stability, health, generosity. Green is invigorating in a subtle way. It does not shout, but whispers all is as it should be. Green is my second favorite color. I feel confident in an understated way when I wear it. I have a lot of green plants in my nest; they clean the air and remind me of the invigorating outdoors.

Orange conveys energy, warmth and joy. It encourages creativity, but too much can be over stimulating. It is a little less bold than red but carries similar messages in a subtler way. Orange is a transitional color associated with the change of seasons from summer to fall to winter.

Purple is associated with royalty and wealth, inspiration and creativity. People either really like purple or can't stand it; there doesn't seem to be a middle ground. It shows imagination. A little purple here and there brings a pop of color to any formal or casual room or outfit.

SEPTEMBER 17

Learn to appreciate your innate sensuality. How things feel. Smell. Look. Taste. Humans are sensual beings. Unfortunately, all too often we cheat ourselves by taking our physical world for granted. The contrasts found in our every-day environment are many and offer pleasure when we use all five senses. The bumpy feel of corduroy pants. Cuddling a soft lap blanket. The healing effects of hot tea when feeling blah or the refreshing taste of cold lemonade on a hot day. Light prevents us from stubbing our baby toe and adds ambiance to our surroundings. Dark encourages togetherness. Sweet appeals to the kid in all of us, no matter our age. Sour sometimes matches our mood and puckers our mouth for a quick kiss. Paying attention to the artifacts we keep around us reminds us of special people, exciting adventures, and the treasures of our well-lived life.

Smelling the food of our particular holidays and family celebrations brings back memories of people no longer with us and times past, our history. For me, cinnamon and popcorn conjure up good times with special people. Sounds also stimulate our memory. St. Augustine said, "When we sing, we pray twice." The birthday song. A special love song from our youth. The wedding march. A particular word or phrase grandma or dad or cousin Joe or BFF Suzanne used. Any familiar noise from our life usually brings a smile and a happy sigh of recognition.

Drumming connects us to the sound of our mother's heartbeat and the vibrations of the earth. All civilizations and cultures use some form of drumming in communication, for fun and in worship services. Drumming is a universal sound that ties us to each other and to Mother Earth. It represents the heartbeat of life itself.

SEPTEMBER 18

The Arts are the expression and language of civilizations and help define cultures. Each in their own way opens our heart, moves our soul, soothes the psyche and stimulates the senses. Life would be boring and sterile without the passion of painting, poetry, literature, music, dance, acting and sculpture. Thoughtfully designed architecture adds form, function and beauty to a community. A carefully laid out system of alleys, roads, streets and highways moves people and products safely from place to place.

The Fine Arts are developed for many reasons. Most artists of every medium would shrivel up and blow away if not allowed to express themselves through their particular passion. A song sung and heard. A book written and read. A painting created and shared. A play and a symphony composed and appreciated. All these art forms bring us together in different ways.

The ancient Chinese art of feng shui is a method of creating harmony and balance in our home. It uses the complementary opposites of yin, a symbol of earth, female, passivity and yang, a symbol of heaven, male, activity. Using objects representing The Five Elements, which are earth, metal, water, wood and fire encourage positive forces to enter and negative forces to leave. When used in proper proportion, they bring peace, prosperity and health to a space.

There are many art forms and practices used to beautify our world, enliven our senses and enhance our life. What marvelous gifts humans gave to themselves. Let's learn to see, hear and appreciate all the hours, work and passion wrapped inside each.

SEPTEMBER 19

Another way to appreciate the beauty in fine art, the performing arts, architecture and nature's bounty is to experience the essence of whatever you are looking at, listening to. "Feel" and "hear" what it is silently saying about its function, form, shape, texture, sound. What is its message? Oh my! Until I read about this approach, I never thought any art of any kind had an essence. Wasn't even sure how to apply the concept.

As is my custom, in order to understand how to apply the term, I needed a definition. The online Microsoft dictionary defines essence as "the intrinsic nature or indispensable quality of something, especially something abstract, that determines its character." A lot of interesting words but it doesn't really tell me how to determine the essence of a particular person, place, animal or thing. I kept digging. After reading a lot of essays and long-winded, written discussions, I decided essence is an elusive quality because it means different things depending upon who is looking or listening, what their experiences are, the emotional baggage they are carrying. In other words, when I look at a painting or listen to a song or read a poem or watch puppies and kittens play, it speaks to me differently than it will to you and you and you. It is personal. What appeals to me may not appeal to you. And vice versa.

So given this conclusion, is it worth trying to determine the essence of an object? I believe it is. It makes it more relatable, more real. Besides, sharing our individual interpretations will encourage a lively discussion and help us learn more about each other. So visit an art museum. Go to a concert or the live theater. Watch a movie at home. And talk about it. Enjoy your art-full experience.

SEPTEMBER 20

The ability to retain tribal experience started with telling stories using hand gestures, body language, movement and sound. The myths and legends of civilizations were passed from generation to generation. The tale usually had a moral lesson or recalled an important event in the tribe's past. Thus, the history of the group was preserved. Through the ages, this important pastime morphed from sitting around the fire to itinerant troubadours moving from place to place to raucous productions in which the audience was as much a part of the production as the actors on the stage. Our modern version of this tradition is live theater and musical performances. From community groups to Broadway and London productions, each tells a universal story to teach, to inform, to entertain. The audience still participates, usually respectfully. We laugh. We cringe. We cry. We sing along. We dance. We applaud. We relate. We learn. For the duration of the performance, the audience, the story-listeners, and the entertainers, the story-tellers, come together as one.

During my high school years, I was involved in speech and drama. I learned the importance of the early story telling in preserving history. I came to understand the human desire to know who we are, where we came from and how we got here started around the campfire sharing stories. We do the same thing through books, movies, music and the theater. As a neophyte writer, I became a student of history because I realized I need to know the rules and rituals of a society before I attempt to interpret their stories with accuracy and make the message believable. I gradually learned using words and movements is integral to preserving our civilization.

The next time your teenagers have the volume of their music at headache-inducing decibels, or your grandchildren bring a story alive using hand puppets, stop, listen and learn. Say thank you to the next generation for reminding you why we have records of past civilizations. Why the Library of Congress is diligently capturing and preserving our music, movies, books and visual artifacts for coming generations. Humans are still making history and preserving it through various art forms.

SEPTEMBER 21

We toss around the words create, creative and creativity with little understanding of their intrinsic meaning. The accepted definition is using imagination to produce something new and original; it is usually applied to some form of the fine arts. But what does the concept mean exactly? My succent definition: Creativity is thinking of novel solutions, sometimes in the moment. Now that opens the door to applying the concept to more than writing and composing and painting and sculpting. It defines the person who invented the wheel. The florist who arranges flowers in an unusual way. The hostess who sets an elegant table using ordinary items. The mechanic who designs a tool to make the job safer, faster or more efficient. The basement inventor who figures a way to reuse old plastic bottles or worn tires in a new way. These people are all creative. They made something useful or beautiful or gave a discarded object new life. They found novel solutions by using their unique imagination to make the world a little prettier or less cluttered or solved a problem. .

Be sure to notice the harried mother with young children who distracts their attention before they have a major meltdown in the store or in church. The salesperson who patiently deals with an irate customer. The nurse who respectfully answers the elderly person's questions slowly, clearly and more than once during the same conversation. The instructor who reaches her class with an interesting example they can understand and relate to. These ordinary people are all creative.

We are fortunate these people are part of our community. In their quiet way without any fanfare or even realizing it, their actions make our world a little better, a little kinder and a lot more loving.

SEPTEMBER 22

Today is the fall equinox. Enjoy the splendor of the change in the season. Even in Houston where the temperature may be in the 90s, we know cooler weather is closer every day. This is the time farmers and gardeners prepare the soil for winter in anticipation of the spring renewal. The cycle of life begins. Each season prepares the earth for the next one, Same with the seasons of the soul. It is a good day to let go of old ways of seeing and feeling. Look at your life with love and appreciate every breath you are given. Accept each lesson prepares you for whatever you need to know. We can't and shouldn't rush the process. Remember, one day at a time.

Just like summer follows spring and winter follows autumn, our psyche, our heart, our soul moves from one lesson to the next. Being aware sets the foundation for growth. Each experience teaches us something we need to know. We never stop growing in wisdom until we take our final breath. So try not to hurry through your day. Appreciate whatever time you are given. Stop. Look around you. Pay attention. Appreciate the people with whom you interact and the adventures you experience, especially the simple and unexpected ones. These are what make up a well-lived life. Savor the gifts from your Higher Power. These are what you will remember fondly as you prepare for your final earthly experience.

SEPTEMBER 23

The Japanese art of "Kintsugi" creates a new piece of pottery from the broken shards of the original. The craftsman bonds the pieces together using a lacquer made of powdered silver, gold or platinum. The breaks are not disguised but clearly show on the restored piece. The philosophy is to treat the breaking and repairing as part of the history of the object; Kintsugi enhances its provenance. It makes the plate or bowl or cup or pot beautiful and useful in a new and different way.

When I read about this ancient art of respect, repair and reuse, it brought broken human beings to mind. How we pick ourselves up and start again when we break into a million pieces. It doesn't matter what causes the emotional damage, we put ourselves back together. The process may take a day, a decade, a lifetime, but we eventually find us again, just in a different form.

My life was shattered when my soulmate of thirty-two years died. I didn't believe I would ever want to or be able to move on and live any kind of normal life. I wasn't even sure what a normal life was supposed to look like. It is nine years since Paul's death changed my life forever. I miss him every day. I love him every day. The hole in my heart hurts a little less every day. I am learning who I am now that I am not a wife. I have created a different life. Not better. Different. I respect our marriage. I repair my heart a little more every day, letting the cracks show, valuing what they represent. Hard-learned life lessons I share in two columns and within the pages of this book of reflections.

My life with Paul was loving, giving, receiving, joyful. My new life is loving, giving, receiving, joyful in a different way. I am me with a new look, a new life, a new usefulness. I am using Kintsugi on me.

SEPTEMBER 24

We are all storytellers in one way or another. By our words and actions. How we act and react. How we relate to others we encounter on our pilgrimage. Our day-to-day behavior. How we live our life. Using human touch to soothe a frantic or worried or scared person, whether we know them or not. Listening with compassion when a friend is hurting or confused or struggling. Sending a loving look across the room when we sense our significant other needs an emotional boost.

Other ways stories are told. The mother who prepares family meals night after night. The man who builds shelves to increase storage in the garage. The committed partners who give birth to or adopt a baby. The loving parents who raise that baby to lead a moral, ethical, thoughtful, giving life. The teen who writes a song or a poem. He or she know instinctively music, rhythm and rhyme soothe the savage beast lurking in all of us, no matter our age or stage. The toddler who fingerpaints with glee, just for the fun and feel of paint everywhere. The child learning to set the table for breakfast and beaming at praise for a job well done. The cheerful person who always smiles and says "please" and "thank you" and "bless you."

Going about our day doing whatever we are doing, we are creating our story, Laying the foundation for a loving, lasting legacy for future generations. What story are you telling? Are you happy with your story? Proud of its message? If not, change its content. Change its direction. As always, it is your choice.

SEPTEMBER 25

There are days when I don't feel like or even want to be positive. Don't especially care what story I am telling today. Not really in the black pit. Just have the blues and the blahs. It takes real effort to pull my weary body out of bed and smooth both mine and the sheets' wrinkles. Make my morning mocha smoothie. Get dressed. Concentrate on the reflections and spiritual readings for the day. My usual affirmations are not working. I'm not saying them because I don't want to feel better just yet. Nothing in particular is wrong or out of order ... except me and my attitude.

Some days, even when I am aware I need an attitude adjustment, my behavior disagrees and refuses to cooperate.

So what do I do if I have to interact with anyone? Via text or email. On the phone. In person. If I have to leave the safety of my cozy nest? How do I cope? Carefully. Very carefully. I am forced to decide if I am going to be cranky to match my mood or will I paste on a fake smile and pretend all is right in my inner world? A dilemma for sure. One I suspect every human faces from time to time. Before I walk out the door, I need to remember the ripples in the water parable. If I am grouchy, my negative mood affects everyone with whom I interact. If I find a smile, even a shaky one, it improves the odds. My decision has the potential to affect a lot more than my day. It may cause the person with whom I was either abrupt or pleasant to pass on the attitude the rest of their day. Do I want to be responsible for giving people a reason to be grumpy or pleasant?

I know what I want my answer to be. I have to remember the positive and put it into action when the blues and blahs attack. I turn it over to my Inner Guide to nudge me when I need a reminder.

SEPTEMBER 26

Quiet is comfortable. Quiet helps me feel secure, isolated in my safe inner world. As an introvert, I prefer not to be noticed. I would rather be the power behind the scenes manipulating the strings, making the decisions, making it happen. I first realized this when I was involved in high school speech and drama. I preferred backstage activities. Put me in front of a live audience and I was an abysmal failure. I had one line in one play. Hated the entire experience. Spent the next three years working behind the scenes: lighting, sound, scenery, costumes, make-up, whispering cues, operating the curtains. Anything but another appearance on stage. The result? I was producer of our senior play. Important for many reasons but especially because it was the first year our all-girls school collaborated with an all-boys school. It was my job to keep everything and everyone focused on the production and not each other. Heady stuff.

During my eclectic career, I frequently found myself second-in-charge of projects. The head honcho had the headaches and took the grief. Fine with me. I did the research; kept my head down and stayed out of the line of fire. The only exception was when I compiled the report or conducted the interviews and wrote the column. I insisted on a byline. I am confident of my way with words and the message within and want the world to recognize my work.

These days, I am involved in various projects. Unless it is my column or a feature article for one of the newsletters, if I include my name, it is tiny letters on the bottom of the last page. Want to add the work to my portfolio, just don't need my name up front, on top, in neon. My ego has been tamed plus I prefer the quiet approach.

Not everyone craves the spotlight; others do. Both approaches are okay. But please remember, whichever describes you, be quiet in your quest for recognition. It is so much sweeter and means so much more when it comes and you are not expecting it, searching for it or shouting about it. It becomes a God given gift.

SEPTEMBER 27

According to the writer, Melody Beattie, "Maybe you don't need to change what you are looking at. You just need to change where you stand." Intriguing idea. What does she mean? How does it work? A common example may help.

Five people witness the same event. When asked to describe, "to the best of their ability" what they saw and heard, there will be five different stories. Each honestly believes their version is the accurate one. Doesn't matter if it is a happy or sad event. Serene or scary. No one "sees" and "hears" the same things. Why? They each viewed the incident through their lens from their particular vantage point. Had they been standing in a different spot, they would have seen and heard and described an entirely different scene.

Maybe we should apply the same principle to our understanding of who we are and where we are standing on our personal path. If we are unhappy with the view, perhaps we should consider moving a tad right or left, a slight step forward. A little each way? Change our perspective, change what we see. Change what we see, change how we feel. Change how we feel, change the results. All because we moved from the spot we were stuck in. How do you think movement would work for you?

SEPTEMBER 28

Let's add something essential to our morning routine. It will only take a moment, but it will have a profound effect on our perception. We give ourselves permission to engage our five senses, to be sensual as we go through our day. Refuse to deprive ourselves the pleasure of seeing, hearing, smelling, tasting and touching our world. Experience the sensations of letting our physical senses run amuck, just to learn what they are, how they make us feel, what they add to our conscious life.

Studies have shown these marvelous sensual gifts relieve stress, encourage emotional stability, improve focus and cognition and enhance problem-solving skills and self-esteem. In some ways, they can be an emotional catharsis and clear any blockage keeping us from finding peace. What a bonanza just from using our five senses. Remember laughter and tears are compatible; both recharge our energy. When we include the energy of our breath, our essence, and add our intuitive knowing, we come closer to conquering our inner demons and quieting the nagging skeptic — ourselves. Watch out, world, here we come!

SEPTEMBER 29

We have discovered the power in paying attention, in being still. We can focus on seeing and listening and being one with our surroundings, if only for a moment. To what the wind has to teach us. What the trees and plants and winged and crawly creatures can show us about appreciating our environment. How human creativity enhances our life. When we give our innate sensuality permission and encouragement to enjoy this precious gift only humans can comprehend fully. If we stop, take a minute to really look and listen. What marvelous miracles are all around us.

Questions to consider:

- Do we understand our seven senses are precious and unique? Yes? No? Why? Why not?
- Why is it critical to use and appreciate our senses to their fullest? What do we gain?
- What have I made my own? What do I plan to carry into October? Into the rest of my life?

Gratitude Entry: I am grateful for the five physical senses: sight, hearing, touching, tasting, smelling. I am also grateful for my breath, the energy, the essence of who I am, which leads me to knowing certain truths about me, my life and my world. These seven senses are marvelous gifts from the Supreme Being. He and She want me to use and appreciate all of them every day.

Reader: Add at least one thing you are grateful for as a result of reading, and contemplating the September reflections.

SEPTEMBER 30

Throughout this month we have been discussing one relationship we frequently neglect and how it nourishes us: Our connection to Mother Earth, the incredible Divine flora and fauna which beautify our existence and sustain our need for fun, food, order and psychic energy. How these precious gifts enhance our appreciation of the five senses.

Supreme Creator, I ask you to help me learn to see, hear, taste, touch and smell my surroundings and everything in it. Help me to see a beautiful sunrise instead of the start of another stressful day. Hear birds singing joyfully instead of a noisy intrusion. Feel the soft fur of a friendly dog or cat instead of a mangy pest. Smell the last breath of a dying yellow rose instead of seeing a flower past its prime. See a suffering soul instead of odd behavior. Hear a needy child instead of a whiney brat. Listen to a wise one's story instead of seeing a crusty curmudgeon, Help me understand how I interpret what I sense in my environment drives how I respond to people and events. Help me answer with love and acceptance. Thank you, God, for the gift of a perfect day.

OCTOBER

Life

"Life is not a problem to be solved
but a mystery to be lived."

St. Irenaeus

OCTOBER 1

The Buddhist teacher, Thich Nhat Hanh, coined the word *interbeing*. He defines it as a deep level of interconnectedness and interrelatedness, which means every single person in the world counts. We are given the gifts and opportunities, indeed a Divine duty, to contribute to a fulfilling life for everyone. We all matter. We all have ideas, words and actions to contribute to the whole of life. Its integrity. Its importance. We are relevant in a world that values the individual for who they are; what they are willing to stand for and stand by.

A word about ego. It is not evil. It is a tool to help us navigate our weird, wacky, unpredictable life. It helps us function *in* the world, but can help prevent us from being *of* the world. So don't be afraid of your ego. It has an important place in your life. It took me several decades to understand its usefulness, one of which is protection from being hurt all the time. When I value myself, I find ways to avoid giving others permission to walk on my sense of self. One of the greatest gifts I gave myself.

As we grow in wisdom and understanding of ourselves and the world, we will bump headlong into issues, problems and situations we can't fix or change, right now. What to do? Accept reality, but keep working on what appears to be unsolvable or unchangeable. Some things take time, the Deity's time. If we can look in the mirror at the end of the day and honestly say, "I did my best and was the best me I can be," our day was successful, even if seemed the universe was conspiring against us and thwarted all our efforts. Diane, one of my closest friends from high school posted this quote from writer and artist, Mary Anne Radmacher, on her bathroom mirror, "Courage doesn't always roar. Sometimes courage is the little voice at the end of the day that says, 'I'll try again tomorrow." Wise words to end our day.

OCTOBER 2

Swiss philosopher and poet, Henri-Frederic Amiel said, "The man who has no inner life is a slave of his surroundings." Hmmm...Let's think about this. What is an "inner life" anyway? There are as many ways to answer this question as there are people. As I keep reminding us, we are all unique individuals. I am me. You are you. Which means each of us has a unique inner life based on our particular needs. As an introvert, I live in my mind most of the time. So my inner life is quite active. It is a challenge to quiet it down, to turn off the noise. It sounds counterintuitive, but turning off my private noise is the only way I can connect with my Inner Being. If I don't get my thoughts to stop shouting, I can't hear what my Deity is quietly trying to tell me. I can't listen and learn.

Maybe our mind is in the closed position much of the time. But in order to integrate new ideas, different opinions, alternate ways of responding to stimuli, we need to be open to hearing them, considering if and how we can use them, make them part of our day. Spend a little time pondering how to develop an inner life which works for you. It will introduce you to a world of wonders to explore, which will lead you to exciting places full of possibilities. It will lead, as my friend entrepreneur, Lanson Jones says, to "An understanding that comes from inner standing." A wise observation, which tells us new knowledge and information becomes a part of us and influences how we relate to all God's creations. What a heady realization!

OCTOBER 3

Sometimes it seems like my life is overwhelming. As if my world is crashing around me. Guilt. Fear. Phobias. Worries. They invade my thoughts and torture my heart. I get stuck until I stop my frantic doing and make myself take the time necessary to deal with and clear away the thoughts and feelings blocking me from moving on, living my life to the fullest. Sometimes it is easy. I give myself a short scolding, then a pep talk, and I am able to set aside whatever is troubling me. Leave it in the past where it belongs. Other times, it takes a lot more than positive affirmations to pull me out of the quicksand of unresolved issues. And a lot more time to restart my enthusiasm, find the way back to the real me. The hopeful, loving me. The me who accepts I am not perfect. I screw up. The friend who makes a sincere apology for an unkind or thoughtless comment. The person who acknowledges mistakes and does her best to make them right. The woman who treats everyone with respect. The kind woman who tries her best to share love no matter how she feels inside or what catastrophe she is facing.

We all need to find our own path to whatever helps us forgive ourself. Heal our hurts. Set aside our disillusionments. Learn to live the life for which we were created. We may begin to discover it in our youth, hone it as adults, finally find peace in the closing act of our life. Whether we find it in an exercise routine, read it in a poem, see it in a picture, hear it from a friend, however and wherever we stumble on it, until we do, we will continue to search for contentment.

The thing we need to remember is to keep searching. Never give up. Always believe our loving Inner Guide will lead us to what we need when we need it. It is worth the wait. Celebrate life. Its joys. Its sorrows. Its triumphs. Its failures. Each offer valuable lessons if we are alert and aware. Live in the sacred now. Your reward will be inspiration to keep on keeping on, no matter what life throws your way. You will learn and grow. And meet the you, your Deity created you to be.

OCTOBER 4

Pay attention. You don't want to miss discovering the real you. "Without accomplishing another thing, you are the complete fulfillment of all those who came before you. How can you doubt yourself?" What a head-shaking, heart-stopping, person-defining statement! Threw my mind into a tailspin when I read this observation from the Zen Buddhist priest, Karen Maezen Miller, particularly because I frequently question my reason for using valuable natural resources. As Charlie Brown said so eloquently, "Good grief!" Sums up my reaction.

Some of us face life using book learning. Some through surviving challenging experiences and emerging stronger. Others use common sense or street knowledge. Some just intuitively "know" how to handle a situation. Some use a little of all four. These are different ways of knowing. Not all are recognized as viable. Or important. Or rewarded by society. But please accept all kinds of knowledge as real and valid. Doesn't matter how we know. What matters is how we use the knowledge. For good. For evil. For others. For ourselves. To help or hinder. To make a difference or not.

Admit what you don't know and voila, the life lessons begin. Some people seem to be comfortable asking questions, others, not so much. Never be afraid to ask a question. Many times those with you are thinking the same thing but don't have the confidence or courage to ask. By posing the question, you help others learn too. Funny how that works. I tell people the only dumb question is the one unasked.

OCTOBER 5

Josh Reeves, Lead Minister of Mile Hi Church, posed this question, "How can I meet my own needs so others can enjoy the fruits of my labor?" My suggestion? Learn to embrace solitude. Not isolation or solitary confinement but a cheerful willingness to spend time alone. You find yourself in moments of quiet. Retreats are popular for this reason. We quiet our mind, settle our ego, leave the noise outside. We open ourselves to just *be*. To discover contentment. Peace. In our frantic world, this is a priceless gift of self-care from which we emerge with our heart bursting with love to share. We have one life. It is our choice how we use it, spend it, share it.

Focus on promises to yourself, not problems encountered in your quest. Acknowledge challenges, just don't let them paralyze you into inactivity. I am a master at falling into that trap! I can come up with a multitude of reasons for not doing something (flying is a current example). It is more difficult for me to list why I should actually do something, anything to move me out of the starting block. Unfortunately, this is one tendency I seem to have taken over from my mom. Unconsciously watched her do this very same thing. The result was she never seemed to be happy with anything, never mind content with her life. How sad it would be to live your life never experiencing joy.

During a Sunday homily, my pastor, Niall Nolan said, "Live your life so you have no regrets." Is this easy advice to follow? Not for me in my early life. It has become easier as I have gotten older. I realized one day, I only have one chance to live my life. Why am I wasting it on regrets about a past I can't change. Fretting about future events which might not happen. When discussing this subject with a friend, he suggested I "live in the sacred now." Joined with Fr. Niall's comment, it defines a marvelous approach to life. I am learning to practice both. Join me. Let's see what kind of life we will create.

OCTOBER 6

Our life is a series of choices, a road with many turns, which means we need a map to our desired destination. Even if it is a wee bit foggy, create a plan to get there anyway. Whether it is what to eat for breakfast; accomplishing your tasks for today. Deciding on a career and how to make it happen. Staying single, being married, having children. Choosing a wandering about itinerary. Writing a poem, a song, a book. If you have no clear view of how you want to live your life, how will you know what choices to make to meet your goals and achieve your dreams?

I would be the last one to tell you your plans will always go as you envision them because they won't. People, events, stuff get in the way. Sudden roadblocks. Unplanned pitfalls. Unexpected side trips. Life poses choices, dilemmas, twists and turns. So be sure to have plans B and C, maybe even plan D. I still live by the Girl Scout motto, "Be prepared." Wise advice.

Through the years, I have learned, although my plans rarely go as I think, hope they will, eventually I accomplish my goal even if it isn't exactly as I envisioned and I reach my destination even if it isn't exactly where I thought it would be. Funny how that works. Why? Because no matter what life throws my way, I believe in me and my Higher Power. If we work together, my goals are within my reach and the place I end up is better than I imagined. So will yours be if you don't give up and remember to lean on your Deity for guidance, support and encouragement.

OCTOBER 7

Like the mythical Phoenix, we can rise from the ashes of broken dreams, disappointing relationships, flagging hope. Even when the love of our life leaves through divorce or death, we can pick ourselves up and begin again. When my husband of 32 years died after a long battle with diabetes and heart disease, I didn't exactly feel my life was over, but pretty darn close. I shut down. Became close cousin to a hermit. Rarely left the safety of our home. Clung to our cat. Avoided making major decisions. It was enough of a challenge to decide whether I would get out of bed, make a meal, any meal, let alone figure out what to do tomorrow and the rest of my life. I didn't exactly stop, but I definitely put my life on hold.

Gradually, over many moons and a drastic change in lifestyle, I understood and accepted wise advice from the inspirational writer, Mary Davis, "No one has hurt their eyes by looking on the bright side." As a result of the major move, I met person after person who showed me how to face life head-on, charge right into the middle of the action and let the consequences come. Don't worry so much about tomorrow. It may not come. We only have this moment to breathe, to smile, to love. I decided to take advantage and enjoy being me, the only version there is, was or will ever exist. And I discovered how much life offers if I just pay attention and take advantage. So can you.

OCTOBER 8

Everyone we encounter as we go about our daily life has the potential to become a momentary mentor. The child studying an ant crossing the sidewalk shows us focused curiosity about the tiniest event. A mom soothing a fretful infant is infinite love. A dedicated teacher who explains the same concept again and again until we "get it" shows unlimited patience. A curmudgeon who smiles at the silly antics of youngsters in the park tells us everyone has a soft side. A group of friends involved in a spirited discussion shows the power of listening and learning from each other. If we pay attention, there are opportunities everywhere to witness people teaching us ways to improve and enrich our life.

There are also those who manage to frequently step on our last nerve. One more feeble excuse for being late to work, with the monthly report, meeting for lunch. The usual excuses. I forgot. The kids were being impossible. My spouse was grouchy this morning. Sound familiar? We want/need to address the behavior. But how?

In day to day life, we meet people with whom we disagree. It goes with being a social species. Just because my opinion is different, it does not give you permission to be nasty verbally, in writing or in behavior. Life is many times about compromise. Sometimes we have to agree to disagree. No shame in that for either person. It means you both are reasonable, caring people who value the relationship and peace and harmony more than being right or getting your way. Be the grown-up in the room. Take the mature path. Be the peace maker. Be the peacekeeper.

OCTOBER 9

Sometimes we need to press delete. Be it a preachy verbal reprimand or a text or an email, we need to stop, reflect and make sure the words are appropriate for the meaning of the message or the inconvenience of the behavior. Once out there, words cannot be erased or unsaid. Maybe we silently count to ten or leave in the draft folder for an hour or refrain from hitting the arrow until tomorrow. Same principle applies to thoughts and feelings. We examine them, learn from them, let them go.

Life is messy. Complicated. Chaotic. Family and friends are precious, but occasionally, they step on our ego or ruffle our feelings. Why make it worse by responding in the first flash of anger or hurt? Give yourself time to cool off. Calm down. Think. Forgive. Then you will be able to answer with understanding and compassion because you remember God dwells within all of us, all the time. And remind our bruised ego, we all make mistakes. Say things we don't really mean. Act in ways we know we shouldn't. Life is messy. And many times, so are we. A reality to ponder.

OCTOBER 10

Don't forget self-forgiveness. Say what? No one goes through life without making mistakes. It is universal to mess up. As it says in Ecclesiastes 7:20, "There is no one on earth who does what is right all the time and never makes a mistake." Some of us are self-critical to the point of getting stuck because we refuse to let go of past errors. We replay them over and over. Guess what? Doesn't change the outcome or make the mistake disappear. It is still part of our history. It is part of what makes us who we are today. So examine it, learn from it, resolve to not do or say it again, apologize if appropriate, let it go and move on. Talk about freedom!

It took me a long time to learn to forgive myself. There are actions and words I still regret. When possible, I have sincerely apologized to the person or performed some kind of private restitution. Doing this usually helps me let the offense go, leave it in the past where it belongs. But I don't forget. I use the memory of hurting a friend and how difficult it was to mend the rift, let it go and move on as strong motivation not to repeat the action or say those words again. My heart remembers even if my conscious mind doesn't.

I continue to work on remembering not to beat myself up for mistakes and indiscretions. I know I am only hurting myself. In all likelihood, the injured party has long forgotten the incident while I am still punishing myself. So I am not telling you this self-forgiveness thing is easy. It isn't. But is worth it. As my wise Gram always said, "It feels so much better when I stop beating my head against the wall!" All I have to do is forgive myself. Besides, life goes by too quickly to waste time on things I can't change anyway. So is yours.

OCTOBER 11

Stuff happens. We make mistakes. Embrace the mess ups. Learn from them. Pick yourself up. Keep trying. Only way to discover and grow into our best selves. Perfection is God's game. She wants to help you be the you the Creator brought you into the world to be. He made us so knows humans aren't perfect. He accepts us as we are especially when we keep trying. Keep getting back up. Keep walking toward eternal life with Him.

Took me many years to accept it is okay to enjoy life. To give in to happiness. Not be suspicious of the proverbial other shoe dropping. To expect I will never make another mistake. Yes, there will be challenges. We will interact with curmudgeons. We will have "those" days. All the more reason to appreciate the unexpected times when our world is operating smoothly and the people around us are at peace. There is joy in the air. We are surrounded by love. Surrender and just be. Ahh...

The challenges of today and the closure of the current stage of life opens the door to a new time. Accept the lessons learned, move on to new experiences. Examples: finishing high school, starting college or trade school, then graduating with a commitment to an employer. Leaving single life for married union. Going from a family of two to a family of three (or more). Retiring to the third phase of life. Saying a final earthly farewell to a spouse, parents, siblings, friends. All closures create change and movement. Embrace each phase with gratitude and move on to the next with excited anticipation. Life speeds by too quickly not to enjoy what each day brings. Remember we learned if we expect to find good things and interact with interesting people, we will.

OCTOBER 12

Communication style is critical in our interactions with everyone. How we offer our message is frequently more important than what we say. I agree with Pastor Rick Warren, "Tact and tone always go together." He goes on, "The more pleasant you are, the more persuasive you are." I learned from my mother nagging doesn't work; it was her default reaction in many encounters with dad and me. We both tended to ignore her as much as possible in those situations. Nothing was accomplished. Same with my children and both my husbands. Didn't apply it as often with my second husband; learned the lesson interacting with my first.

If we practice the *Four Elements of Right Speech* as taught by the Buddhists, we will enhance and improve our relationships. We need to: clear the clutter from our mind; speak clearly; cultivate kind calm conversations; and practice mindful listening. Simple instructions with powerful consequences.

Life is unpredictable. You never know when it may be the last time you are with a loved one, a special friend, a casual companion. Make sure to part with a kiss, a hug, a smile. Any or all three. Make your parting moments gentle and loving. Even if the encounter was tense, unkind words were exchanged and neither of you likes the other in the moment, part with love. Separate the annoying behavior from the cherished person. You will be grateful you did, especially if anything happens before you meet again. A friendly reminder: If you listen to and heed your heart, it will never lead you astray.

OCTOBER 13

As my practical, plain-spoken husband always said, "No one gets out of this life alive." The first time I heard it, my immediate reaction was a grimace and a train of thought something along these lines. How maudlin. How can he think that way? How can he say it out loud? Is he trying to tell me something? Wait. Maybe in his particular way, he is giving me a message...from God, perhaps? He really was stating a fact of life many of us don't want to think about, never mind prepare for. We all will die. There, I said the unsayable. And the sky didn't fall. Nor did the world end. At least not today for me or you.

As I ventured down that sort of scary path, I examined why I didn't want to contemplate my death. I wasn't ready. Too much still on my to do list. But what are the real reasons lurking behind my fear? After thinking about my reaction, I realized it wasn't fear of death so much but rather fear of how I would face the manner of my passing. Will there be pain? Will I go to sleep one night and not wake up in the morning? I finally decided it was fear of the unknown manner and reaction to the cause of my passing, not the passing itself. I believe in an afterlife spending eternity in God's presence, His special home. With a contented sigh, I thanked my sweet husband for yet another tangible gift I didn't know I needed and didn't ask for; Peace of mind about my death.

OCTOBER 14

Death is a fact of life. We Americans are afraid of even thinking about let alone discussing the final adventure in our human life. I have been blessed, yes I say blessed, to have been with those making the transition from this life to eternal rest. To meeting their Creator and rejoining those special souls waiting for them in our eternal home.

Dad passed peacefully after waiting until I could travel from Texas to Michigan to hold his hand and be by his side. Mom's passing was a lingering death; she was in and out of the hospital for three years. With her indomitable will, she lived to see her beloved granddaughters graduate from college; she died nineteen days later. After receiving a notice from her doctor she couldn't live alone any longer, Gram spent the next four days gently saying goodbye to her family. She went to sleep and didn't wake up; she died as she lived, her way. My beloved husband, Paul, battled diabetes and heart disease for ten years. He was in the hospital and a rehab center for six months before he passed. He lovingly waited until I was with him before he let go and went to meet God. It was his final gift to me. He knew I would never forgive myself if I wasn't there and he died alone.

I share these experiences to assure you death doesn't have to be scary. While we are never truly prepared for someone to leave us in death, whether it is quiet and gentle or an unexpected, untimely passing, eventually we come to understand we had no control in life and we have no control over the time or manner of our death. No point fretting about the inevitable. You will not make the journey alone if you believe your God will be waiting for you.

OCTOBER 15

Be sure not to ignore or avoid the practical tasks in preparing for your death: a will, medical and financial powers of attorney, funeral plans. These vital items will save loved ones from making decisions during a difficult time. My attorney told me I could still be in charge after death if I have "my legal and financial affairs" in order. As a control freak, I whole-heartedly accepted that idea!

Start a file, an envelope, a box with important information. Include a personal letter to those closest to you: parents, grandparents, significant other, children, grands, BFF, friends. Doesn't have to be long. Just words of wisdom you want to pass along. Don't forget I love you. Add something fun that screams YOU. Think mine will be a small bear or maybe a flash drive with a few special essays, maybe both. Label *To Be Opened At My Death*. Tell someone where it is stored. Now set aside that worry knowing you have left your affairs in order and your passing will be easier for those closest to you.

Are there special things you want certain people to have after you are no longer around to use and enjoy them? Think about doing what my beloved gram did. She started giving those things away while she was still alive. Why? She wanted to be around to watch how we would use them, display them. Her wise words, "Use what I give you. They are not meant to be stored or just looked at. If you break it, mend it as best you can. If it can't be mended, throw it away. It has lived a useful life. Let it rest." I still follow her sage advice. And have passed it on to my girls.

As the oldest grandchild, I am privileged to have received several cherished items. One in particular fascinated me as a child. It is a set of four pale blue cups, saucers and luncheon plates with a matching creamer and sugar bowl. I would stare at those cups and saucers for hours. When I bought my first dining room curio cabinet, gram carefully packed them and sent the set via UPS. What a wonderful surprise! The set had a prominent place in all my homes until I gave it to my older daughter on her 50th birthday. It was time to pass it on. Gram split her jewelry and other belongings between her daughter, daughter-in-law and four grandchildren and the two great grands who knew her. My mom did the same. I am continuing the tradition. One more way to celebrate our family history and keep the memories alive.

OCTOBER 16

There are days' life overwhelms me. The noise paralyzes me. I can't think clearly. I don't know which way is up, down or sideways. I feel if anyone says anything to me, I will burst into a million teeny, tiny pieces and never come back together. Worse than Humpty Dumpty. I just want to hide in my closet and never come out. Other days I am convinced I am an abysmal failure. Everything I attempt goes awry. I can't seem to do anything right. You ever have impossible days like these? I see you nodding in understanding and agreement. Didn't think I am alone feeling like I am treading water as fast as I can and still starting to sink.

Failure is not the end of life. What brings life to an abrupt stop is when we don't get up, dust our egos off and try again. Everyone makes mistakes, messes up, throws a monkey wrench into plans. It is called being human. When the inevitable happens, apologize if needed, learn a lesson and vow to do better next time. That is all anyone should expect from us. It is all we should expect from and for ourselves. Take responsibility, but don't allow a failure to derail your life.

I am an expert at beating myself up again and again for mistakes and failures and storing them in my memory bank, never letting them go. What have I accomplished? Nothing but piling on guilt and being afraid to take a chance when the next opportunity comes. Another self-defeating activity. How sad. Who knows what I might discover if I come out of my self-imposed isolation? What I might accomplish if I forgive myself, learn a valuable lesson and give life another try. This is me peeking out the slightly ajar closet door.

OCTOBER 17

Traumatic events cause a seismic shift in our life. They can have either positive or negative effects, depending on the event and how we react to and process it. Whatever the outcome, we change. Become different. But as we learn to navigate this part of our personal path, we will eventually accept the new version of our self. As Trappist monk, Fr. Thomas Merton said, "A tree gives glory to God by being a tree," so too we are still the person we were created to be, just a different iteration. Usually an improved version, if we so choose. Remember, as we put ourselves back together, cracks, crevices and lines included, it is our choice who we are, how we act and react, what we do with the priceless gift of our life.

Life holds the potential for events which transform us. Graduating from high school or college; earning an advanced degree. New city. New job. New responsibilities. What about a promotion or the misfortune of being caught in a downsizing. Retiring brings its own set of adjustments. Marriage. The decision to have a child. Ending a long-term relationship. Death of a loved one or a close friend can begin a personal reassessment of the direction in which our life is headed, potentially a healthy nudge. These occasions will have a profound effect on our choices for many years to come.

Life is unpredictable even when we willingly choose a particular event. Think clearly. Tread carefully. But don't be afraid to take a calculated chance. Life will be so much more fulfilling and fun. I wonder what's around the corner today?

OCTOBER 18

Trust the in-between times in life. Between the end of one chapter and the beginning of the next. When you don't know what is going to happen, when you're not exactly sure where you want and need to go, whom you will meet when you get there and what your assignment might be. The in-between time can be scary or it can be exciting and full of anticipation of what is to come. It all depends on your mind set.

As we discussed yesterday, there are many transitions in life. Graduation and the first meaningful job. The end of a relationship by dissension, divorce or death. Engagement leading to a marriage commitment. Arrival of the first baby. The last one going off to college. The decision to write a book, a song, a poem or build the bookcase or the fence. These are but a few of the events in life that can bring on the in-between time.

If you trust this mystery time, your intuition, the universe or whatever source you believe in, will lead you to whom and what you need to proceed doing to reach where you need to be. I am not suggesting you shouldn't do your homework and due diligence. I am suggesting to remember you are not alone on your path. Family, friends and your Higher Power are reliable guides as you move to the next chapter. How comforting! How exciting! When do we start?

OCTOBER 19

Be careful not to let guilt and recriminations keep you from living your life, becoming unstuck from one chapter and turning the page to the next one. From releasing an old way of thinking to embracing a new perception of your purpose, your Divine duties. As there is an ebb and flow to the ocean's tide, there is transition and transformation to life. Don't fear the growth you are experiencing on your pilgrimage. Decide if your life is really too busy or is your mind too afraid to stop, look and learn? It is your decision to accept and move on or stay fearfully stubborn and stuck. Which will you choose?

Another obstacle is giving control of your life to someone else. This transfer usually happens slowly and subtly. Most of the time, we are not aware we are allowing another person to pull or push us into thinking and acting as they desire. As the Danish philosopher, Soren Kierkegaard said, "Every human being comes to earth with sealed orders." We cannot and should not give our responsibilities away because they require our special attention and touch, not someone else's. When we discover our Divine Duties, what we do with them, how we use them is our choice. We have a free will. If our Deity won't force us to do anything, we shouldn't give another human the wheel either.

Our Divine Guide will provide us with the talent, the tools and the guidance required, but we each need to make a conscious decision about how we respond. We can ignore them. We can turn them over to another. We can use them for good or for ill. We can give it our all or we can do a mediocre job. May I remind you, these particular responsibilities are assigned to only us. If we don't fulfill our part, they will not be done as they were conceived. Think about that for a minute. Each of us has a purpose in life, a job to do. If we give them to another, ignore them, turn our back, or walk away, these special assignments stay undone for all eternity. Oh my!

OCTOBER 20

Find your passion in life. If you misplaced it in the midst of the noise and responsibilities of day-to-day living, give yourself the gift of picking up a long-lost hobby, a favorite pastime, a secret delight. We all have these special activities even if we left them behind in our youth. If you haven't consciously thought about what your passion is, take time to remember what you lost yourself doing when you were young. What always captured your attention as the hours flew by? Bet there is a passion buried deep in your memory. Maybe you need to give yourself permission to be that young, enthusiastic person again, if only for a day or a few hours.

My passion is reading and writing. I have always taken time to read. It is my default way to relax and just be. I've always been a writer. The difference these days is I am able to write whenever my Muse whispers (or sometimes shouts) in my mind and heart on any topic I yearn to explore. These are the two gifts I rarely deny myself anymore. One of the special perks of my "retirement" years. Reading and writing bring me a special kind of joy because they are my passions. I thank my Creator for blessing me with a way with words, to both use and understand them. I will continue to cultivate both until my final breath.

Find and embrace your passion. Whatever it might be. Sewing. Crafting. Golfing. Fishing. Tennis. Swimming. Running marathons. Stamp collecting. Wandering through antique emporiums, book shops, hardware or junk stores. Life is too short to forego, what I call, our purple passions.

OCTOBER 21

Learn to integrate prayer life, home life, work life, play life into one life, your life, lived with joy, radiating love. As Indian spiritual leader, Paramahansa Yogananda says, "I will do everything with deep attention: my work at home, in the office, in the world — all duties great and small will be performed well." Don't live a schizophrenic existence. I did for many years. It caused untold harm to me and everyone around me. I didn't know who the real me was. I was one Jan at home, another out in the world. It made it difficult to decide what the right reaction was in many situations. When I was finally able to begin to integrate all the parts of me into Jan, I was amazed at the woman who emerged from the disparate pieces. I actually liked her. More importantly, I respected her. As I have moved along my personal path, I like and respect her more as I get to know her better. What a precious gift!

Making every part of life work together smoothly, can be a dauting challenge. And when you are determined to carve out time for me, it just adds to the tension. I didn't figure it out until I was well into my eighth decade. If I want to be honest, I'm still working on it. Some days I'm successful. Others, not so much. The difference is I now recognize the importance of a balanced, integrated life. Please note: The statements made at the end of the above paragraph are my way of practicing hopeful gratitude. If I tell myself I have accomplished a goal, I give myself a mini-pep talk and an emotional boost. And I keep trying because it feels good to believe it for even a moment. Encourages me to believe I will one day reach and practice the goal every day.

OCTOBER 22

Emotion contains *motion* so let's think of an emotion, any emotion, as an invitation to movement. A way to energize us to face whatever life tosses in our direction. On this day. In this stage. During the only life we have. Even when the world seems to be conspiring against us, remember what the French writer, Albert Camus said, "In the depths of winter, I finally learned that within me there lay an invincible summer." To me, he is suggesting we have the power to face any obstacle with passion and persistence, overcome any challenge with grace and grit and reach our ultimate goal, whatever it is at this moment in our life.

And we can repeat the process with each goal on our ever-expanding to-do wish list. What an intoxicating idea!

I want to add a suggestion many of us, me especially, forget to include in our plan: Have fun. Moments of levity replenish and restore our psyche as much as moments of learning excite and energize our mind. Don't take yourself so seriously, you neglect to notice the sheer joy of laughter. Doesn't matter if it is a smile, a snicker, a giggle or a deep belly laugh, we produce endorphins, those feel good hormones make the day a bit brighter and, well, more fun.

I am blessed to have friends who encourage me to take a day off, let my inner child out to join them for a play date. Whether it is a quiet conversation with a cup of tea, shopping therapy and lunch, a walk around the lake, watching a movie or listening to music. Indulge in some kind of fun at least once a week; more often if your life seems to be going off the rails. I promise you will feel better and your world will be a nicer place.

OCTOBER 23

Put your oxygen mask on first is another way of saying self-care is essential for the smooth functioning of our individual world, which in turn affects the wider world. It's called the Butterfly Affect or when the wings of a butterfly flutter in Beijing, the atmosphere changes in New York City. So too, our emotional minefield has a direct bearing on everyone in our space. No one is immune. All are touched by our attitude as we interact with the world. If I am positive, I radiate joy. If I am negative, my behavior brings everyone down. This is where self-care enters. When I feel good about me and my place in the grand scheme of life, I spread good will to everyone.

So ease up on yourself. Take a break. Walk away. Come back refreshed. I suggest self-care behavior a lot because it took me into my eighth decade to truly grasp its importance and necessity in my life. I don't want you to wait that long to discover its bounty. And if you are in your 70s or beyond, remember, it is never too late to adopt a new habit, especially one which will bring so much peace into your days. Under 80, over 80, it will bring peace and, dare I suggest it, contentment into your mind, heart and soul. Your Inner Spirit approves.

OCTOBER 24

Your life goes where your attention goes so learn to say goodbye to: people, places, things, beliefs, behaviors, dreams from yesterday. Live in and appreciate today, while you prepare for tomorrow. Embrace all your experiences, the good and not so good. They add richness and texture to life. Having a plan is good, but be willing to wander and wonder too. And don't fear the unpredictable. What is the old saying? The only thing we can count on is change. So why not accept it and learn its lessons. "Intelligence is the ability to adapt to change." — Stephen Hawking

Life rushes in, stays put for a moment, then backs away to begin the process all over again, These thresholds offer a new way of acceptance, peace and love. Don't be afraid to step off the planned path of your life. Take that trip. Have that adventure. Walk into that new group. These are the times and places you will learn about yourself. How to relate and react in unfamiliar situations with unfamiliar people. When you let yourself stay in your safe rut, you can't see or feel or learn beyond the same scenery.

I'm good at staying in my safety zone. I'm getting better at saying, "Yeah. Sure. Why not." I finally discovered, while it may be a little scary to venture from my safe nest, when I do, I am rarely disappointed. There is a big, crazy, wonderful world out there just waiting and beckoning me to experience it, learn and grow. What am I waiting for? Only have one life. Experience all it has to offer. Celebrate everyday joys. Those who spend time with people at the end of life tell us one of the biggest regrets they have is what they failed to do, to try. I don't want to feel that way. Do you?

OCTOBER 25

The sun does not revolve around you. It isn't all about you. Who put you in charge of the world? Sound familiar? All have been directed at me. Bet you have heard them too. All are true statements. Or are they? In the macrocosm of history, they are factual observations. In the microcosm of our corner of the universe, maybe not so much.

Outside weather events can cause widespread devastation. Inside storms can cause seismic shifts in our thinking, our feelings, our relationships. Both types of storms take us out of our usual lives and suddenly dump us into new ways of relating to reality. We are always changed in some way. How we react to these changes is what is important. Storms come. They move on. The weather is rarely perfect, so enjoy the beautiful day while it is here. Life isn't perfect either. So embrace the small joyful moments. Store the memory for when the storms come again as they will. In the final years of my time on earth, I remember the good weather *and* the not so good and relearn a valuable lesson: This too shall pass. So too internal storms pass and offer a moment of clarity, if you stop and accept it.

We all fail. Part of life. As Pastor Rick Warren says, "Only when we let go of the fear of failure will it release its maddening grip on our lives." Our unrealistic fear can lead to being a perfectionist, a workaholic, avoiding calculated risks. Limits our lives in many ways because we always play it safe, never venture out of our comfort zone. When we remind ourselves our Higher Power is behind everything that happens [sin too?] and what doesn't, it is easy to accept, as Zen teacher, Thubten Chodron says, "...not sure wakes us up from complacency...and also wakes us up to smiling at whatever life brings." I want to smile. How about you?

OCTOBER 26

Intellectual Humility allows us to learn and grow. Admitting we don't know something or we made a mistake, gives us permission to progress on our inward journey of intellectual enlightenment. How we fit into the Grand Plan, the Creator's Plan for the universe, His purpose for our personal universe.

If I am not intellectually humble, how will I realize I am wrong about something I believe to be true? Especially something which profoundly affects my life, the life of those in my inner circle and those who read my columns or listen to my presentations. Someone once told me I am an influencer in my community. I never thought of myself that way. After some soul-searching, I realized it is true to the extent my columns for two newsletters reach a variety of people in diverse situations. People I may influence by my words and my behavior. Momentarily I forgot the ripples in the water parable.

Just because you are intellectually humble doesn't mean you lack confidence. In actuality, it means you are sure of what you know and just as sure about what you don't know. You recognize if you stop questioning, you stop learning, you stop growing, you stay stuck. I have been stuck. It is not a comfortable place to be. Adopt intellectual humility and you will unstick from whatever is holding you back from becoming the best you, the you your Supreme Being created you to be. So you can move into the next chapter of your unique pilgrimage.

OCTOBER 27

The universe, working in concert with our Higher Power, sends us what we need, when we need it and not a moment before. We are learning, growing, becoming who we are meant to be our entire life. But we are not allowed to see, know and understand before we are ready. We are not given too much too soon in this life. It is not in our timing but in the Unknowable timing we receive our greatest lessons, our most important gifts, our truth.

It took me into my eighth decade to understand this phenomenon. Why? I wasn't ready. I had to get my ego in line. Had to learn to be patient. Had to accept I wasn't the one in control. I am still working on accepting I need to (gulp!) surrender. It is a challenge to even type that word, never mind practice what it means. My spiritual mentor used the word when introducing me to the concept of quieting my thoughts so I could listen for God. I balked. Nope. Not me. I don't surrender to anyone or anything.

Every time I have surrendered led to disappointment, disillusionment and incredible pain. I am not willingly walking into that trap. The only concession I would make is to stop fighting the idea. Even that seemed an impossible move to make. But gradually, I have come to accept there is One to whom it is safe to surrender. God. She loves me unconditionally and will never do anything to harm me. I'm working on accepting it while I keep on keeping on. She will wait until I finally agree to trust Her completely, let go and surrender...no matter how long it takes me.

Recently during a discussion on this subject, another friend suggested we could substitute the word "allow" for the word "surrender." I am contemplating the subtle difference in meaning. Semantics? Perhaps. But maybe I have finally found a way to turn myself over to God's care completely. Time, eternal time, will answer that question. What I know for sure: I am still searching. Still questioning. Still learning. Still growing.

OCTOBER 28

Knowing our heritage tells us where our family began and helps us understand who we are and why we react the way we do. We all carry genes and innate knowledge from our ethnic ancestors. However, neither defines us. We have a free will, which gives us permission to decide who we are now, how we respond to our personal and collective history, how we behave today.

Are you ready, willing and able to be who you want and have what you desire in this life, the only life you will have? You are the only one who can answer this question. Will you use your God-given talents to achieve what your heart desires and your soul yearns for? If your answer is a resounding yes or even a tentative maybe, either response demands you do what is needed to prepare yourself to reach your Nirvana.

Even though I didn't consciously realize it until a few months ago, my life-long dream has been to write a book. To share my thoughts, my life lessons, dare I say it, my wisdom with others. I have lived through challenging times. I emerged knowing who I am. More importantly, I like who I am becoming. I am comfortable in my skin. I smile when I look in the mirror. I still endure "those" days now and then, but I know my Deity loves me for who I was yesterday, who I am today and who I will be tomorrow. I want to share my lessons and my joy with others as encouragement not to give up, to keep on keeping on. Remember, God wants you to reach your earthly pinnacle and find contentment as much as She wants to welcome you into your heavenly home. What are you waiting for? Go after your dream. I did. So can you.

OCTOBER 29

Life happens when we are busy being and doing. Toddler. Child. Teen. Adult. Mid-years. Young-old. Mid-old. Old-old. All of a sudden, the end of earthly life is close. We are able to review our years through the lens of learning and wisdom. What do we see? Do we approve of what we see?

The wise Native American, Crazy Horse, said, "I see a time of Seven Generations when all the colors of mankind will gather under the Sacred Tree of Life and the whole earth will become one circle again." Sometimes I'm sure my entire family will never gather around my table again. How can all cultures, all nations, all people ever come together? Maybe if we stop talking and truly listen, we might actually hear and understand what the other person means, how he feels, what she thinks, what they need. Maybe if we share our honest thoughts and real feelings, we will understand and respond with compassion. And our lives will change for the better, which will alter our world, if just for a moment. The 12-step programs have one thing in common, they acknowledge we may not be able to do something for the rest of our life. But if we practice One Day at a Time, we can manage.

What I know for sure, there is freedom in knowing who we are, what we believe. We intuitively know how we will behave because we have a firm set of beliefs and act with integrity. I am not suggesting we will never abandon, adopt, adapt or adjust a belief or a behavior, but we will only do so after doing our due diligence. We won't change just for the sake of change. We will know why we are making a shift in perception. We will be convinced deep in our mind, heart and soul, it is right and proper for us at this time. While it may often be scary and sometimes painful, it is necessary. It is growth. It is loving ourselves enough to know it is a message from our Inner Guide whispering, "It is time."

OCTOBER 30

Don't fear change, it is part of life. Learn the art of reinvention. I have experienced it many times in my life. I just didn't always recognize it until later: Stay open to life and its people, places and possibilities. Never say never. Change means life is moving. Maybe it seems like it's sideways but it still movement from one place to another, which is good. New ways to learn and grow, so embrace the slightest move as a positive nudge from the universe, from your Inner Guide of wisdom and truth.

Just like we don't pay attention to our physical body growing, our spiritual and emotional growth happens gradually too. Most of the time, we won't be aware of the change until after it happens. One day, we realize we have grown into the wonderful, beautiful person we have always been. We were just too busy living life to notice her or him. Make sure to appreciate who you are. Who you are still becoming because we all keep growing and learning until we take our final earthly breath. Life is a gift to be opened, lived joyfully and treasured always. Experience life, don't limit yourself. As it says in 1 Corinthians 14:1, "Go after a life of love as if your life depended on it — because it does."

Questions to consider:

- Do we understand what our life is for, is meant to be? Yes? No? Why? Why not?

- Why is it critical to appreciate my uniqueness? What only I bring to the table of life?
- What have I made my own? What do I plan to carry into November? Into the rest of my life?

Gratitude Entry: I am grateful for my unique life. The opportunity to engage in and enjoy the people with whom I interact; the places I encounter and events I experience. I am grateful my Inner Spirit will provide all I need when I need it to complete my assigned Divine Duties because if I don't do them, they will remain undone for all eternity. Thank you for who I am becoming. I like me.

Reader: Add at least one thing you are grateful for as a result of reading, and contemplating the October reflections.

OCTOBER 31

One of the earliest Irish festivals in the Celtic tradition, the Feast of Samhain, was a liminal time. An in-between time when the boundaries between this world and the netherworld were blurred; bonfires were lit to protect and cleanse. Livestock was slaughtered. The harvest was gathered. Winter was near. The veil between the earth and spirit worlds was very thin. Food and drink was set out to appease any evil spirits who might be roaming, but the good spirits were near too. The souls of dead kin were thought to visit so extra places were set at the table.

Concentrate on inviting the good spirits and those of your loved ones into your life as you celebrate All Hallows Eve. Open your mind, your heart and your soul to the good and positive in life. When you expect and ask for what you need and want, the universe, the Creator, Adonai, God, Allah will respond.

Dear Higher Power, I accept my life is dynamic, always moving, changing, growing. It is not finished until I take my final breath.

This means my potential is always expanding offering new and different opportunities. Going forth, I will remember to help, to encourage, to spread joy, to love. I vow to be the best me I can be every day. I promise to ask for Your help.

NOVEMBER

Gratitude

"Gratitude begins in our hearts and then dovetails into behavior.... "

Anne Lamont

NOVEMBER 1

The month we celebrate Thanksgiving should be the month we celebrate the gift of gratitude. Start today to make a list of what you are thankful for. Add one entry each day. Maybe you can start a new tradition and share your list with those gathered for the family and friend feast on the fourth Thursday of this month. The entries on your list don't have to be big and showy and important. In fact, the list should include the tiny happenings we usually don't notice, we ignore or take for granted. Using the days leading up to Thanksgiving to start a gratitude list is a wonderful way to begin the habit of adding a gratitude entry to your journal.

Number one item on my November gratitude list is breathing. I am blessed. I don't have to remember to take a breath. Many do. A dear friend of forty-five years has emphysema and COPD. He needs oxygen all the time. He inspires me to be thankful I can breathe without needing artificial help or even thinking about whether I will have a next breath.

I'm going to cheat and add another: I am grateful for this moment. Not everyone will make it through the night to have one. We all know many who didn't. If I think of each moment as an opportunity, they all become special. How fortunate to have them one at a time.

I've given you two examples. We'll check in later in the month to review our list.

NOVEMBER 2

Giving is easy for me. It is part of my DNA. It was passed from my grandmother to my mother, then to me by example in their daily interactions. I grew up knowing it is the right way to act. I tried to pass the joy of giving on to my girls, now my grandsons. My list includes: time, attention, praise, gratitude, things. Notice things is last on the list. No further comment needed.

Learning to receive is trickier. Even now, I frequently cringe when someone gives me a gift, comments on my startling blue eyes, or compliments one of my newsletter columns or oral presentations. I have learned to smile and say, "Thank you," but it is a challenge. Inside I am still battling the I'm-not-worthy-of-praise demon. When you grow up with criticism and could never do anything "quite right" or "quite enough," it is difficult to put the feelings of unworthiness aside. It is hard to believe what I do or say is proper and appropriate and has earned acknowledgement or, heaven help us, praise.

What helped me get to the point of being able to outwardly accept graciously was a friend suggesting I was hurting the other person's feelings when I rejected their generosity with some lame comment. Wow! I trained myself to receive with appreciation so I don't deny the giver the pleasure of their act of generosity. Don't think you are being humble when you murmur "I don't deserve" whatever is being offered. All you are doing is disrespecting the giver, demeaning the gift and destroying a special moment. Giving and receiving work together seamlessly when both are done with love. No strings. No expectations. Just because.

I am still learning and still trying. It is becoming a little more comfortable and a little less intimidating to receive graciously.

NOVEMBER 3

Be grateful for who you are. Acknowledge the special qualities and gifts you bring to the table of life. There is only one you. Be authentic. Don't try to be someone you are not. Eventually the mask will slip and the true you, the real you, the human you will be visible to everyone in your corner of the world. Whether you are headstrong and ornery, kind and loveable from the first encounter, you don't have to remember which persona you use in a particular situation or with a certain person. It is being honest about who and what you are.

The real you is the person staring back from the mirror, not the perfect avatar conjured in your online fantasy universe. Besides, from what I have read, even the saints were human, had challenging times and were far from perfect. So be who are. Be grateful for your gifts and your faults and idiosyncrasies. They are what make you unique. Why be an imitation when you already are a genuine jewel. Wrinkles, bulging middle, messy hair, scruffy clothes and all. You are you. Smile. Walk tall. Be proud. You light up every room you enter. Spread your special kind of joy everywhere you go.

Be grateful for where you are. Know you are in the place you are supposed to be acting as you are supposed to. Friend. Student. Spouse. Parent. Employee. Each place and persona is part and parcel of loveable you. Even when you mess up, you are given chance after chance to repair the broken relationship, rewrite the report, make the meatloaf a second time. Say I'm sorry. Start again. We are given a lot of do overs. We just need to recognize the opportunities and take advantage of them.

NOVEMBER 4

When I have an off day, whether it is emotional or physical, I try to be grateful the malady isn't worse. As I write this reflection, I have a nasty head cold. Coughing. Sneezing. Stuffed up sinuses. Headache. Mild laryngitis. Sound like a barking seal complaining about sore fins. Not sleeping restfully because of the above. I feel like roadkill. Been hiding for the last few days for two reasons: As much as I want to feel better, I don't want to risk giving this crud to an elderly neighbor. And I just don't want to interact with anyone, friend or not.

Yesterday, after a twenty-minute coughing session when I could finally breathe again, my conscience got my attention. My better angel reminded me how much worse I could be. I could have bronchitis or pneumonia or chronic emphysema. Or who knows what else. It is a common cold. I will feel miserable for a few days but eventually, I will feel myself again, able to go back to my normal routine (whatever that is). Many will not "get better." They continue to suffer day after day. After my sobering realization, I told myself to stop moaning. and feeling sorry for poor old me. I said a prayer for all the suffering in the world and added a grateful one knowing I will get better when I am supposed to.

Note to self: Remember whenever you feel crappy, physically or emotionally, this too shall pass. You are blessed to be reasonably healthy for your age. Be grateful. Stop complaining. You will get better. Thank you, Inner Guide, for reminding me to be grateful.

NOVEMBER 5

Be grateful for your imperfect self. Doubts. Fears. Warts. Idiosyncrasies. Who you are. Your unique way of interacting with the world. What you believe deep in your heart and soul. Many of us learned early in life to hide our feelings. There were lots of words used and reasons given, but I believe we were told to "be quiet, you don't know anything" because people either didn't understand or didn't want to understand. Why? Because instinctively they knew we were speaking our truth and they found it unacceptable or scary or didn't want to think about our message, so they quickly hushed us. Shut us down. After being squashed for so many years eventually, we didn't believe or trust our own truth. We were being carried by the prevailing wind instead of holding fast to ours. I know I did.

Be grateful for the small gifts. Letting you into the long line at the market. Waving you from the parking lot into the traffic lane during rush hour. The beautiful bunch of weeds lovingly offered by a smiling child. The cherished coffee mug given because it reminds you of a favorite spot. Don't wait for the expensive present or extravagant gesture to say a sincere thank you. Any act of kindness or thoughtfulness offered is an opportunity to express gratitude. When we say Gracias, Dunka, Merci we acknowledge our appreciation someone, even ourselves, recognized us for the unique person we are. Alleluia and thank you!

NOVEMBER 6

"Gratitude for the past is forgiveness. It allows us to take the best of what we have gathered, while we allow what's done to be done, so we can move on." So said, Josh Reeves, one of the pastors of Mile Hi Church in Denver. It is an intriguing view of both the past and gratitude. Never thought of either from this perspective until I read this quote.

One of the reasons I save quotes that speak to me in the moment is because they provide inspiration for examining why I say, act and react as I do. Food for thought I sometimes explore in my journal. Be sure to thank yourself for your personal practice of giving, not only physical things, but your time and undivided attention. Your warm smiles and cheerful nods of recognition. Sharing your thoughts, feelings, hugs. Intangible but priceless. Free of charge. No complications. No strings attached. The actions and attitude that start in your heart and soul become a tangible sign of love. What a gift! Everyone benefits. Your significant other. Family. Friends. Colleagues. Strangers. You. The world is a little better, a little kinder, a little gentler because you gave of you. Thank you!

NOVEMBER 7

As many young girls of my generation, I kept a diary. It even had a tiny lock on it; I kept the key with me at all times. It was my special place to talk about my day, my fears, my joys, my crushes, my dreams, my disasters. I was eleven or twelve. That in-between age: not a child any longer but not quite a teen either. An adolescent with raging hormones, which caused confusion and questions. It was also about the time I discovered I could use words to express myself. When I wrote them down, they sounded so much better than when I said them out loud. I was working on my craft before I knew I had found my life-long avocation. Then I caught my mom reading my diary.

I was devastated! When asked why, she merely commented, "I am your mother. I have a right to know what you are doing and thinking." She wouldn't tell me how she opened it. I never wrote another entry in that diary. I didn't give myself the gift of working through my feelings and fears in a journal until a few years ago. I unconsciously harbored the fear someone would violate my privacy as mom had all those years ago. I turned to writing essays and cringe-worthy poetry. I could express my feelings, hiding them in plain sight. To read my compositions with an open heart is to know who I am.

Why did I start journaling in my early seventies? I was seeing a therapist for prolong grief syndrome and PTSD; she recommended it. When told of my history, she reminded me I wasn't a little girl any longer and my mom has been dead for twenty-five years. Furthermore, I lived alone and no one had access to my laptop files unless I gave it to them. Sound reasoning. I started journaling in December 2018 and have been writing entries ever since.

NOVEMBER 8

Some would argue the difference between a diary and a journal is semantics. I disagree. The online Microsoft dictionary defines a diary as "a book in which one keeps a daily record of events and experiences." The definition of a journal is "a private place to write down your thoughts, feelings, experiences and reflections on a regular basis." To me the difference implies journal entries are of a deeper, more reflective nature than daily diary notes. Besides, journal sounds more grown-up. In my case, I think of my ramblings as journal entries because of the painful experience with my girlhood diary. The word diary has a very negative connotation in my vocabulary.

Whatever you call your ruminations, writing down your thoughts, feelings, and frustrations is a cathartic way to work through them. I use my journal to discuss the pros and cons of a particular option, opinion. attitude or response. I talk freely, openly, no holds barred. I use words and phrases I would never utter outside the pages of my personal journal. As an editor, I instinctively use proper grammar and sentence structure but really don't fret if I break a rule or two or four. The purpose is to record my thoughts and experiences so I can clear my mind, my heart and my soul of good, bad and indifferent thoughts and actions. I also fuss about people who stepped on my last nerve or hurt my feelings or otherwise messed up my day. It is a cathartic way to dump unwanted and unnecessary baggage without causing a personal war with someone. There are many folks who were spared my wrath because I worked out my issues with them in my journal!

I also talk about the good experiences. I want them in the record too. Too often in the past, I would gloss over the happy and positive because I didn't think I was worthy of anything good happening or believe anyone special, man or woman, would come into my life and actually stay around. My motto, "If it ain't wrote down, it ain't real and it ain't happenin," applies here too. The only rule I have for journal entries is they must be honest and true. No make believe. No stretching the truth. No one is going to read it. If anyone finds my journals after I'm gone...well, all I can say is "I warned you,"

NOVEMBER 9

There is no right time to journal. I write in my journal whenever I have something to share, a vexing problem to work out or I am having an exceptional day and want to write about it while I remember the details. Rarely do I write on a daily basis. Some make an entry faithfully every day. Some people start the day journaling; others end the day noting their thoughts, feelings and experiences. Some begin and end the day with their journal. Whatever works for you is okay. Just remember to include details and be honest.

If you write in the morning, think of the day ahead as a blank page. Decide how you will interact with people. With a smile or a frown. With patience or irritation. Plan errands in some logical order; it will save time and frustration. Depending on your schedule, you may need to give yourself a pep talk. Or detailed instructions. Ask for grit and grace. Remember, you are not alone. Be thankful you have been given another day, not everyone receives one.

If you write at the end of the day, examine how you used the time. Instead of admonishing yourself for what you failed to do, congratulate yourself for what you accomplished, even if it was lots of little to dos. Even if you took a me day. Note the fun moments as well as the exasperating ones. Both make up a life well-lived. Be grateful for the people you encountered and the experiences you had. All provided some kind of lesson.

This is your journal. Your story. You're his-story. You're her-story. Open your heart, share your thoughts and feelings, accomplishments, and screw-ups. Don't leave out the messy parts, the parts you aren't especially proud of. Those are part of life too. A journal is your safe space. Your special space. Your sacred space. It is your life. Appreciate this marvelous gift.

NOVEMBER 10

One of the ways counselors suggest we learn to face and deal with our messy, unpredictable life, is to write down three things every day for which we are grateful. Through the years, I have tried it, but never got into the habit. Seemed kind of silly and many days I couldn't come with one item, let alone three. After a couple of years keeping a journal, I had a flash of insight: Add something for which I am grateful to the end of my ruminations for the day. Since I rarely write in my journal daily, surely I could come up with one or two things. Ah-ha! Two birds, one stone approach.

When I started adding a separate gratitude entry, there were days I couldn't come up with even one. I would resort to family, friends, a roof over my head, food, clothes. Not that these are small or unimportant, but surely there are other people and things for which I am grateful. So I assigned myself the task of paying attention to the small, seemingly random happenings. Surprise! When I consciously look for the kind, the pleasant, the pretty, I discover the phenomenon everywhere. They had been right in front and beside me the entire time. I just hadn't noticed. The clear, blue sky. The smell of newly mowed grass. Ripples on the lake. The honk of the ducks. The cashier's cheerful "good morning!" The tiny baby's gurgle. Random smiles and nods from strangers. Switching my mindset switched my world. Minor miracles were all around me. Once I trained myself to see and hear, to observe, my cup of daily life runneth over. I had lots of things for my gratitude entry. Whatever I record, the memory always brings a smile of appreciation for the positives in my life. Imagine that.

One day I was reading an essay on visualization; had another flash. Add a "projecting gratitude" entry. Something I want to happen or a project I want to finish: I have lost 25 pounds. I finished the book of reflections. I found a publisher for my book. My friend doesn't have cancer. My cousin's grandchild was born whole and healthy. You get the idea. I am sending a positive conclusion into the universe expecting whatever I named to happen. I am confident it will occur as long as I do my part. Kind of a variation on Gram telling me I can accomplish what I set out to do, if I am willing to put in the time and effort to achieve success. Suspect Gram was behind the insight on this idea.

I highly recommend you add both a gratitude entry and a projecting gratitude entry to your journal whenever you write in it. It is a wonderful way to summarize your activities in a positive manner. And end your day with a smile of appreciation.

NOVEMBER 11

As I have thankfully grown older, and by necessity, move slower, I notice and experience my environment in a new way. I pay more attention to the sights, sounds and smells. Because I have recovered my lost perspective, I have gradually rediscovered my childhood sense of awe and wonder. The sky seems bluer. The grass greener. The water clearer. The sun brighter. The rain more refreshing. The stars twinkle faster. The people friendlier. Or maybe I am just more aware. Whatever the reason, I am grateful I finally opened my senses to the beauty and serenity surrounding me.

As I am prone to do, I asked myself what I have gained, other than appreciation for all I see, hear and smell. Then I stumbled on this quote from the Rabbi mystic, Abraham Joshua Hershal, "Awe is more than an emotion; it is a way of understanding, insight into a greater meaning than ourselves. The beginning of awe is wonder, and the beginning of wisdom is awe." The proverbial two-by-four again.

In the last chapter of my life, I have regained my child-like awe and wonder of the universe, which is leading me to wisdom. I finally have enough years and time to appreciate the beauty and specialness of all the Creator's handiwork. I am grateful for realizing peace and serenity resides in my backyard. All I need to do is step outside my door and there it is in all its splendor; I just need to stop, look, listen and take a deep breath. Mother Nature in all her glory. What an amazing gift! Thank you.

Awe, wonder and wisdom is there for you too. All you have to do is pay attention.

NOVEMBER 12

As I have gotten older and, I like to believe, a little wiser, I am thankful I am able to use the written word to share my thoughts, tell a story, pass along hard-learned lessons. I write to clear my mind, to work through a dilemma, to practice an apology. Occasionally there is a message in one of my columns only a friend will 'read" because it contains a veiled reference to a shared experience. It becomes part of my broader message. I do that as a way to reinforce what my friend taught me by sharing it with my readers. It is a subtle way to say thank you to a valued teacher.

I have completed one volume of memoir essays. I am telling my story in short essays, one person, one incident, one memory at a time. I have always regretted I didn't ask my parents, grandparents, family members and close family friends more questions about their early life, the one before I came along. I am answering those questions to leave a written record of life in my "dark ages" before my descendants came along. I started a memoir-writing class for residents in my retirement community to encourage them to do the same. What a history lesson for all of us as we listen to each other's recollections and ruminations.

I use my journal to clear out mental and emotional clutter. To kickstart creativity. Track my transformation. It is a treasure trove of me growing, changing, stalling and moving forward. I think of it as focused writing. I write my way through a vexing or perplexing issue. List the dos and don'ts, the rights and wrongs of a decision. The first couple of times I did this, I felt a little silly. Then I reminded myself, these words and ruminations were for me, no one else. If I can't be honest, even feel a little silly with and to myself, I won't learn who I am, what I want and where I am headed. Wow. A life-changing insight I need to remember and practice.

There are a multitude of ways to share your story, to preserve your history. You just have to decide which one(s) to use and then start.

NOVEMBER 13

Be grateful for your life as it is today. Celebrate it. The joys, The sorrows. The triumphs. The failures. The ambiguities. The uncertainties. Each offer valuable lessons if we are alert and aware and thankful for them. Appreciate this time, right now, no matter what you are doing, facing, enduring, anticipating. Your reward will be inspiration to keep on keeping on, no matter what life throws your way. You will learn and grow. You will meet the you God created you to be. Pay attention. You don't want to miss discovering the real you.

Marilyn Monroe said, "I believe everything happens for a reason. People change so you can learn to let go, things go wrong so you appreciate them when they are right. Sometimes good things fall apart so better things can fall together." What a wonderful and wise way to view life in general, but particularly those times when you feel overwhelmed and don't think you can take one more step, get through one more hour, make it to the end of one more day. For the most part, I am fairly optimistic, but as I shared, I suffer from depression. When I am in the black pit, I can't see sunshine, never mind the good and the love in the people around me. One of the positive mantras I mutter is, "This too shall pass." The next one is, "Everything happens for a reason." Seems Marilyn and I are in agreement on that one. Perhaps it would help you to adopt the same view. Try it. You might surprise yourself with a positive turn around, even on "those days."

NOVEMBER 14

Be grateful for time to rest, to relax, to play. Play? Yep, play. Maybe we aren't really suffering from chronic fatigue. Maybe we have misplaced play, locked it in the closet of our memories. You know the time when you lose yourself in some activity that chases away the weariness, the worry, the world and brings pure joy.

I have two girlfriends who give me permission to play. I know when either suggest we spend time together; we're going to have a play date. It doesn't matter what we do, it will be fun. We shop. We lunch. We talk. We laugh. We cry, but that is more than okay. We all crave a place where we feel safe. We all need a person we know deep in our bones will always accept and respect whoever we are in the moment. We expect each other to be real. No masks. No pretense. Just vulnerable us. What a relief! How grateful we are to be friends. Be sure to tell them, "Thank you." Add a warm hug for emphasis. You will part knowing you are respected, appreciated and loved. What a glorious blessing.

NOVEMBER 15

Feeling swamped? As if you don't have the energy to decorate one more room. Search for one more gift, let alone wrap it... Forget about making one more batch of cookies or loaf of holiday bread. It is all too much and you just want to hide in the closet, under the bed or maybe run away from your life, if only for today. This is one state with which I am intimately familiar! Too many to-dos. Too many people demanding my undivided attention. Don't know which way to turn. What to do next.

The happy holiday season is in full swing. Happy? Yes, happy. No matter what your traditions, the final two months of the year are supposed to be filled with family, friends, food and frivolity. Not stress, strife and wishing it were January 15th already. Stop. Breathe. Count to ten (or twenty). Define your priorities. Do you know what they are? Have you written them down? Are you checking your list? Paying attention to it?

Today in the messy middle of planning, baking, shopping, wrapping, take some me time. Remember the list you started back on the first? The list of all the things for which you are grateful? You have been adding something every day? Right? Now is the time to fix a cup of tea or coffee or pour a glass of wine or open a beer and pull out that list. Review all the wonderful, special people, places and events you have enjoyed this month. Smile as you remember the laughter, the conversations, the hugs. Read it as many times as you need a reminder over the next forty-seven days (the end of the year) all the work, all the frustration, all the doubts about getting "it" all done are worth every second. Because as you anticipate your loved ones' excitement as they enjoy the fruits of your loving labor, it really will be worth it. Honest.

NOVEMBER 16

Be grateful you are learning to believe in life, your life, all life. Be grateful you are learning to let go of loss, disappointment and disillusionment. You are learning to record, not judge. To respect your particular path through life, the people, places, experiences. You are beginning to understand everyone and everything is connected. You know when it is necessary to look for places of repose; you know they are around you and within you. You are confident you are right where you need to be, where your Creator wants you to be, doing what She assigned you.

Be grateful you recognize one comment or one diagnosis does not define who you are or determine how you behave. Labels given us by others do not make us who we are. We make those decisions by our choices and the roads we walk. We know we can, with thought and preparation, take calculated risks with confidence, because if we fall on our face, we will pick ourselves up, soothe our ego and try again. As the poet and philosopher,

Mark Nepo said, "Embedded in the edge of risk and fear is the authenticity that makes life worth living."

Knowing we are being our authentic self as we are growing in knowledge of the Spirit within, the firmer and deeper our roots are planted in reality. We are aware we need an anchor, a place of safety (maybe two) in order to reach our potential. To become who our Creator made us to be. And we know we do not have to walk alone. Our Deity puts the right people on our path exactly when we need them, for as long as we need them. We acknowledge these human angels are God's emissaries as we are for others. God works in mysterious ways. We are blessed.

NOVEMBER 17

Be grateful you know how to set boundaries. They protect you and frequently keep you from making silly or stupid mistakes and living with unnecessary hurt. Also be grateful you know when it is time to toss those barriers aside because you no longer need them; you have outgrown them. They were meant for a younger you, a different time in your life, a different phase. You are ready to move on in a particular area of your sense of self.

You have been presented with an opportunity for growth. If you refuse to lower a boundary out of uncertainty or fear, you will miss making a needed change in an essential part of who you are becoming. View the chance as encouragement from your Inner Guide saying, "It is time to grow." Listen to the whispering, or maybe shouting, of your conscience to accept the challenge. Go into this new phase with your whole self: mind, heart and soul. Let go of whatever barrier you have erected or boundary you have set. Go. Do. Be.

While there will be roadblocks and pitfalls, believe you will find a way to conquer them by yourself and with the help of those around you. You will achieve your goal, whatever it is. Because you trust your Spirit Guide and your intuition. Accept the opportunity. Research what you need to accomplish your objective. Gather the appropriate tools. Ask for help. Then do it! Don't forget to congratulate yourself when you reach your goal. Accept the results with a grateful heart. Be sure to thank those who helped. It will be satisfying to know you made the transition successfully. Bravo!

NOVEMBER 18

The 4th Thursday in November we celebrate Thanksgiving. As we move toward that special day, let's give thanks for life. Right now. Today. My life. Your life. All life. Be grateful for the people in your life. Ancestors who paved the road. The lessons learned from my maternal grandmother continue to be important. Gram taught me it is good to dream because when I do, I am really preparing for who I will eventually become. My parents provided an excellent education. I learned the value of asking questions and thinking for myself. I wasn't blessed with blood siblings, but I manage to find friends who let me "adopt" them as my sisters and brothers of the heart. They never disappoint me. Both husbands taught me about life and how to relate to a male partner in an intimate relationship. My children and grandchildren are the best part of my life and bring continuous joy. Through them our family lives on. My extended family gave me a sense of belonging to something greater than myself.

I have been blessed with incredible, unique friends from whom I learned the meaning of being there when you don't have to, but because you want to. Enlightened educators who opened the doors of learning in a classroom setting. Professional colleagues who introduced me to the ins and outs, rights and wrongs and how to behave and not behave in a business environment.

Strangers who smiled and nodded and improved my day and didn't know they did. I am grateful for the people I don't like because they cause me to look inside myself and determine why I don't like them. That exercise always teaches me something invaluable about me. I am grateful to the door openers, the ones who paved the way, my mentors. Now it is my turn to pick up the mantle, to start opening doors for others.

There are many people for whom to be grateful. Most provided opportunities to learn and grow, how to be, how not to act. Some may have introduced yummy food, or wonderful books or exciting adventures. Whoever they are, whatever part they played in our destiny or how they affected our particular path, they were sent to us for a reason. Be grateful when and if you figure out why. I'm still working on that part. Since I may not have the opportunity to thank everyone in person, I will tell them now: Thank you to everyone who touched and impacted my life at some time and in some way. I wouldn't be the me I am today without you. And I like me.

NOVEMBER 19

I am grateful for all the angels in my life, past, present and those I haven't met yet. The Creator assigns everyone a guardian angel while we are in utero. Sarah (the name I gave mine) has been with me through all good, not so good, challenging and joyful times. When I was born, Graduated from high school and college. Married. Gave birth to two beautiful daughters. As I waited for my two precious grandsons to enter this crazy, wonderful world. As I watched them become fine, loving, caring young men who gradually grew very protective of their Ga, their loving name for me. Sarah was with me as I watched over and cared for my beloved Paul. She helped me through the years of my prolonged grief. She was with me when I made the painful, exciting transition from a we to a me. As I moved from our shared home to my very own retirement space; embarked on the last chapter of my pilgrimage and met the special souls accompanying me. I felt her presence when I made the decision to return to the church of my childhood. As I write this book of reflections, I feel her steady encouragement. As I tell you about her place in my life, I sense she is smiling softly as we remember our days together. Thank you, Sarah, for never abandoning me, for always looking out for and loving me. Thank you, God, for giving me my special spiritual angel.

The Creator also sends human angels at the exact moment I need one. I don't even have to ask; they always appear when I am about to give up. Sometimes I recognized Who sent them at the time, but often it is years later before I make the connection. Whenever and however, I figure out their Sender, I am grateful they were provided and continue to arrive at the most opportune times.

I am grateful I finally learned to appreciate the sacred now. I have my editor to thank for the introduction. Linden and I were talking one day when he used the phrase "sacred now." I stopped him and asked what he meant. He lovingly explained the sacred now is this moment right now and it is all we are promised. We will never have this exact one again. I immediately understood the marvelous gift he was giving me: He was telling me in his special Linden way, to be grateful for who we are with and what we are doing because it is the only time we will have this particular experience. Now I view my days through a different lens, a positive lens, thanks to understanding the sacred now.

NOVEMBER 20

This is a challenging day for me. It is the anniversary of the passing into eternal life of my beloved best friend, husband, soulmate, Paul. It gets a wee bit easier as the years pass. I have learned to be grateful for the thirty-two years we shared instead of continuing to mourn we were not granted the privilege of growing old together. Do I like it? No, but I have learned to accept it. I am grateful for the soft sighing in my soul; it is my Spirit telling me Paul continues to look after me as he enjoys being in God's presence; his reward for living a life of sharing, caring and loving.

Paul was not outwardly religious or particularly spiritual. Nonetheless, he was a good man with a strong understanding of right and wrong who treated everyone fairly and honestly. He loved me, our children and grandchildren with every fiber of his being. Was he prefect? No. He was human. He was a simple man with an incredibly optimistic outlook on life and our crazy world. One of his frequent comments, especially when I was fretting, "The sun is going to come up in the morning!" He truly believed it. Raining? Not a problem. "The sun is just hiding behind a cloud." Hard to argue with that belief. Do I miss him? Everyday. But I feel his presence especially when I am sure my world is about to implode. His eternal love whispers, "The sun is going to come up." I smile through my tears.

I would never suggest it is easy to accept the passing of a loved one. Nor predict how long it will take. I do say you will get through the pain and be a stronger version of yourself. If your significant other dies, you will discover you can have a rewarding life as me instead of we. Will it be easy? No. But you will do it.

Everyone you care about will always be a part of your unique history. They live on in your memories and have a permanent place in your mind, heart and soul. In my faith tradition, I know we will be together again someday. Until that time. Paul's love is with me all the days of my life as your loved one's is with you. Amen.

NOVEMBER 21

As the Irish priest, poet and philosopher, John O'Donohoe, said, "If you would listen, you will hear what your heart would love to say." What is his message? The holiday season is here. For many it is a joyous time. For others, maybe not. Perhaps they are going through an emotionally challenging time. Missing a loved one. Lost their job and with it, their dignity and sense of identity, of purpose. Enduring a medical crisis or walking with someone who fears a scary diagnosis.

Suffering has many faces. Some with no relief, many times with no answers, often without someone to stand by their side. What to do? First, let them know how grateful you are for their presence in your life. How unique they are. How much they bring to your world. Do something practical. Give them your undivided attention. Listen with your heart. Invite them to join you for a meal. Offer to take over carpool for however long they need it. Give them a week of your PTO (personal time off). Ask mutual colleagues to volunteer a day or two. These are a few concrete ways to help. To let someone know you appreciate them. You may only be one person, but to one person, right now, you might be the only one helping them hold their world together. Be grateful you are.

NOVEMBER 22

Today is the anniversary of the day John F Kennedy was assassinated. I have always viewed this tragic event and its aftermath as the day America lost its innocence. The world seems to have tilted off its axis and hasn't been able to right itself since. Maybe it was my age. I was a senior in high school. I was on the precipice of womanhood. As most young adults, I was full of optimism and convinced I would change the world. I wasn't sure how, but knew I would. Murdering the leader in the world of Camelot wasn't supposed to happen. A myth isn't supposed to leave a grieving, young widow and two preschool children. Fairy tales don't end that way. It's supposed to be all sunshine and roses with a positive happily ever after.

At seventeen, I didn't understand. My parents, grandparents and other adults didn't either. Neither did the rest of the world. I wish I could tell you I have learned whatever the lesson dropped on me sixty years ago was, but alas, I can't. I still haven't figured it out completely. Gradually, I have come to believe I lived through those traumatic days to teach me life is fragile. We never know when earthly existence will end for anyone. I try to be present in every encounter, every conversation because I don't know if it is the last time I will be with my companion. I am grateful for this time, this minute. I celebrate the priceless gift of the sacred now. It is all I have. It is all any of us have.

NOVEMBER 23

The Thanksgiving holiday is all about being grateful. As I have been writing the reflections, I realized I mistakenly thought dedicating this month to journaling and gratitude was my idea. Fell into a familiar trap...again...of believing I am in control. I was reminded of the error of my ways.

One morning during my prayer time, My Inner Guide whispered quietly, "I walked you to the choice of gratitude and journaling for November. Wasn't your idea at all." God needed the two by four...again. As I have confessed before, I am a slow learner! With my ego firmly in check, I said, "Thank you," and wrote this reflection. Couldn't help wondering if I will ever learn, and remember, I am not in control and never will be. So very grateful God hasn't given up on me.

She hasn't given up on you either.

NOVEMBER 24

Black Friday, for many, is about getting up before dawn to stand in impossibly long lines to score a deal on a gift, if someone doesn't receive, will have absolutely ruined their entire holiday and their life — forever! Bah! Humbug! Don't misunderstand. The final six weeks of the year is my favorite season. I enjoy everything about it except shopping. Come again?

Shopping is my least favorite way to spend time; even trumps wrapping. As an introvert with claustrophobia, crowds are anathema to my feeling of good will, so when I venture into the shopping wars, I try to make the trek when the stores aren't quite so crowded. I come prepared with a list. I smile at fellow shoppers and say "thank you" to the store clerks. These days, I am grateful for online buying. Saves me from the crowds and I complete my gift list with minimal angst and frustration, quicker and with no sore feet. All good in my world.

To me, the real purpose of the season is not exchanging gifts, but spending time with family and friends. Eating and drinking more than is healthy and playing board and card games. It is about being together talking, laughing, teasing, taking walks with my grandsons and their dog, sharing time and smiles and kindness. The end of the year holidays are about gratitude for all the many blessings I enjoy throughout the twelve months. The season starts with Thanksgiving dinner and ends New Year's Day at bedtime.

This year let's adopt the attitude the holidays, however you celebrate, are filled with spreading kindness, good cheer, joy and hugs, lots of hugs. I promise you will dread the whole scenario less and recapture the "holy" in your holidays. What a marvelous gift to yourself and those you love.

NOVEMBER 25

Be grateful for the seemingly small things and minor everyday events. The sun. The moon. The stars. The trees and flowers and grass and lakes, oceans and mountains. Getting up in the morning when many don't. Slipping into bed at day's end knowing many don't have a safe place to sleep. Eating a healthy meal when many have little food and do not receive adequate nourishment. Sipping clean water when many don't have access to this potable, life-sustaining necessity. Going to any place of worship when many are denied this basic right. Listening to favorite music or watching an entertaining film or reading an interesting book knowing many cannot enjoy these simple pleasures. Sharing a loving hug with someone special. Many are alone in life. On second thought, maybe these small and simple things and events aren't so inconsequential after all. Maybe we need to rethink what is important in our daily life. All those things we take for granted.

I want to share a few random memories this side trip led me to. Sitting in my car waiting to collect the girls from some event when they were in elementary school. I was daydreaming. I noticed the tall pine trees. I saw them as three dimensional, living beings. Momentarily, I was in awe of my discovery. One evening wondering and worrying why the girls had missed their curfew, I was relieved by their phone call. I was grateful for mobile phones in a visceral way. After five years believing I was going to be in deep mourning forever over the death of my best friend and soulmate, I slowly began to understand it is okay to miss Paul. To be grateful for our years together instead of being disappointed he doesn't physically hold my hand anymore. Knowing with certainty, he is with me in my memories and in my heart all the days of my life.

Continued tomorrow.

NOVEMBER 26

I was as guilty as anyone else for not always seeing the bounty in my life. I didn't always appreciate the abundance with which I am blessed. I was too busy being and doing and sometimes complaining. I needed to stop, take a moment, to really be aware of what is silently present day after day, night after night. I am not exactly sure when I began to take notice. When I began to truly take time to appreciate the awe and wonder all around me.

The realizations I shared yesterday are a few of my moments of recognition and grateful acceptance. I am indeed blessed, not only by the small and simple, but for the insight to be grateful for all I had in the past, have now, and will have in the future. For all the exciting, enlightening and educational experiences, past, present and future. I am grateful for the awe and wonder in the universe. I am grateful I have the ability to know how blessed I am to be able to recognize the joy all around me. Because God used the two-by-four when necessary, I have reached my eighth decade older but also a little wiser. It inspired me to share lessons learned. Awe helped me on the road to the me, my Creator envisioned I would be. And I like the me I am becoming.

Thank you, God, for giving me the life You designed just for little ole me and no one else. The ups, the downs, the side trips, the potholes. The people, the places, the events. What a marvelous gift. I promise to do my best not to forget these lessons and to pass them on. And to pay forward all the help I received from Your human angels.

NOVEMBER 27

One lesson I had to learn many times is to address unfinished business. I don't like confrontation. Of course, the issue doesn't go away just because I refuse to face it. It usually grows and festers becoming worse with neglect. Carrying unnecessary emotional baggage drains our psychic energy. Taking care of unfinished business frees us to move forward on our personal path. I know it is not easy, but I also know it releases us from the bondage of regret and guilt and fear. Eventually even risk-averse me knows she has to address the elephant in the room before it destroys everything in its path. In my experience, the encounter is rarely as bad or traumatic as I imagined.

If the person is unavailable for a one-on-one conversation, write them a letter in your journal. If you have contact information, reach out with a card, a text, an email. Better yet, pick up the phone and call. Whatever your method of communication, speak from your heart. Do your best to mend the rift. Take responsibility for your part of the problem. Even if the other person refuses to let go, be grateful your Inner Guide encouraged you with permission to let go and move on.

What a relief. What a gift to the friend and to yourself. Don't leave unfinished business unresolved. It hurts both of you. Reaching out in humility and love will help both of you heal and grow, find peace and move on in gratitude knowing you did the right thing, made the honorable move.

NOVEMBER 28

Be grateful for belief in and acceptance of your Higher Power. No matter your understanding of the Entity greater than you, your faith tradition or what you call Him and Her, be thankful for The Presence in your life. Whether you know your Deity as God, Adonai, Jesus, Allah, the sun, the universe or some other name, He and She are available twenty-four seven. Whenever and however you need help, guidance, hope and love.

Your Higher Power will never abandon, neglect or forget you. Knowing that immutable fact has always brought me strength and comfort in the worst, most desperate, most fearful times in my life. I knew I wasn't alone, even when I momentarily misplaced hope. When I didn't think I could take one more step, make one more decision, live through one more day or make it through one more night. My God always wrapped loving arms around the frightened little girl deep inside who needed assurance I would make it through whatever challenge I was experiencing. God sent a friend or maybe a stranger into my life. Or I read a quote, a saying, a book, a poem. Listened to a song. Watched a film. Something let me know I was not alone. He was carrying me and She was walking along side of me. As we are reminded in Isiah 40:31, "...those who hope in the Lord will renew their strength. They will soar on wings like eagles; they will run and not grow weary, they will walk and not be faint." I held on to this promise as one holds onto a life preserver, because it is a spiritual life preserver all the days of our life.

NOVEMBER 29

This month we have been thinking about gratitude on both the good and the challenging days. It is easy to be grateful for the positive people, events and things in our life. It is difficult to remember the stress, the hurts, the disappointments, the failures all teach us about who we are and how we work through these times we all endure. No one is immune from the trials and tribulations, just as we all experience the fun and joy in our days with people we trust. We learn we are capable and resilient. We land on our feet stronger than before. We celebrate our victories and our failures because both are part of a well-lived life.

Questions to consider:

- Do we understand how important gratitude is and how it enhances life? Yes? No?
- How does keeping a journal, with gratitude entries, help me understand me?
- What have I made my own? What do I plan to carry into December? Into the rest of my life?

Gratitude Entry: I am grateful I decided to keep a journal. It is helping me sort through my jumbled feelings, explore my good and not so good decisions and plan the next step on my unique pilgrimage. I am grateful for a safe place to vent at anyone and everyone, especially me. I also give myself a pat on the back when I conquer one of my demons or give up a habit affecting my physical or emotional health. I thank my Inner Guide for inspiration and guidance.

Reader: Add at least one thing you are grateful for as a result of reading, and contemplating the November reflections.

NOVEMBER 30

The German philosopher, Friedrich Nietzsche said, "He who has a *why* to live can bear almost any *how*." Thinking about this quote, I decided when we add gratitude to daily living, it changes the trajectory of our lives in positive ways. Keeping a journal contributes to our knowledge about ourselves. We can see the why more clearly and understand the how better. Our life is an irreplaceable mosaic gradually built through the years by the people with whom we interact, the places we visit, the events we experience. When we reach the end of our earthly life, we have created a unique mosaic of who we are and what we believe to be true. We are a genuine jewel in God's firmament.

God, into Your wisdom, I place my path, my goals, my decisions. And if today I lose hope, please remind me Your plans are better than my dreams. Help me learn from all the people, possessions, places and events in my life. Help me appreciate the bounty of the universe and be grateful I need only stop, look, listen and take a breath to experience it in all its splendor. Strengthen my faith so I keep on keeping on and don't give up, just tor today. Amen.

DECEMBER

Love

"Love is the ultimate and the highest goal to which man can aspire."

Viktor Frankl

DECEMBER 1

An established tenet is belief in love of and for God comes first. Almost as important is love of self before others. Self-love is not selfish. It is necessary. Devote the day first to God in prayer, then to self in care. Before we can be kind to and love others, we must nurture and love ourselves for the person we are now, not who we once were or who we are becoming, but who we are today, right now.

Love of self is not permission to be an egotistical jerk or expect the world and everyone in it to cater to your every whim and desire. It is permission to be grateful for your personal past, your story; the good, the so-so, the ugly, the fun, the lessons. You are who you are today because of your experiences, the people you have encountered, the places you have been. You are optimistic, positive, kind and compassionate. You spread happiness and joy just entering a room. You bring sunshine everywhere you go. You are love in action.

All goodness flows from love. If you love yourself, you trust yourself. So if a person, place or situation doesn't feel right, leave. It is called self-preservation. It is as simple as that. You don't owe an explanation to anyone. You are responsible for your own physical, mental and emotional well-being. It is also being honest with yourself. Don't make excuses. Don't talk yourself out of doing what your heart, your Inner Guide is telling you. If you operate with self-love and listen to Divine Love, your decisions will always be right. You may not understand at the time, but you will "know" you did what you are being guided to do. Remember, God works in mysterious ways.

DECEMBER 2

Learn to say no and stick to it. It is a critical element of self-love, especially during the last six weeks of the year. Revise your shopping, baking, cooking, cleaning and decorating self-demands so you actually experience love and joy instead of yearning for peace and quiet. As you quickly scan holiday cards, paper and electronic, slow down a bit, take time to read and appreciate them.

No matter how you celebrate the end of the year traditions, take care not to drive yourself to the looney bin as you prepare for the actual day(s). If you are too tired and frazzled to enjoy family and friends, you have missed the reasons for the season. Peace. Joy. Love.

Since I turned the majority of the holiday arrangements over to my daughters. I don't have to do as much. Meal planning and preparations is a biggie I happily released. I still do a bit of baking, but not nearly as much as yesteryear and mostly with my grandsons beside me. Pure fun. Never stressful. Even though my retirement space is smaller, I clean and decorate. Shopping and wrapping takes planning and mountains of time. Remember, enough is always achievable, perfection is not. So why drive yourself to exhaustion by expecting the holidays, or more importantly, you, to be perfect. Not gonna happen. So relax. Enjoy a glass of wine, a cup of eggnog or a special holiday tea. The peace, The quiet, The knowledge you did your best. That is all anyone should expect from you. Especially you from you.

DECEMBER 3

If we listen and speak with compassion and love, with no hidden agenda except to pass along information, we will maintain control of ourself and the conversation will not go off the rails into the weeds. Our partner in the interaction will feel heard and respected, no matter the message. Pediatrician, Dr. Kelly Franklin suggests using what she calls the "teach back" method of communication. Ask the listener to repeat what you just said. It sends a couple of messages. I acknowledge I may not have explained myself as clearly as I thought I did, It also provides an opportunity to fix any misunderstandings or misinterpretations of your message. It opens the door to improving communication and encourages us to learn from each other. A win-win.

As a pediatrician, Franklin advocates using this method with children, but when I read the description I immediately recognized it as an effective method to use with everyone. Anything we can do to prevent misunderstandings and potentially hurt feelings is worth a try. A lesson I learned early on is poor communication is almost always at the core of relationships going sideways, sometimes coming apart all together. So anything we can do to help us focus on hearing someone correctly is a step in the right direction.

An old adage I used to tell my kids is important here. Many times, it is not *what* we say but *how* we say it, that may convey an unintended meaning. Not only the tone of voice but the look on our face sends either a positive or negative signal. Especially when the message may be sad or is a much-needed lesson, it is critical to be aware of how our demeanor may be perceived. With love as our baseline, the message will be conveyed properly from the heart.

DECEMBER 4

Whether we want to admit it or not, we all indulge in gossip from time to time. Even if the information seems benign, gossip has the potential to be hurtful, harmful and destructive and leave a life-long scar. Do you gossip to make yourself look important? Bring someone down? Start a rumor? No matter the motivation, the ego is involved. And love is hiding in the closet.

How do you react to and handle gossip when you hear it? Do you listen gleefully, planning to pass it on? Or do you dismiss the comment as soon as you realize its intent? Makes me wonder if the person talking to me about someone who is not present, what are they saying about me when I am not around? Sobering thought to consider.

I would much rather be thought of as a worthy listener who never betrays a confidence. I want people to trust me. I don't want them to question my love and loyalty. As it says in Proverbs 11:13, "A gossip betrays a confidence, but a trustworthy person keeps a secret."

DECEMBER 5

There are many ways to show love. In my humble opinion the best way is two-fold: giving your undivided attention and listening with love. These two actions work in tandem; can't have one without the other. If we practice this behavior consistently, with everyone we encounter, we radiate our love to the world, one person, one conversation, one interaction at a time. We quietly help soothe the effects of trials and tribulations and spread acceptance and joy in our corner of the world.

Since I firmly believe in the positive effects of the pebbles in the water parable, little ole you and me, with our seemingly small efforts, become the Butterflies of Change in the universe. Wow! Talk about unintended consequences of our personal power. When my Inner Teacher helped me understand this amazing concept, I humbly accepted my Divine Duty to be present with and for everyone with whom I interact. Offered with love, there is no better gift.

DECEMBER 6

One day while reviewing the copious notes for this book, my mind suddenly jumped to my age. Where I am on my path, my personal pilgrimage. What the? I had no clue why I had this abrupt thought. Having learned to acknowledge these seemingly random thoughts are messages from my Inner Guide, I closed my eyes and pondered.

Seventy-seven isn't exactly old. Two thirds down the path toward my eternal reward is all I will accede to, as I stumble and fumble my way through the days. I have lived longer than I have left to live. What I know for sure is many things and tasks I once considered critical, are now barely a blip on the windshield of my life, most are in the rearview mirror where they rightfully belong. Priorities have changed.

My life has taken many interesting turns and challenging twists. Some were scary. Some disappointing. Some enlightening. But all offered valuable lessons. I took what I needed and discarded what I didn't. I was able to unstick myself from uncomfortable physical and mental places. I moved forward, sometimes sideways, but I always moved. In retrospect, I know I grew in wisdom and became stronger and more resilient. I became a better me.

Do I wish I hadn't had to carefully pick my way through some perilous minefields? Of course. But I accept the tests, tasks and trials were gifts from God. Ways for me to learn and grow into the woman I am becoming as I rapidly approach my ninth decade. I learned God works in mysterious ways.

DECEMBER 7

We all have fears. I fear flying. I fear making an unfixable mistake. I fear dangerous animals and unsafe places. But my biggest fear is not loving enough or in the right way. Sometimes I misread a person or a situation. Or don't listen as closely as I could. Or stumble with words and end up hurting someone, These are some of the ways I don't love as I expect myself to love. I let myself down because my behavior led me not to show love as I am capable of showing it.

What do I do? I beat myself up instead of recognizing I am human and I made a human mistake. I can't turn back the clock and rewind time. What I can do is remind myself, as an imperfect person, I won't always read the situation correctly, say the right words, act appropriately. Love won't erase what I said or did, but it will make the apology sincere. Love will encourage both participants to accept and forgive. The bonds of love will grow and deepen and become stronger. And I will learn a valuable lesson: No matter how hard I try or how diligent I am about my motivations, I will make mistakes. I will hurt people. My recourse? Learn from my mistake. Apologize from a place of love. That is the best response in the midst of human frailty.

DECEMBER 8

Respect is first cousin to love. I don't know about you, but I can't love if respect isn't standing alongside. Early in my life, I realized the importance of respect in a relationship. If I don't "feel" the other person's respect, it is almost impossible for me to interact with them on anything other than a superficial level. If it is someone in my inner circle, I have trouble letting them get too close. I put up impenetrable barriers. I am wary of their intentions.

I also realize if I don't respect myself and my behavior, I can't love myself, therefore I am incapable of loving others. The two form an unbreakable circle in my life. It helps explain why it takes me time to learn to love someone. I have to respect them first. It means I have to try to understand their behavior. This was a life-changing insight for me. For a time, my world tilted off its axis while I wrestled with this knowledge. Now I am grateful for the understanding. My friendships are stronger, more meaningful because love and respect are both an integral part of all my important relationships. Learning this lesson was worth the uncertainty. It makes a tremendous difference in my life.

DECEMBER 9

Love requires trust. When I love someone, it is a forever commitment I take very seriously. It is difficult for me to let go and love. First I have to be confident I can trust the person. Trust takes time. If someone breaks my trust or takes advantage of me once too often, I have learned to step away from the relationship. It is a difficult decision, but one I have to make and then stick with my resolution of putting space between us.

Another lesson I learned the hard way is if I don't end the relationship when trust is broken, I always pay emotionally in painful ways. Trust is the foundation on which my relationships grow into love. When trust is gone, the structure crumbles into meaningless dust. I don't stop loving the person, but I do step away and put a safe distance between us. I would be foolish to continue to be close to and spend my limited time with a person I cannot trust to be honest with me. Because the people we are the closest to are the ones who can hurt us the deepest, why would I consciously set myself up for pain? Self-defeating behavior of the highest order. I quietly and deliberately move away from having much contact. I wish them well and continue to lovingly pray for them. I just don't spend time in their company.

DECEMBER 10

Love has many languages. Sometimes verbal. Sometimes actions. Sometimes listening. Sometimes silence. Sometimes just being present. Love always wins no matter how it is shown or how it is offered. The trick is identifying and appreciating the language being used and the one that is needed.

I need words, actions and listening. I respond to all of these, depending upon my mood in the moment. I suspect most of us are the same. But communication can break down or be strained if we are not aware of, not only our love language, but the language of those to whom we are close and with whom we spend the most time.

Wash their car. Fill it with gas. Bake a favorite cake or make a special meal. Have coffee or morning tea ready. The evening beverage waiting. Spend time with their family and friends. Engage in their hobby or favorite pastime. Listen quietly and attentively. Be there. Be silent when life is overwhelming. A warm hug. A loving kiss. A cuddle on the sofa. Turn whatever you are doing into an act of love. It will make even the smallest word or act a special gift. Whatever you do or don't, say or not, these behaviors tell your loved one they are important. They send an important message: I acknowledge you. I care about you. I love you.

DECEMBER 11

Loving someone is work. Maintaining a loving relationship of any description requires diligent attention. The closer the twosome, the more work required. Saying and showing are both essential.

Being there in mind, heart and soul, not just in body. We need to pay attention and listen. The only way to love is to accept people in their wholeness as they are, not as you would like them to be.

"According to Ernest Holmes, an American New Thought writer, teacher and leader, "Love heals, forgives and makes whole." Because we radiate love, we heal ourselves and those around us. Practice is required but no special equipment is needed. Love shared in our corner of the world changes the entire universe in profound ways. Our love makes a difference in small and big ways. Never discount the power of love in action.

Be sure to tell people you love them. Say the words. Something wonderous, definitely divine happens when the three little words. "I love you" are said from the heart, seen in the eyes and shown in the body language. Mr. Rogers, the beloved children's television host, offered a shortcut, a code if you will: 1-4-3. Great way to express your love quickly, quietly, privately. Let it be your special message. I (one) Love (four) You (three).

When someone has left their earthly life or you are close to making your final journey, don't regret not telling someone you love them. It is the best gift you can give. Don't let "I love you" remain unsaid. 1-4-3.

DECEMBER 12

"To love someone deeply gives you strength. Being loved by someone deeply gives you courage." This comment by Lao Tzu was in a card a close friend gave me when he somehow knew I was not in a good place. I hadn't said anything to him; he just knew I needed a gentle reminder I had love in my life, even if I couldn't see or feel it in the moment. It is an amazing view of love between two souls, especially ones who are committed to being there for each other in all kinds of weather. I was touched in a way I had not been before.

Then I realized who had made the observation. A rather obscure Chinese philosopher who practiced a form of Daoism. He lived in the 6th century BCE. He taught the importance of inner calm and purity of mind. I find it fascinating a recluse came to this understanding of love. It suggests a couple of interesting concepts. Humans haven't changed much over the millennia. And love is as old as the universe itself.

When we share love, it grows exponentially. Funny how that happens. Love for self. Love for others. Doesn't matter. Love expands and colors our view of ourselves, our family, our friends, our sacred space. It spreads like a joyful wildfire consuming everyone in its path. Light someone's fire today.

DECEMBER 13

John Dodinsky, a writer and blogger said, "People who uplift you are the best kind of people. You don't simply keep them. You have to treasure them." What a marvelous way to describe the special people in our life. The friends who make us laugh. Help us recognize the best part of who we are. The ones who keep on forgiving us. Feed our souls and our psyche. The people with whom we want to spend our precious time. I am blessed with several friends who make me feel I am loved and needed. Make me feel special. Overlook my faults and foibles. Who encourage me when I believe I won't make it through another day. The friends who catch me when I am falling, physically and metaphorically. The people who love me unconditionally.

I am a firm believer God sends us the people we need when we need them for as long as we need them. They hold our hands and join us on our journey. They build us up when the world tries to tear us down. They use positive words and avoid the negative ones. They are honest. If they see or even suspect, we are doing something potentially destructive, they step in and gently, but firmly point out the error of our thinking. They don't walk away. They stay and help us through, to use a saying by Charles Dickens, "the best of times and the worst of times."

I love these wise and gentle souls. I know they are a very special gift from God. We can never repay them. All we can do is pass it on and pay it forward. I believe they approve. So does God.

DECEMBER 14

Hanukkah, the Jewish Festival of Lights, is celebrated in mid-December. The date is based on the lunar calendar so changes each year. However, it is always on 25th of the month of Kislev on the Jewish calendar. It is a joyous remembrance of the defeat of the tyrant Greek King Antiochus by the Maccabees, a ragtag army of reverent Jewish soldiers. The Maccabees regained control of the Temple in Jerusalem, but discovered only enough oil for the sacred Menorah for one day. Miraculously, the lamp stayed lit for eight days. Hence, the holiday is celebrated for eight days. Gifts are exchanged. Special food is prepared. Families get together for lively singing, dancing, eating and conversation.

Although there is no solid proof concerning the deeds of St. Nicholas, we do know he was born in the 4th century near modern-day Demre, Turkey. He is known as the protector of the young and impoverished and is the patron saint of sailors. Legend has it small gifts of food and fruit were left on the windowsills of poor children, especially during cold weather. Today, In many countries, gifts are exchanged on December 6th, his feast day. The spirit of St. Nicholas lives on in the German iteration, Santa Claus.

Kwanzaa is a Swahili phrase meaning "first fruits." This secular holiday is a celebration of African American culture, which begins on December 26th and ends January 1st. It is recognition of African heritage, family and unity. It was introduced by Maulana Karenga, an African studies professor, in 1966. The festival honors seven principles: unity, self-determination, collective work and responsibility, cooperative economics, purpose, creativity, faith.

The three Muslim holidays celebrated in December are based on the lunar year so the dates change. Mawlid commemorates the birthday of the prophet Muhammad. The Islamic New Year is in December. Ashura marks the martyrdom of Imam Hussain during the Battle of Karbala. Mawlid and the Prophet's birthday are celebrated by Muslims world-wide with readings from the Quran and family get togethers. Asura is a day of mourning for Shia Muslims and a time for fasting and reflections.

DECEMBER 15

As discussed yesterday, each of the Abrahamic faith traditions have holidays in December. All are spent with family and friends. I would venture each family; no matter their holiday traditions have memories of disasters. At the time, they were not funny, but as time passes, we look back on these occasions with a smile, a chuckle, maybe even a belly laugh. Here are a few of my family's holiday disasters, or as I prefer, treasured memories.

I was six or seven and went with Grandpa Al to pick out their Christmas tree. Our choice was much too tall for the small living room. It had to be trimmed. It is December in Detroit, Michigan. Gramps carefully put newspaper over the living room carpet and proceeded to saw off the bottom of the tree. I remember suggesting he might want to put that end on the porch. He replied, "It's cold out there!" Even as a youngster, that didn't make sense because the front door was wide open. In the middle of this process, Gram comes home. Needless to say, she was not pleased with the mess or grandpa's explanation. Even her regular evening martinis did not change her opinion of his decision.

My mom and her sister-in-law used to trade hosting the family for the holidays. Mom and her brother continued to squabble, even as adults, with children of their own. One year they had a huge argument on Christmas Eve. Mom refused to go to their home the next day. Having made no dinner plans and with no grocery stores open, we had no holiday meal. The only place open on Christmas Day was a Chinese restaurant. Not exactly traditional fare but it is one of the only Christmas meals I remember from those years. I had my parents all to myself. I didn't have to share their attention with anyone. What a treat for me!

More memories tomorrow.

DECEMBER 16

These holiday memories weren't exactly disasters, but did cause frustration and hurt feelings in the moment. Our local bakery offered red and green dinner rolls as a treat for holiday dinner. I thought it would be fun as well as a festive touch to the table. What I failed to do was take into account teasing teenagers. All four of the dears had something to offer about the "yucky" looking rolls. None of the comments were flattering. No amount of explanation was going to convince any of the charmers to even taste one. The only reason Paul tried one was to make me feel better. Even with his assurance they tasted "normal." I ended up freezing them and eating them one by one myself. Took months to finish the job.

One year I discovered the Incredible Scissors. Great stocking stuffers for young adults on their own for the first time. Oh boy, did I take ribbing about these gadgets. All four went around Christmas day hunting for things the Incredible Scissors wouldn't cut. Mom (me) was not amused.

Mustn't leave the four-legged furry children out of these memories. We were living in a small townhouse. My parents came for the holiday. Luckily we gave them our bed. The decorated tree was at the foot of the sofa bed in the living room. One night about 2:00 am, the two cats decided to inspect the tree. Do you have any idea how loud a falling Christmas tree is or how heavy it is or how big a mess it creates when it lands in the middle of the bed you are sleeping in? I do.

Our male cat decided to eat the tinsel from the tree. Of course he did. What respectable cat can ignore a dangling, sparkly string hanging right in front of his nose. I should have known after shooing him away and replacing the tinsel several times, eventually, he would swallow some. This disaster could have proven fatal. Instead, I ended up pulling tinsel from him as he tried to pass it on his own. Not a pretty sight and the sounds were horrible from him and me.

These are but a few of the holiday disasters that have become fond (?) memories of family holidays. Take a few minutes and remember yours. It will bring a special kind of happy to your day.

DECEMBER 17

Even with your eyes closed, your feelings hurt and your mind in a whirl, your heart knows love. Never forget your life message is unique. No one can be you because you are already taken. Body. Mind. Heart. Soul. Psyche. You have been given a special set of

343

instructions and divine duties, created just for you. There has never been another you and there never will be.

You are you for a reason. It is your life-long responsibility to become the best you possible. Your Deity gives you all the assistance you need. All you have to do is ask for Her help and guidance. And then listen with your heart open. The answers will appear. Maybe not in exactly the way you thought they would or hoped they might, but they will come. One thing I know for sure: You will know love in all its majesty. It was a breath-taking joy when I realized and accepted God's promise of eternal love is true and will never be withdrawn.

I also realized I am never going to figure life out. In some ways life is simple, in others, not so much. There is evil in the world but it doesn't have to include me being mean or uncaring. There is ignorance all around me, but it doesn't mean I should stop searching, questioning and learning. There are self-important people everywhere I look, but I can stand up straight, declare my truth and follow my ethical choices without being an egotistical know-it-all. There is indifference around every corner, but it doesn't mean I should stop loving. It is always my choice as it is always yours.

DECEMBER 18

Buddhism teaches to adopt a can do, why not, no problem attitude. It also cautions knowledge comes first and wisdom comes later. Fr. Richard Rohr suggests, "There is humility in accepting how much we don't know." The trick here is to keep asking questions especially when you think you have figured life out and can now coast along. Got news for you. Life doesn't work that way. I know. I tried. Several times. The world always knocked me down. I had to learn life evolves as I grow in age, experience, book learning, street smarts and wisdom.

As I am quickly closing in on my ninth decade, I know I have more to learn about what I don't know; more to discover about the world; more questions to ask; more dilemmas to face. None of these activities will end until I take my final breath. How I decide to live whatever time I have left on earth is my choice. I refuse to leave it to chance. Or worse, let someone else decide for me.

What I know for sure: I have love in my life. Love of blood family. Love of family by choice. Love of close friends. Most of all, love from God. With Her love and guidance, I will stay grounded in reality. I will live simply and deliberately and gratefully embrace challenges. I will see the big picture but nurture individual ties to my community. I will stay in touch with myself physically, emotionally and spiritually and make time for stillness, silence and solitude, I will remember the Zen proverb, "No snowflake ever falls in the wrong spot."

DECEMBER 19

Reverend Josh Reeves suggests we say, "I release my attachment to who I think you should be, and I accept you as you are. I love you as you are." Wow! If we could all accept that belief and practice it, just imagine how much better, kinder, gentler our world would be. Boggles the mind! A shift in thinking can make an enormous difference in our interaction with and relationship to everyone we encounter.

Our attitude determines how we view the world and everyone in it. If I insist everyone believe the same way I do about religion, politics, how to raise children, which neighborhoods are appropriate, what should be taught in the schools, beef is better than chicken, which is better than seafood and definitely better than veggies, the country is better than the city and on and on and on. First, it would be a really dull world, but more importantly, we would never be exposed to new thoughts and ideas and all learning would stop. No advances in science, medicine or understanding how and why people behave as they do. Think about that for a moment. We would all still be living in caves. No music. No art. No wine. No chocolate. No motor vehicles. No television. No Internet. Oh my gosh! I admit sometimes a little less of all the things listed might be a good thing, but a world without them would certainly mean a challenging existence.

If all we have to do to avoid living in caves again is learn to love one another, I do believe I will choose to love all whom I encounter, no matter their ethnicity, gender, religion, politics or socio-economic level. I will love because it is the right way to live my life. Because my Higher Power is love personified.

What would be your choice?

DECEMBER 20

Your only true possessions are your ability to love and to make choices using knowledge, reason and judgement. I believe all creatures have a soul, so it is our free will, which elevates the human animal to a thinking, feeling being. Even in the worst situation, we decide what to say, how to act, where to go and how to get there. Unless we give them the power, no one can take away our ability to choose good over evil. Right over wrong. Compromise over stubbornness. To help or to hurt. To love or be indifferent.

Yes, you read that right. Hate is not the opposite of love. Indifference is. When love is not present, we are indifferent to the person. We just don't care one way or the other what happens to them. Whether they are happy or hurting. High on life or falling apart. No matter what their emotional state, it does not affect us in any way.

In my way of thinking, when someone is indifferent, they have lost, or maybe never had, real love in their life so they are unable to feel much of anything. I honestly believe love really does make the world go round. That is why I choose love every time, Admittedly, sometimes I need to remind myself to love a particular person. When I don't, all kinds of negative emotions flood my head and heart. My behavior is not my best. I don't like me very much. So I consciously choose to "love my neighbor" because I believe it is the right way, the only way, to live my life.

Which choice do you make?

DECEMBER 21

In the northern hemisphere, today is the Winter Solstice. It is the shortest day and longest night of the year. The center of the earth is the farthest from our sun. (In the southern hemisphere, this phenomenon occurs in June.) In my part of the hemisphere, the change is not as dramatic as in more northern areas, but even in Houston, we are beginning to feel the change. If we haven't experienced the first cold front of the season, we will soon. The trees are bare. The fields are fallow. There is little color except when we are blessed with a clear blue winter sky or spy the welcome sight of a brilliant red cardinal. The early spring tulip and crocus bulbs are using this time to prepare for their glorious, colorful appearance in the spring.

We have pulled out the warm blankets for the beds and the cozy throws for the sofa and chairs. The A/C is off. The furnace is on. The lamps are turned on earlier. As my beloved gram taught me, I "put my house to bed" as I close the curtains and blinds earlier in the evening. More soups and stews are eaten. Sweaters are donned. Coats and jackets are warmer. The outside world may not slow down much, but our inner world does. We just don't move as fast this time of the year.

This is a good day to clear away the clouds in our mind, heart and soul. Use the cold as the reason to slow down mentally, wrap up warmly and snuggle with someone special. Think about the ways we are fortunate. Count our blessings. Focus on the people and possibilities for which we are grateful. Take time to say "thank you" for all the positive in our life.

Pope Francis said, "However dark things are, goodness always re-emerges and spreads. Each day in our world, beauty is born anew. It rises transformed through the storms of history." What a marvelous message to remember and hold on to every day, but especially during the dreary days and long nights of winter. I would add one more thought: Spring will come in its time just as winter follows autumn and summer follows spring. It is the Creator's loving promise to all of us.

DECEMBER 22

Michelle Medrano, a leader at Mile Hi Church in Denver, Colorado said, "What can love do. How can love express. How can love be. How can love show up. It starts with each one of us." This comment caused me to stop, take a deep breath and decide how my love could show up. What can I do to share my love? After some thought, I wrote a *Daily Manifesto of Promises to Myself*. I plan to add them to my morning quiet time in the new year. To help you appreciate your love's impact, I suggest you write promises to yourself or use mine until you do. As always, it is your choice.

- I forgive myself.
- I forgive all those who have hurt or misled me.

- I put away my mistakes and do the same for others.
- I notice and appreciate the awe and wonder in the world.
- I will be the best me I can be today.
- I will live in the sacred now with joy and appreciation.
- I will smile real smiles.
- I will use soft and gentle words.
- I will offer warm hugs.
- I will remember my Deity dwells within all persons, including me.
- I will love myself and all I encounter with the love my Higher Power has for me.
- I will remember to honor me and my fellow humans as children of God.

DECEMBER 23

Martin Luther King, Jr. said, "Everyone one can be great because everybody can serve. You only need a heart full of grace. A soul generated by love." Any service, large or small, performed with the proper mindset is love. If asked to participate in decorating your church, temple or mosque for a coming special service, do it with joy. Share the time with laughter as you help untangle the lights with someone you meet this morning, a potential new friend. Bake the extra batch of cookies to help a beleaguered, over committed mom. Shovel the snow in front of the houses on both sides with a smile and a cheery wave for passers-by. Help haul the toboggan up the hill for the neighborhood kids with a merry ho-ho-ho. Take out the trash for your elderly neighbor.

If the next few days have no particular meaning for you, offer to cover a shift for someone with kids who want mom and dad with them. It is a kindness both of you will remember long after you may have been financially compensated for your time.

These acts of kindness are love in action. When you mirror the joy of the season, you smile, others smile, God smiles, however you know Him and Her. Love radiates from you with every large or small service you perform because you want to, not because you have to. If you can't take on one more thing, say so. This is self-love. It is okay to give yourself permission to react to what you need; a few quiet moments to catch your breath, to remember the reason for all the activity. We are preparing to celebrate the day Love personified entered the world. Halleluiah! Hosanna! Amen!

DECEMBER 24

Certain holidays are on the calendar for everyone. Personal "holy" days are special and important too. Birthdays. Our own. Loved ones. Intimate friends. Family by choice. Anniversaries. Graduations. New jobs. Promotions. Moving. Beginning of a friendship. Stopping an addiction. Reaching a target weight. Confirmations. Bar and Bat Mitzvahs. Weddings. Deaths. Put these dates on your calendar too. Make a call. Send a card, a text, an email. Some recognition you remember and cherish the memory of the occasion.

Changes and leavings can be a challenge, but we carry the people, the places, the experiences in our heart, no matter where we end up or how old we are. In the final chapter of my life, I savor my recollections as a comment on my choices, my changes and the progress on my personal pilgrimage. So will you.

DECEMBER 25

No matter your faith tradition or spiritual philosophy, celebrate this day as the anniversary of the birth of Universal Love entering the world. The Love that was, is and always will be. Believe sacred spaces are anywhere and everywhere we spend time with those we love. On this day of blessings and joy, be with the special people in your life. And hold the ones who have moved on to their eternal home in your heart because they, too, are with you in your sacred space.

Make time on this holy day to be grateful for the gift of love. Family. Family of the heart. Friends. Life. Laughter. Music. Lights. Quiet. Memories. Faith. Hope. Yourself. Be grateful for the gift of grace to keep on keeping on. The gift of an abundant life. If you believe you have all you need, you will be content. You have Universal Love in your heart, so you are blessed beyond measure. Inhale peace. Exhale love, the greatest gift you have to share. You change the world with your love. Thank you.

DECEMBER 26

In five days, this year ends. In six days, we begin a new one. In preparation for these annual events, make two lists. On one, write down the self-destructive thoughts and habits you have accumulated in the past twelve months. Think about why you need to be rid of them. Take your time. Savor the lessons learned. Remind yourself of the human angels who helped you move through these challenges. Thank them with a short note. Pen and paper is best, but a text is okay too. Just express your gratitude with the written word. Once this solemn ceremony is finished, burn or bury the list. These thoughts and habits are now part of your history. You are ready to move on.

The second list is the good thoughts and habits you have acquired this year. The results of trying new ways of viewing yourself and your world, meeting new people, going on planned and unplanned adventures, taking calculated risks and saying an enthusiastic "Yes!" to interesting opportunities. Include specific ways you have grown. Side trips you have taken on which you learned about yourself. Smile as you remember special people, places and events. Store this list in a safe place, perhaps in the beginning of next year's journal. When you have one of "those" days, you will be able to remind yourself how awesome you are, how far you have come on your personal pilgrimage. We all need a boost in confidence now and then. A pat on the back. This list will provide it.

These healing rituals offer quiet moments for you to do a bit of soul-searching. Include your favorite beverage. Sit in your special spot. Thank your Higher Power for the gifts and blessings of the year. Tell Her you appreciate Her presence in your life. Be sure to write about this end-of-the-year ritual in your journal. In the twilight of your earthly life, you will treasure the memory of your growth. You will know you were important, that you made a difference in your corner of the world. Because you do. The mystic, Fr. Thomas Keating said it this way, "Every moment and every event of every man's life on earth plants something in his soul." The journey is just as important as the goal.

DECEMBER 27

Let's make today a rest day. To stop, take a breath and just be. Since we probably overindulged the last few days, make simple, healthy meals instead of fancy calorie-laden ones. In the early evening as the sun slowly sets, sit in your favorite chair, maybe with a comfy lap blanket over your knees. Relax. Listen to soft, soothing music as you enjoy the lights and decorations with a cup of tea or a glass of wine or the final mug of eggnog. Maybe add a cookie (or two) or the last slice of holiday bread. Ahh... The simple joy of peace, quiet, solitude and serenity.

Remember the gleeful noise and happy chaos. The dog barking. The cat batting the tree ornaments when no one is watching.

Someone saying, "What I really wanted! Thank you!" Grandma smiling and nodding fondly at the familiar confusion. Aunt Barbara giving the coolest gifts. Nancy preparing a marvelous meal for family and friends. Everyone playing the new games laughing, but still competitive. Someone quietly taking pictures. Witnessing the joy of giving and receiving. People sharing love. These are the scenes and sounds you will take into your twilight years. How do I know?

I am the grandmother in the middle of the mayhem. I am remembering the last few days with family and friends. I am also remembering missing family and friends. Those who are far away. Those who have gone to their eternal home. I am feeling their loving presence in the room. I am remembering past holiday celebrations when I was the one who did all the planning and preparations. I am "seeing" my girls unwrapping gifts as I watch my grandsons open theirs. I also remember fond scenes from my childhood with my parents, grandparents, extended family and close friends. Younger cousins shouting gleefully, just because. These are just a few of my memories from long ago holidays.

No matter your age, I know you have your own memories you are savoring as you read this reflection. The feeling of love from the past is overwhelming, but more so today. That is why the sacred now is called the present. Enjoy today as you experience the love and remember the reason for the season: the birthday of Love Personified. Amen.

DECEMBER 28

Love your personal path. Your pilgrimage. Your destiny. Where you are now. How you got here. The people. The places. The events. The experiences. They are all unique to you and your life.

If you had not met the people, visited the places, had the experiences, you wouldn't be the person you are today.

The wonderful person God made in His and Her image and likeness. The creative person who is improving your corner of the world. The person who radiates joyful confidence. The person who knows love is the most powerful force in the universe. The person who shares their incredible gifts with everyone in their sacred space. The person who listens with their heart. The one who cares, gives and receives with love. The person who accepts the gifts and responsibilities assigned to only them by their Supreme Being, by whatever name and however you understand Him and Her.

Thank you for being you. Thank you for sharing you with everyone you encounter. What a gift you are to all

DECEMBER 29

Love is transformative. Your love. My love. All love. We carry it in and with our Inner Spirit. It is our moral guide, our reason for existing. When we love with our whole being, we not only make a difference in ourselves and our loved ones, but we change our little corner of the world for the better. There is nothing on earth or in heaven more powerful than love. Love transcends everyone and everything.

If we believe in love, nothing is impossible. We can lose everyone dear to us, all our possessions, even our freedom, but if we share our love, we rule the world. Never doubt the power of love. It is the ultimate gift from our Creator. It is who we are meant to be. It is who He and She are. Love brings healing light. Let your love radiate every day in everything you think, say, do. You will change the world with the light of your love.

Will the world know you by your love?

DECEMBER 30

The only true, lasting virtue is love. Lean on it. Tap into its power. Let love loose. It will always conquer whatever evil you encounter in whatever form it takes. I am constantly amazed when I stand back and watch what happens. The miracles begin. Mind, body, heart and soul respond. Anger abates. Tension lessens. Tempers simmer down. Tears slow. Thoughts are gentler. Words are wiser. The atmosphere cools. The mood changes. Compassion stirs. All because love is present. Our Creator is present. As Psalm 136:4 says, "To him who alone does great wonders, for his steadfast love endures forever..."

Questions to consider:

- Do we understand how important love is? How it enhances all life? Yes? No?
- Do we understand the power of love in our life? In the world? Yes? No?
- What have I made my own? What do I plan to carry into the rest of my life?

Gratitude Entry: I am grateful for the powerful gift of love. I am grateful I learned to be still and Be, because that is when I find my calm center of love. I find my Creator. I find Pure Love.

Reader: Add at least one thing you are grateful for as a result of reading, and contemplating the December reflections.

DECEMBER 31

May you find peace, hope, contentment and love in the New Year.
Be still and find your center of Love.
Dear Lord, help me remember:
When in doubt, to be silent.
When in doubt, to be kind.
When in doubt, to be gentle.

When in doubt, to be forgiving.
When in doubt, to be thoughtful,
When in doubt, to be hopeful.
When in doubt, to be helpful.
When in doubt, to be prayerful.
When in doubt, to be loving.
When in doubt, to be me.
When in doubt, I will remember
I am a conduit of wisdom, light and love from the Divine Healer.
Amen.

YEAR-END
Reflection

"With acceptance, we find wisdom.
With peace, we find serenity.
With love, we find God."

The Garrulous Grandma

This reflection is a summary of what we have learned, separately and together, during our yearlong pilgrimage. When we invite a Higher Power into our life, we have a reliable guide, all day, every day. There is no time limit for or cap on our Deity's unconditional love and forgiveness. Life is a gift. Age is just a number. We have no regrets about yesterday. We don't fret about tomorrow. We enjoy where we are: In the sacred now, in our sacred space. If we remember to focus on what is right with us and in the world, instead of what needs fixing, we know: We will find happiness in the small events, experience joy in the everyday and live in comfortable contentment. With peace in our heart, Voila! Peace in the world.

We have learned ways to bring light to other people's day, to always be honest in our interactions, to share love no matter the person, their behavior, or the circumstances. We are no longer resistant to gradual change. We take pride in progress at our own pace. We tell ourselves and other people how well we are doing to improve everyone's life in our limited time on earth. We accept being a cheering chorus for ourselves and others is necessary for everyone to achieve success and to grow in wisdom and faith. We are learning to offer unconditional love to everyone as our Higher Power always has and will continue to do; we believe He and She expect us to do the same.

We recognize we are unique. No one can be us or take our place in God's heart or do what our Higher Power assigns us. We expect the positive, so we find it. We expect to see kindness, so we do. We treat people with respect, even if we don't like them or want to spend time with them because we recognize the Divine dwells within all of us. We live one day at a time and shine brightly in our corner of the world. We embrace the knowledge no one cares, gives and loves like we do, except our Deity.

I have never kept a spiritual journal. As I was writing the April reflections, I realized this book has become my first one. After pondering this revelation, I recognized I needed to wait until my eighth decade before I could write these reflections. It took me 77 years to gain the wisdom and insight needed to put my thoughts in order and the lessons learned into words to share with you. I thank the Holy Spirit, my Inner Muse, for providing the inspiration to tackle this daunting project.

My Gratitude Entry: A special, heartfelt thanks to you for joining me on this pilgrimage and walking part of my journey as my partner. It has been a privilege to have you as a loving, spiritual companion on my personal path. Please always remember to: Stay curious. Be loving. Share hugs.

EPILOGUE

Throughout this Pilgrimage, I reference my daily prayers. Occasionally I quote a short section, so you may recognize parts of them. After pondering and asking my Muse for guidance, I decided to include a few of them in their entirety. Some I have written, others I borrowed from various sources. But all speak to me for one reason or another. As I have throughout these reflections, I offer them as a guide only. You certainly may use them as is. Better yet, please consider writing your own prayers and choosing sacred writings which speak to you. My goal is to encourage you to make your daily conversations with your Deity personal, to speak and listen from your heart;

Blessings on whichever way you decide to proceed; maybe you will decide to use a combination or none at all. As always, it is your choice.

MORNING PRAYERS:

My prayer for today: To be the best me I can be. To face my faults, failings, hurts, and destructive habits. Remember the least, the last, and the lost and always interact with love, compassion, and empathy. I offer my thoughts and actions as a humble gift to you, God. The small and great ways in which I experience suffering, hardship, and pain, laughter, joy, contentment, and love. There is sacred in everyone and everything. Yoda reminds us, "Do or do not. There is no try."

Since I am living one day at a time, God, all I need and ask for is strength, courage, and wisdom, just for today. Help me recognize if I am in fight, flight, or freeze mode, so I am able to avoid paralyzing anxiety. Help me embrace your gifts of humility, simplicity, and sincerity in all my encounters. Help me be grateful for who I am and all I have. Maybe most importantly: Lovingly accept I am enough, just as I am. God values integrity over image. Psalm 23:1 reminds me, "The Lord is my shepherd; I shall not want."

God, grant me the serenity to accept the people I cannot change, the courage to change the one I can, and the wisdom to know it's me. Help me accept the things I cannot change, make the choice to change the ones I can, and find the wisdom to turn the rest over to you.

Native American Proverb
Listen to the wind. It talks.
Listen to the silence. It speaks.
Listen to the heart. It knows.

Note to the world and reminder to me to accept myself for who I am and be accountable for the woman I am becoming. I am who I am, and I am enough. People will know and remember me by my love and heartfelt hugs. David Grahl said: "Trust yourself. You'll find your way." Chris Lorenzo said, "Take me as I am or watch me as I go."

As Thomas Merton so humbly suggested, I believe I am following your plan for me, God. Even when I misinterpret or mess up my mission, I believe you accept my sincere efforts because I am performing them with love.

Wise words to remember and practice today:

I have all the time I need for all I need to do.
Be actively calm.
Be calmly active.

Stay steady.
Stay aware.
Stay loving.

MID-DAY REFLECTIONS:

Progress is being connected, attentive, and listening to my inner voice. Living in the sacred now. If I feel I must DO something, I will remember the Buddhist way: nowhere to go, nothing to do, no one to be. Mark Nepo says, "Accepting this, we can do everything and go anywhere."

To live in the sacred now:

- Keep showing up.
- Keep an open mind.
- Keep listening.
- Keep noticing.
- Keep believing.
- Keep showing compassion.
- Keep being humble.
- Keep loving.

Be open. Be alert. Enjoy the scenery as I walk my unique path. I will get there when I get there.

With the Holy Spirit's loving support, I have the desire and the courage to take one more breath, move one more step, and keep on keeping on. Michelle Medrano says, "Don't give up. Keep going. Keep listening. Keep moving. You are loved."

Remember:
One day at a time.
One hour at a time.
Hugs soothe the soul.
Hope doesn't let the story end.
No matter how dark,
I am never alone.

I am loved.
Life is a gift.

My lasting legacy is determined by the choices I make each day.
- What I share and with whom.
- How I act, react, and interact.
- How I show love.

EVENING PRAYERS:

God, my day is done. My body is tired, and my mind is weary. This morning, I asked the Holy Spirit for Her wisdom and guidance. I did my best to listen and follow Her suggestions.

I am learning to let go and let you. I am learning not to snatch back concerns about my loved ones and the emotional and physical issues I am facing. I am learning to accept I am not in control of anything or anyone, sometimes not even me. I am growing as a woman because I am paying more attention to my spiritual life.

Please forgive my mistakes and indiscretions. I am an imperfect human asking for Your mercy, your forgiveness, and Your love. I promise to be better and do better tomorrow. As Thomas Merton humbly suggested, I believe I am following your plan for me, God. Even when I misinterpret or mess up my mission, I believe you accept my sincere efforts because I am performing them with love.

Thank you for the gift of today. I appreciate all my experiences and lessons. I will carry them with me into the tomorrow I pray you give me. I am grateful for each day I have the opportunity to live, love, and share heartfelt hugs.

"Finish every day and be done with it. You have done what you could."
Ralph Waldo Emerson

If my time on earth is done, please comfort my children, my grandchildren, the family of my heart, and close friends. Encourage them to follow the Irish tradition and celebrate my life rather than mourn my death. Holy Spirit, be with me and help me meet the Father and Son with courage and humility. Thank you.

FAVORITE VERSES FROM SCRIPTURE:

"God does speak, sometimes one way, sometimes another, even though people may not understand." Job 33:14

> Are you listening, Jan? Are you hearing the divine messages meant just for you?

"Be still and know I am God." Psalm 46:10

> Pause. Listen for divine guidance. Hear what She wants me to change and accept. Acknowledge mistakes, learn from them, ask for and accept forgiveness. Leave hateful words and unacceptable behavior in the past. Learn what God is calling me to do in the sacred now. Remember: Stop before starting to give my mind, heart, and soul a moment to determine the right response and prepare for the process of holistic healing and gentle growth.

"Be careful how you think; your life is shaped by your thoughts." Proverbs 4:23

> Since I live in my head, it is critical for me to be mindful of the meaning in this message. It is too easy to let my thoughts go down destructive paths, stumble over hidden pitfalls, and sink into unseen potholes. Holy Spirit, keep reminding me I am responsible only for myself. I am enough as I am. More importantly: God doesn't make mistakes or junk.

"No one who follows me will ever walk in darkness." John 8:12
> Help me remember and cling to this divine promise before I slide into my black pit.

"Above all else, guard your heart, for everything you do flows from it." Proverbs 4:23
> My heart is overflowing with God's love, but hurts because of all the pain, ignorance, meanness, disillusionment, and insecurity I see in the world. I treasure being an empath, and ask for wisdom to use this God-given gift to be there for the people with whom I interact. And remember to apply it to me as well.

"Lord, help me control my tongue; help me be careful about what I say." Psalm 141:3
> As a wordsmith, I accept I have a responsibility to choose my written and spoken words carefully and lovingly. To use my special God-given gift to uplift and educate, never to put down or intimidate. To think before I write or speak. To first hear with my caring heart rather than respond immediately with my logical brain. To remember Namaste. St. Benedict of Nursia said, "There are times when good words are to be left unsaid out of esteem for silence." St. Arsenius said, "I have often regretted speaking, but never being silent." Help me remember these wise words when I need them the most."

DAILY EMAIL REFLECTIONS:

- Bishop Baron Daily Gospel Reflection: wordonfire.org
- Daily Catholic Wisdom: catholicwisdom.org
- My Catholic Life: mycatholiclife.org
- Mile Hi Church Daily Pearl: pcc@milehighchurch.org
- Richard Rohr Daily Meditations: cac.org

- Rick Warren: connect@newsletter.purposedriven.com
- Reflections on Buddhism: dailyom.com
- Lessons from the Stoics: dailystoic.com
- Fr. Laurence Freeman Daily Wisdom: wccm.org

ABOUT THE AUTHOR

 Jan Masterson is a sassy senior woman, widow, mother, grandmother, nana, friend, confidant. She has a Bachelor of Arts degree in English with a minor in social science. More importantly, she is a student of life with an open mind and an open heart. She has an insatiable curiosity about the world and is always listening, learning, growing, sharing, reading and writing. A friend dubbed her "Hugger in Chief." It is a title she wears with pride.

Jan has edited books on faith and science, travel adventures and faith and culture and slide presentations for a graduate course on faith and science, including a companion teacher's guide. She writes a quarterly column, *The Garrulous Grandma,* and for six years was the Features Editor for the *Eagle Vista* newsletter. She facilitates a memoir writing seminar and offers editing services for various groups in her community. She is founder, reporter and copywriter for the online newsletter, *News and Views from Contemplative Network.* As Managing Editor writes, *Musings from the Editor.* She is also Director Communication for Contemplative Network (www.contemplative.net).

Jan lives in the independent living section of Eagle's Trace, a continuing care retirement community, in Houston, Texas. She reads all kinds of material, does research for articles and writes something every day. She doesn't want her writing "muscle" to get rusty from disuse and neglect or her Muse to desert her. She spends time with family, family by choice and two-legged and four-legged friends living life to the fullest, at least as full as her sometimes uncooperative body and always unpredictable memory allow.

Contact Jan at:
thegarrulousgrandma@gmail.com

Follow Jan on:
Substack.com@TheGarrulousGrandma

ABOUT THE EDITOR

Linden Price did his undergraduate work in social studies education with a concentration in history. His favorite genre was historical research. One of his more memorable writing experiences was a required senior year course in research taught by the Ph.D. archivist at the New Mexico state library. This course allowed access to original documents stored at the library. The research topic was the establishment of the Santa Fe Trail. He relates it was an academic thrill of a lifetime to be touching and reading those documents. Not only did he ace the course, the professor suggested he should consider a career in historical research. Even though he did not follow her advice, the experience and outcome bolstered his confidence in his writing skills.

Many years later, enter Jan Masterson. Shortly after the COVID lockdown was lifted, he invited himself to the Legacy in Words writing group she leads at Eagles Trace Senior Living. The welcome mat had not been put out and resulted in his rather awkward departure from the meeting room. She later sent him an email opening the door to participation. He counts himself privileged to have listened to many essays in his time with the group, including Jan's. Her communication skills extend beyond writing and are clearly evident in *A Pilgrimage to Find Acceptance, Peace and Love Within.*

Linden relates, prior to his participation in Legacy in Words, his editing experience was limited to essays written by his children for high school classes. The challenge there was making sure his input didn't make the essay read like it was written by someone else. He gives his assurance to readers of the Garrulous Grandma's work her writing style has been left untainted. Her invitation to edit her book has been a privilege he has greatly enjoyed. It is his belief readers will find her work to be thought-provoking and motivational as they take the daily walk with her on a journey of a lifetime.

You can contact Linden at lhp@contemplative.net.

BIBLIOGRAPHY

Technically this list is not a bibliography, but rather a selection of books, columns, apps and web sites I recommend because they all spoke to me, taught me, touched me and ultimately inspired me to write *The Garrulous Grandma's Daybook: A Pilgrimage to Discover Acceptance, Peace and Love Within.* It was different ages and in different stages of my life's journey and on my spiritual quest when I read the books and discovered the columns, apps and web sites; all had a profound impact on my thinking and understanding of me and my inner world and helped me navigate my outer world. If you decide to read any or all of these titles and columns, use the apps or visit the web sites, my prayer is you might gain insight into your two worlds as I did. Enjoy!

BOOKS

Ban Breathnach, Sarah, *Simple Abundance: A Daybook of Comfort and Joy*, Warner Books, Inc. 1995

Beattie, Melody, *Journey to the Heart: Daily Meditations on the Path to Freeing Your Soul*, Harper One, 1996

Carlson, Kristine, *Don't Sweat the Small Stuff for Women*, Hyperion, 2001

Davis, Mary, *Every Day Spirit: A Daybook of Wisdom, Joy and Peace*, Rich River Publishing Company, 2017

Gawain, Shakti, *Reflections in the Light: Daily Thoughts and Affirmations*, Nataraj Publishing, 1988

Helminski, Kabir editor, *The Pocket Rumi,* Shambhala Publications, Inc., 2001

Hesse, Robert J. *Faith and Science: A Journey into God's Mystical Love*, (New York: Crossroad Publishing, 2022).

Hesse, Robert J. *Face to Face: Divine Encounters in God's Earthly Kingdom,* (New York: Crossroad Publishing, 2025).

Kabat-Zinn, Jon, *Wherever You Go There You Are: Mindfulness in Everyday Life*, Hyperion, 1994

Lewis, C.S., *Little Book of Wisdom: Meditations on Faith, Life, Love and Literature,* Compiled by Andrea Kirk Assaf and Kelly Anne Leahy, Hampton Roads Publishing Company, 2018

Nepo, Mark, *The Book of Awakening*: *Having the Life You Want by Being Present to the Life You Have,* Conari Press, 2000

Nouwen, Henri, *Bread for the Journey: A Daybook of Wisdom and Faith*, Harper One, 1997

Palmer, Parker, *On the Brink of Everything: Grace, Gravity and Getting Old*, Berrett-Koehler Publishers, Inc. 2018

Patton Thoele, Sue, *The Woman's Book of Courage: Meditations for Empowerment and Peace of Mind*, MJF Books, 1996

Rohr, Richard, *Falling Upward: A Spirituality for the Two Halves of Life*, Jossey-Bass, 2011

Schiller, David editor, *The Little Book of Prayers*, Workman Publishing Company, 1996

Strelecky, John, *The Café on the Edge of the World: A Story About the Meaning of Life*, Aspen Light Publishing, 2020

Thubten Chodron, *Awaken Every Day: 365 Buddhist Reflections to Invite Mindfulness and Joy*, Shambhala Publications Inc. 2019

Young, Wm. Paul, *The Shack: Where Tragedy Confronts Eternity*, Windblown Media, 2007

NEWSLETTER COLUMNS

- "Heard it from the Eagle's Beak" by Becky Ogle in the Eagle Vista newsletter
- "From the Board" by Contemplative Network Board in the News and Views Newsletter
- "Mining Truths More Precious Than Gold" by Bill Gorsky in the News and Views Newsletter
- "From Science to Soul" by Deborah Klesel, RN, PhD, MSN in the News and Views Newsletter
- "A Recommended Read" by various contributors to the News and Views Newsletter
- "The Women of Angela House" by various Residents in the News and Views Newsletter
- "An Interesting Journey Godward" by Alex Torres in the News and Views Newsletter

WEBSITES

- Center for Action and Contemplation, www.cac.org
- Contemplative Network, www.contemplative.net
- Daily Hope Devotional, www.pastorrick.com

APPLICATIONS

Always Positive
Centering Prayer
Daily Jewish Quotes
Daily Mass Readings: Reflections
Jewish Sayings
My Positive Outlooks
Suggested pages to follow on Instagram:
        Brene Brown
        Contemplative Network
        Daily Om

Deepak Chopra
Eckhart Tolle
Positive Thoughts
Richard Rohr
The Tiny Buddha

www.ingramcontent.com/pod-product-compliance
Lightning Source LLC
Chambersburg PA
CBHW070906130626
46555CB00001B/20